PLAYING COMMEDIA

Barry Grantham is a performer, director and teacher of *Commedia* and related physical theatre. His background is professional theatre: his maternal grandfather was a music-hall artiste and his father a classical actor, who first aroused an interest in the *Commedia dell'Arte* in his son. Barry trained as a dancer with Idzikowski, a famous Harlequin in the Diaghilev Company, and was coached by him in that role.

An early career working in almost every form of theatre from fringe to the West End and in films such as *The Red Shoes* and *The Tales of Hoffman* prepared him for a return to his first love, *Commedia dell'Arte*. In the 1970s he began a series of workshops and performances at the Oval House Theatre and the City Lit, London, and formed the nucleus of the Intention Commedia Company, which has continued to give performances up to the present time.

He has performed and given master classes in Norway, Sweden, Holland, Germany and in Italy itself at the Teatro Municipiali Reggio Emilia. Recently he has made visits to Latvia and Estonia. He currently writes, directs and appears as guest artiste with various companies while still running the Intention Commedia Company.

1

BARRY GRANTHAM

Playing Commedia

A Training Guide
to
Commedia Techniques

London
NICK HERN BOOKS
www.nickhernbooks.co.uk

A Nick Hern Book

Playing Commedia
first published in Great Britain in 2000
as a paperback original by Nick Hern Books Limited,
14 Larden Road, London W3 7ST

Playing Commedia © 2000 by Barry Grantham

Barry Grantham has asserted his right to be
identified as the author of this work

Typeset by Country Setting, Kingsdown, Kent CT14 8ES

Printed and bound in Great Britain by Biddles, Guildford

A CIP catalogue record for this book is available
from the British Library

ISBN 185459 466 4

For Joanie
in whom the muses
nine combine

ACKNOWLEDGEMENTS

I would like to thank the following people
for their encouragement and support

John Ballanger of Fools Paradise; Martin Burton, Director, Zippo's
Circus; David Drummond of Pleasures of Past Times and Chairman
of The Clowns Gallery; Desmond Jones of The Desmond Jones
School of Mime; Mrs Thérèse Kitchin, Director, Quercus Theatre
Company; Ms Rona Laurie, Drama and Speech Consultant;
Jean Marlow and Eamonn Jones of The Actor's Theatre School;
Mitch Mitchelson of Original Mixture Theatre; Brian Schwartz
of The Off-Stage Bookshop; Barbara Segal of Contretemps,
early dance and music theatre

PREFACE

This is a book to help the performer, director and teacher gain a knowledge of the technique of modern *Commedia* which is a style of theatre based on, and inspired by, the ancient *Commedia dell'Arte*.

The book is addressed to anyone who wants to learn and hand on the traditions. It can be a 'self-study' book and the individual should find it useful. The aim, though, is towards performance; *Commedia* is a group activity: it cannot be done alone, so you will find some sections of the book addressed to the workshop leader, the teacher or the director. If you are a performer rather than one of these, it would be helpful to get with some colleagues to work the games and drills together. I feel that *Commedia* is a theatre form of wide possibilities; and today's creative artists are turning more and more away from a naturalistic approach, looking for a formal background and training method to suit the new mood. Unlike its ancestor the *Commedia dell'Arte*, it is not restricted to either stereotypes of doubtful relevance or male-dominated orientation. In the games and exercises that follow, the *'Masks'* of the *Commedia dell'Arte* are often called upon, but they should be a starting point, not always an end in themselves. However, those wishing to create a *Commedia dell'Arte* revival in one of the different period styles will find the subject covered extensively in Part Two.

One really nice thing about *Commedia* is that no one is debarred; you can never be too young or too old, too fat or too thin, too tall or too short, too ugly or too beautiful. Oddness of form or feature, even disabilities, can be turned to advantage, and if you show the ability to play *Commedia*, the troupe welcomes you.

CONTENTS

ILLUSTRATIONS

INTRODUCTION

WHAT WAS
THE COMMEDIA DELL'ARTE?

Since classical times there have been two great traditions of Western theatre, which developed on separate but parallel lines. Sometimes one would predominate, occasionally they would meet, and they would often influence each other, but in the main they coexisted independently. We can differentiate them as (a) *'the Written and Memorised'* and (b) *'the Spontaneously Improvised'*. To the first belong the plays of Sophocles and Shakespeare, Molière, Wilde and Shaw, and this tradition continues to flourish as audiences fill theatres to listen to the written word, memorised and reiterated by the actor.

On the other hand that other great tradition – the improvised – languished and all but disappeared during the eighteenth century, leaving what? A few prints, some scenarios buried in the great national libraries, some accounts in ancient memoirs and of course a few indestructible, if much altered characters: Harlequin, Columbine, Pantaloon, who still hold a place in popular imagination. But in the sixteenth and seventeenth centuries, improvised theatre rivalled the drama of Shakespeare in popularity and esteem. Noble and royal personages patronised it at great expense, and the coins of the populace provided a livelihood for countless small troupes performing in streets and market places throughout Europe. The most highly developed form of this type of theatre came to be known as the *Commedia dell'Arte*.

We should perhaps start by asking just what was the *Commedia dell'Arte* – but it's not altogether easy. Experts disagree on how Shakespeare's plays were first presented: how much more elusive, then, must be the *Commedia dell'Arte*, for which there is not even a written text to guide us, nor a living heritage continued into our own time as with classical ballet.

Such a form of theatre, once vital but now shadowy, is open to any number of interpretations, so that the very words 'Commedia dell'Arte' conjure up something quite different for each of us, from those who would have a romantic dreamland inhabited by ethereal and poetic figures, to those who would seek a biting satire tilting against oppression. Naturally it did vary considerably as it adapted itself throughout its long history to the changing tastes of audiences ranging from the jostling crowds of Venice's Piazza San Marco to those of the Sun King and his court at Versailles.

The Italian words *'Commedia dell'Arte'* do not translate into a simple English equivalent; *'Commedia'* is obvious enough, though it is used in a wider sense than our word 'Comedy': for the *'Commedia dell'Arte'* companies also presented Pastorals, Fantasies, Tragicomedies and even Tragedies, in the same way that the *Comédie Française* plays Racine as well as Molière. **'Dell'** is straightforward – 'of the' – but **'Arte'** can lead English-speaking people astray. One can't easily escape the idea that one is talking about 'Art Comedy' or even worse 'Arty Comedy'. 'Arte', though it can mean 'art', also translates as 'Skill' or 'Craft' in the same sense as we use 'artisan' for one skilled in his or her trade. *'Commedia dell'Arte'*, then, meant comedy or other plays presented by skilled professional actors. This was to distinguish it from the *'Commedia erudita'* or written comedy performed by amateurs at the learned academies or at the cultivated courts of the nobility. In the early years it was also known by other titles, which give an indication of some aspects of its make-up, such as *'Commedia improvviso'* (improvised comedy), *'Commedia alla maschera'* (masked comedy), *'Commedia a soggetto'* (on a theme), and *'Commedia a braccia'* (off the cuff).

In recent years students and actors have used the shortened form *'Commedia'* to define a way of performing inspired by the historical *'Commedia dell'Arte'*, but not necessarily using the traditional characters or scenarios. Although this new *'Commedia'* includes worthy attempts at correct historical re-creation, it also allows for innovation, experiment and application to other, perhaps modern, themes. It has proved a fertile source of inspiration

2

for all types of physical and stylized theatre and a useful training tool for performers in many fields. So a distinction can be drawn between 'Commedia dell'Arte' – a long defunct theatrical form – and its modern descendant 'Commedia'.[1]

Before we consider this new 'Commedia' – what it is, what it might include and how we may apply it – we will look at a couple of examples of its great predecessor at its most idiosyncratic and, I hope you will agree, inspiring. For anyone not familiar with the development of the Commedia dell'Arte, an outline of its history is given at the beginning of Part Two and may be referred to at any time.

The Capocomico's Briefing

If we would be surprised today by the unfamiliar skills and style shown in performance by the major Commedia dell'Arte companies, we as actors, with our three or more weeks of production, would have found their rehearsal methods alarming. Given that, as a company, they may have spent years together working as a team, and that a proportion of what they were to present on stage was as familiar to them as a variety artiste's own act would have been, the achievement was still extraordinary. Let us visualise the scene: the venue for a performance being given later that day. The commedians, including the actors who are to play Pantalone, Doctor Graziano, The Captain, the leading ladies Isabella and Flaminia, the young leads Oratio and Flavio, the soubrette Franceschina, the comic servants Arlecchino, Pedrolino and Brighella, and the innkeeper Burattino, are all gathered round their actor/manager, sometimes grandly referred to as the **Chorogus** or **Capocomico**. He tells them that later that day they are to present 'La Finta Morta' (The Lady Supposed Dead), which they have not performed before. They listen attentively as he reads to them the **'Argumento'**, the outline of the story:

> Pantalone wishes to marry his daughter, Flaminia, to a Captain Spavento whom he imagines to be wealthy and a suitable consort, but she is in love with the worthy young Oratio, son of Doctor Graziano. Graziano and Pantalone are rivals for the affections of

---

1. In this book I use the word 'Commedia' to indicate this wider meaning; and 'Commedia dell'Arte' to denote the historical form and its traditional 'Masks'.

Franceschina, the innkeeper Burattino's attractive wife, and so there is no love lost between them. With the help of the servants of both households, the young couple devise a plan to thwart her marriage to The Captain. She is to take a sleeping draught that will make it seem as if she is dead. How she is rescued from the tomb by Arlecchino and Pedrolino, how Pantalone and Graziano fare with the provocative Franceschina, and of the love affair between Oratio's sister, Isabella, and his friend Flavio, the play will tell.[2]

Next the *Capocomico* will make certain the cast is quite sure to which 'household' of the 'three-house-set'[3] each of them belong. This is important because in other scenarios Isabella might be Pantalone's daughter or even his wife, Arlecchino might be the Captain's man instead of Pantalone's servant, and Franceschina, as was more usually the case, might play the role of maidservant to Isabella. In *'La Finta Morta'*, Pantalone, Flaminia, and Arlecchino would normally enter from Pantalone's 'house' on stage left. The Doctor Graziano, Isabella and Oratio would enter from Graziano's 'house' on stage right. The Captain and Arlecchino have taken rooms at the inn run by Burattino and his wife, which would occupy the central position.

The play will be divided into three acts, with about twelve scenes in each act. The *Capocomico* will next elaborate on each scene detailing who is to be in each one and what advance of the story-line has to have taken place before they leave the stage, or before they give a cue for the next actors to enter and take over. He will have prepared this *'Scenario'* with great care, as the entire progress of the play will depend on it. He will have developed it anew from the *'Argumento'*[4] or from his own or others' previous attempts. He will have written out lists from the *'Scenario'*, which will then be pinned to the wings and backstage as a guide for the performers, when they come to improvise the per-

---

2. From a scenario published by Flaminio Scala in 1611, probably from the same story by Matteo Bandello that was the source of *'Romeo and Juliet'*.

3. Whether in a purpose built theatre, or on a trestle stage in the open air, the setting, unchanged throughout the play, would usually indicate three houses: one house to the left, one to the right, and one centre stage, through which the actors make their entrances and exits. Two further directions would be implied: off right – 'to town', and off left – 'out of town and beyond'.

4. *Argumento* – a précis of the basic plot. *Scenario* – a development of the *Argumento* dividing the production into scenes, indicating the characters involved, and giving some basic moves.

formance a little later in the day. He now leaves it to the actors, who may consult with their partners for a particular scene, considering what comic business can be interpolated, and which *Uscite* (exit lines) and *Chiusette* (endings, see page 218) to use. The whole procedure will have taken up only a couple of hours shortly before the performance!

The '*Lazzi*'

Let's consider the **Lazzi** (*Lazzo* is the singular). These are, roughly speaking, prepared visual gags slipped in at an opportune, or even better, inopportune moment. They are 'prepared' in the sense that they are rehearsed beforehand and 'slipped in', meaning not scheduled. The *lazzo* may be a single action, like the **'Lazzo of Parting Legs'**; an unobserved signal from one player would indicate: 'Part your legs so that I can dive through and make a comic escape'; or it could last several minutes. The *lazzi* are usually physical, but can also involve wordplay. They may well have nothing to do with the further-ance of the plot, as in this famous solo, **'Lazzo of Arlecchino Eating Cherries'**.

3

Arlecchino comes on stage, and mimes eating cherries and spitting out the stones. Why did this become famous? Why is it so well remembered? Try it – the most brilliant mime will find it hard to get little more than a titter. No, it wasn't Arlecchino's miming alone that got the laughs, it was the nature of the team-playing within the company. Let's imagine this:

> The Company know that Arlecchino is likely to introduce the *Cherry Lazzo* at some point, but they have no idea when. Today he chooses a love scene between Lelio and Isabella, the romantic leads. The actor playing Lelio is annoyed that the actor playing Arlecchino has chosen this, his best scene, to introduce the *lazzo*, and the actor playing Arlecchino knows that the actor playing Lelio will be annoyed. What is more, the audience knows that the actor playing

Arlecchino has done it just to annoy the actor playing Lelio. Arlecchino sits on the edge of the stage, holding his bowl of cherries. Lelio looks at Arlecchino with the thought, 'Please don't spit the cherry stones at me'. Arlecchino doesn't even eat the cherries; he just plays with them. He dangles them; he uses them for earrings; he takes them off the stalks; he juggles with them. And all the time Lelio goes on with his attempt to propose to Isabella. Arlecchino throws a cherry in the air, and catches it in his mouth – 'Ah, delicious'. He rolls it round in his mouth! Lelio is getting more and more apprehensive. From the corner of his eye he sees Arlecchino take the cherry stone out of his mouth; he is trying to work out what to do with it. Like a child he tries to put it up his nose, then in his ear. 'That's got rid of it!' Then he gets worried . . . It's stuck! He shakes his head violently, until it comes out. The audience is now laughing out loud and paying little attention to the love scene. Arlecchino eats another cherry and this time spits the stone directly at Lelio. Lelio's hand goes to his neck. 'Ow!' (Remember it's only a mimed cherry stone.) He shakes his fist at Arlecchino, who lets him get on with the scene for a few moments. Then Arlecchino goes on the attack again. A stone hits Lelio on the cheek. Then one on the arm, another on the neck. Arlecchino is stuffing them into his mouth. He spits another out and hits Isabella by mistake!!

'Oh dear!' You can do anything with impunity to the Innamorato (the hero) but the Innamorata (the heroine) is quite different. She comes towards him. He stands up facing her, his cheeks bulging with cherry stones. With both hands she slaps the sides of his face, and with a gulp he swallows the stones! He runs off in alarm. She returns to Lelio: 'You were saying . . . ?'

WHAT IS 'COMMEDIA'?

We have looked briefly at what the *Commedia dell'Arte* was; now perhaps we are ready to say what '*Commedia*' is.

The Characteristics of *Commedia*

(a)   It is a style of performing, broad and non-naturalistic, in which the visual element is given equal, if not greater, emphasis than the verbal. It includes the audience as part of the performance, and their presence is frequently acknowledged.

(b)   It makes use of the multiple skills of the performer – the spoken word, mime, dance, acrobatics, music and other abilities to tell a story or create a dramatic situation.

(c)   It may be improvised, but employs memorised and rehearsed material (including *lazzi*) to back up the spontaneous invention of the actual performance.

(d)   It may feature permanent characters that can be carried over from one play to another: either those drawn from the Italian Comedy, or new ones developed on the same principles.

(e)   It can make use of facemasks for some or all of the characters.

Not all of these elements need be present at the same time: the conventional characters may be seen in a fully scripted play; the performance could be solely in mime; a play could be improvised, the style and technique present without the traditional characters; all could wear masks or they could be totally dispensed with; an existing play (such as a Shakespeare comedy) can be done in *Commedia* style.

The *Commedia* Style

Style is easier to recognise than to describe. We have said that it is broad and non-naturalistic; that it is larger than life. But even when it employs its greatest excesses of ridicule and parody, it must remain true to the underlying forces of thought and emotion. *Commedia* compares with straight acting as caricature with representational drawing. Caricature is the art of exaggerating the truth; *Commedia* is the same. Emotions and ideas expressed must be recognisably genuine and sincere, and as strictly motivated as any follower of Stanislavski could wish. Only then will the audience be moved by the externally broad playing of the actor.

For anyone who has never seen a *Commedia*-based performance, how would one describe these exaggerations and magnifications of the playing? If a character is in a hurry he will move four times faster than a straight actor, and if someone gets in his way he would more likely jump over them than go round them. If the character is stupid, he could spend an entire scene on one leg staring at the audience. If he is afraid, his knees will visibly knock together. Isabella and Lelio virtually dance as they play a love scene (see page 217). As Columbine flirts, her fan tells a different story to the words she uses. The boastful Captain is in fact a disgraceful coward, so, when he is at length forced to face his adversary, he approaches toes first, leaning back at an almost impossible angle, his sword straight in front of him, his eyes averted. He soon turns tail, and, bent over double, retreats attempting to protect his backside with his sword.

Let us say The Doctor wishes to ingratiate himself with a superior. He will bow till his chin reaches the floor; however, the motivation will be as genuine as that which promotes the straight actor to tilt his head. Pantalone kicks Arlecchino: not only must the kick appear to be hard enough to make Arlecchino's subsequent somersault seem the result, but Pantalone must be sufficiently full of anger to provoke him to action, and the anger must have been initiated by the previous situation. Arlecchino, as an incompetent waiter, juggles with the dishes as he serves. Again each move must be motivated; he keeps the dishes in the air because he is uncertain who is to have which, not to show off his juggling dexterity.

Although it is this exaggerated playing that is the fundamental stylistic distinction of *Commedia*, the player has at his disposal the whole gamut of emotions and reactions and is not expected to play the entire performance *fortissimo*; he can reduce to the subtlest of *pianissimo* when the occasion and the audience's attention permits it. Even though he may stamp his foot, fling his arms about and turn his head away to say 'no', he might suggest 'yes' by a mere flick of his nose.

Mime and Speech

The *Commedia* style developed principally because of the audiences for whom the actors performed. This factor was magnified by the itinerant nature of the early players. In those days, even more than today, there were wide differences in local dialects: subtleties of language used by a player from one district might not be readily understood by an audience in another. The problem was increased when the players travelled outside Italy, which happened at an early stage. Also to be taken into consideration were the open-air conditions under which they usually worked. As any present-day street entertainer will tell you, it is not the easiest thing to get dialogue across in a busy thoroughfare. The open-air and language factors caused the players to develop a method of miming the main purport of their dialogue *simultaneously* with the spoken words. As they said 'you', they would point to the person addressed; and on 'me', point to themselves. If they were to say 'I am very happy', they would make sure by their 'stance' that this would be clear to anyone who failed to hear or understand what had been said. This might seem a coarse and unsophisticated approach, and not worth reviving before a modern audience, but in fact it can add to the humour and vitality of the performance: a skilled actor will be able to introduce niceties of subtlety, as when the body language is made to contradict the spoken word: e.g. 'I am very happy!' in a 'stance' of utter despair. Incidentally, as the actor may well be masked, the emotion frequently has to be told by the body rather than by facial expression.

4

In Partnership with the Audience

By no means exclusive to it, but especially evident in *Commedia* is the actor's direct communication with the audience. It is the very antithesis of naturalistic acting where the spectators form a 'fourth wall' to the proscenium stage, observing but unacknowledged by the actors. The *Commedia* player addresses the audience in monologue, frequently employs the 'aside', interrupts dialogue to solicit sympathy, and even encourages backchat and comment. *Commedia* acknowledges the audience because it *is* there. It accepts reality rather than striving after realism. If a player tells us he is walking through a field of tulips, he knows, and knows that we know, that there is nothing but a bare wooden stage, and the tulip field is a game of imagination we are asked to share.

He will make us share in the pretence that his wooden sword is glistening steel, and extend the make-believe to incorporeal objects plucked from the air, which he will make us see by his skill as a mime. But if he mounts a high-back chair and tells us that it is his trusty steed, he will make us aware of the reality of the *chair* by commenting on the unusually long neck of his horse! This is similar to Bertolt Brecht's 'alienation': the continual reminder to the spectators of their environment, and the puncturing of the make-believe. If a player is not involved in the action he will not necessarily hide himself in the wings, but might remain in view, even joining the audience, enjoying and encouraging the efforts of his colleagues.

The *Commedia* Masks

Most other theatrical and ceremonial masks cover the entire face, which greatly limits the actor's use of speech; the *Commedia* mask, however, is a 'half-mask', restricted to the upper part of the face. These half-masks obey different rules from those of full-masks and demand a very special technique, which we'll be going into in detail later. For the moment, we are just concerned with the way masks affect the nature of *Commedia* itself. The way the actor behaves – the way he stands, moves, and reacts – is profoundly influenced, not only by the particular character-mask he is wearing, but also by the general rules governing half-masks. The half-mask hides and reduces some aspects of the performer's portrayal while greatly exaggerating others, so it is important to know its strengths and limitations.

The character the actor plays only exists in the mask, and could be said to be born through the mask. It would be impossible to rehearse a production, until a few days before the opening, and then hope to put the mask on with the costumes for the first time at the dress rehearsal. The character is collaboration between the actor and the mask, and the actor can never entirely superimpose his will on the mask. In the *Commedia dell'Arte*, so essential was the facemask in the creation of the role that it became customary to refer to the 'character' as **'the Mask'**. An actor would take on, appear in, become, or play the Mask of Arlecchino, or the Mask of Brighella – or the Mask of Pierrot. And in this last case, there is cause for possible confusion, for Pierrot is a Mask (character) although unlike, say, Pantalone, he doesn't wear a facemask.

But why did our Italian predecessors look with such favour on the use of facemasks? They were employed from the very earliest days, and the nature of the open-air performances made the mask the most dynamic and clearest way of giving identity to the character. We should also think of the mask as just part of a total image, which comprised not only costume, make-up and hand props, but also the way the character spoke, moved and reacted. Because of these attributes, the Mask would be instantly recognised on entry, no matter in what play, or what actor was playing the role, and his comic reactions to the scene predicted. Charlie Chaplin is a good example of an 'identifiable image' of more recent times. The little moustache and the bowler hat make a more acceptable image than a facemask would on screen, but in all other respects Chaplin's 'Little Tramp' is a Mask – a clearly recognised individual who raises certain expectations in the audience. As Chaplin's 'Little Tramp' is identified in one film after another so the *Commedia dell'Arte* Masks would appear again and again in the different comedies. The Marx Brothers provide another example, and here we have a *Commedia* team of clearly distinguished and identifiable Masks whom we have got to know and whose reactions to each other and to situations of the scene we anticipate with pleasure.

These Masks are sometimes referred to as stereotypes but this is not entirely accurate. A stereotype is a character sketched in broad outlines representing a class of persons about whom there are generalisations and sometimes prejudices – for example, 'tramps are lazy, dirty and untrustworthy vagabonds'. Chaplin's Mask may include these traits but they do not limit him. He doesn't represent a class but is highly individualised. 'Old men are lecherous and avaricious' – Pantalone is both of these, but he too is an individual, and he is unlike any other character in life or fiction. The term 'stock' figure can also be objected to; the villain of melodrama is the same two-dimensional role, whether his name be 'Sir Percy' or 'Baron Hardcastle'. He exists to fill a place in the demands of the plot. In *Commedia*, on the other hand, it is the play, whether written or improvised, which will grow as a result of the behaviour of the Masks.

Improvisation

There remains to be discussed the spontaneous nature of the performances given by the *Commedia dell'Arte* troupes, and it is this aspect of the *Commedia dell'Arte* that has proved most difficult for present-day actors to emulate.

The difference between two distinct meanings for 'improvisation' must be clearly understood. There is *'Impro'*, in which a group of actors start rehearsals with no written script, and then improvise on an agreed theme until a play has been constructed. It is then fully rehearsed and remains more or less constant throughout the run of performances. This often produces good and naturalistic dialogue, born from the interaction of one 'real' person with another, but sometimes suffers from lack of construction. This form of *'Impro'* can really only be distinguished from normal drama in that it is a play 'written' by a group rather than by a single author.

Then there is *'In Performance Impro'*. Here the actor makes up the dialogue, and develops the drama before the eyes and ears of the paying public, and it is for a 'once only' occasion; tomorrow's performance must be new again. This kind of presentation has a very special quality, suiting particularly the realm of comedy. A line that would not seem even amusing on the written page convulses an audience when used by a talented actor extemporising in response to the stimulation of the situation and of his fellow performers.

It was this style that the Italian 'Commedians' used and perfected over some two hundred years. Working only from the scenario and the list of entrances and exits prepared by the **Capocomico**, they would improvise a different play at each performance – but it would be a mistake to think that they depended on inspiration alone. They had at their command a technique that could be relied on to work on every occasion. It was based on two principles; firstly to create a situation where inspiration

was likely to flower, and secondly to give the actors command over a vast repertoire of usable material that could be brought into play should inspiration flag. So the *Commedia dell'Arte* didn't dispense with 'memorisation' but, on the contrary, had at its disposal a prodigious stock of memorised speeches, phrases, aphorisms, rhymed exit lines, puns and visual and verbal gags, all of which were appropriate to the individual Masks, and could be introduced into the action to enliven, develop and sometimes save a scene. This method is employed in an elementary form by today's quiz show host who would have us believe that the quips he employs are the creation of the moment, and not recalled from his stock of memorised gags. The skill of the *Commedia dell'Arte* player rested in his ability to alter the material to exactly suit the situation at hand. As a comedian nowadays often keeps a 'gag book' so the actor of the *Commedia dell'Arte* used a 'day book' in which he collected items suitable for future use. These might contain ideas for comic business (**lazzi**) or speeches culled from the best authors of the day and antiquity. Some of these actors' notes, in a form polished up for publication, have survived, and are a useful indication of this aspect of the performances. Also surviving is a large number of the scenarios, published and in manuscript, from which the actors worked.

Multiple Skills

The mime element as *'simultaneous mime'* and mimed sequences has always been so important that it has led to the frequently held erroneous belief that the *Commedia dell'Arte* was, and always had been, silent. It remains none the less an essential part of *Commedia*, and will be much drawn upon in the following pages.

Closely integrated into the style, also, is dance ability. The *Commedia* player's body must bend and sway, leap and prance, stride and stamp, skip and hop. Acrobatic dexterity will extend *Commedic* possibilities. Like traditional circus folk, the *Commedians* learnt to play instruments from an early age, and any musical or vocal expertise that the modern performer can add to the presentation will be of value.

Above and beyond any additional skills the performer can bring to the part are three essential qualities: the willingness to work as a team, the gift of being able to seize the 'moment of opportunity' in improvisation, and the ability to act with truth and sincerity.

PART ONE
TRAINING DRILLS

WARM-UP GAMES

An Introduction to Commedia Games

There have been major changes in approaches to an actor's training over the past decade or so, and two of the methods now commonly used are 'improvisation' and 'acting games'. Both concepts are fundamental to the training programme that follows. 'Improvisation' was always a major component of *Commedia dell'Arte*, and **'Commedia Games'** introduce that element of play in which *Commedia*, more than any type of theatre, needs to be undertaken. Our English words 'player' and 'play', for the actor and his activity (although not duplicated in Italian) are a happy corroboration that our approach should be in a playful spirit. Like acting games (of trust, confrontation, collaboration, role playing, etc.) **Commedia Games** start simply, childishly, even foolishly. The *Commedian* in his role is not far from the Fool, and until one is prepared to be foolish the difficult 'Art' can't be mastered. The aim of *Commedia* training, like that of the actor, is first to lose inhibitions, and secondly to gain skill. With **Commedia Games** the student will pass rapidly from one to the other.

Game 1   Ha!

The workshop (perhaps we should call it a play-school at this stage) starts with a circle, everyone facing inwards. The instructor then warns the class that he/she is going to make a lunge forward and cry out 'Ha!' expecting the class to do the same, and at the *same* moment. Once some degree of synchronisation is achieved, the group is told that anyone may initiate the action. After some reticence the cries come thick and fast.

> The initial purpose of this exercise is to raise the attention and energy level of the group, and as such it works well. It can also introduce newcomers to a bit of fundamental stagecraft. The 'Ha!' of the leader should resemble that used by acrobats to demand applause (arms outstretched, palms up) and this pose must be *held* for a few beats before releasing it. You will notice that many of the group, instead of striking the position and holding it, tend to 'jab' at it and retreat. This should be resisted, as an ability to hold a position long enough for it to register with the audience is important in *Commedia*, as indeed it is in all types of performing.

Game 2   Silly Noises

Next, the leader asks for one of the students to step into the circle and make a silly sound and accompanying gesture that the rest of the class must copy. Each student should do this, coming forward of their own volition.

> The aims here are that the duplication should be as exact as possible and follow the original immediately (two important aspects of later improvisation).

Game 3   Silly Walks

This is an extension of Game 2. One person crosses the circle doing an eccentric or comic movement, again accompanied by vocalisation. He or she then takes the place occupied by another person in the circle who immediately moves off with their own invention, until all have had a turn.

> Games 2 and 3 should help the players to feel free to invent and not be inhibited in doing something foolish before their colleagues. The longer term aims of **Game 3** (all aspects of *Commedia*) are **(1)** using vocal sound and movement simultaneously **(2)** inventing instantly – as each takes over, no time must be allowed for 'thinking' **(3)** using rhythm in the crossing; that is, repetition of a movement and sound: e. g., a hen clucking and flapping wings, etc.

Game 4   Glee!

This begins with everyone raising their shoulders and tensing all muscles as much as possible, screwing up their faces and saying the word 'glee' in a very tense and restricted tone. This is held for a few moments and then, on the instructor's command, 'Deadpan', all relax the body and assume a 'deadpan' expression. When the class is comfortable with this, they are asked to point at each other (still retaining the tension) as they say 'glee'. The pointing should be as inventive as possible, such as over the shoulder, between the legs, etc. When in 'relaxed mode' they should be able to look at each other without losing the 'deadpan' in laughter.

The purpose here is to encourage the use of unusual body positions; to practise tension and relaxation and to be able to confront without laughter.

Game 5   Make Yourself Laugh

If the aim of the previous game is to practise 'not laughing', this one is exactly the reverse! Take a big breath and then, with a sigh, exhale every bit of air from the lungs. When you think you've done that, raise the shoulders and with a 'Ha!' exhale some more. Then bounce the shoulders and shake the body, with 'Ha! Ha! Ha! Ha! still without taking a breath. Time now for a big breath and a repeat of the sequence, a little quicker, this time varying the pitch of the 'Ha's', high and low. If everyone does this together, the infectious nature of laughter ensures that the room soon shakes with genuine laughter.

Game 6a   Harlequin Knees Bend

Stand with the feet fairly wide apart and turned out (ballet 2nd position). *Take approx 2 seconds for each count.*

Count 1.   Bend the knees slightly (ballet *demi plié*).
Count 2.   Increase the bend.
Count 3.   Increase the bend even more (ballet *grande plié*).
Count 4.   Straighten the knees, back to original position.

On the first of the bends assume an expression of irritation or annoyance, which increases on each bend. Go to 'deadpan' on the rise. Repeat several times.

> This introduces the concept of movement associated with a particular character. The *pliés* are also a necessary part of any physical warm-up.

Game 6b   Harlequin Surprised

Stand with the feet apart and turned out as above. Arms by the sides.

Count 1.   Raise the shoulders. Mime: 'sudden surprise' (jaw drops).
Count 2.   Sudden drop into full knees bend ('I don't believe it').

Count 3. Sharply drop shoulders (mildly aggressive).
Count 4. Slowly straighten knees, and at the same time 'wobble' the head from side to side (look of nonchalance: 'See if I care!').

Game 6c   Harlequin Hears No Good of Himself

Stand with feet a little wider apart than in Game 6b: arms by the sides.

Count 1. Raise right shoulder only.
Count 2. Lunge[1] the right leg to the right, head and body still facing front (but advancing the right ear as if listening).
Count 3. Drop right shoulder suddenly ('Fancy saying that!').
Count 4. Slowly return to upright position (mumble, mumble).

Repeat to the left.

Game 7   Smart Walking

For this the students walk briskly round in a circle. (Start with the right foot.) As they walk they count aloud in 'eights'. This number is used because of its musical affinity, and the following is a helpful method of counting, often used by dancers:

1/ 2, 3, 4, 5, 6, 7, 8.   2/ 2, 3, 4, 5, 6, 7, 8.
3/ 2, 3, 4, 5, 6, 7, 8.   4/ 2, 3, 4, 5, 6, 7, 8.
5/ 2, 3, 4, 5, 6, 7, 8.   6/ 2, 3, 4, 5, 6, 7, 8.
7/ 2, 3, 4, 5, 6, 7, 8.   8/ 2, 3, 4, 5, 6, 7, 8.

Then start again with: 1/ 2, 3, 4, 5, 6. 7. 8. etc.

When all find this easy to do, they can begin counting silently to themselves, and then we make it more complicated by taking 8 walks forward, before making half a turn (turn towards the left shoulder (anti-clockwise) and walking 8 steps backward, still continuing in the same direction. Then, turning toward the right shoulder (clockwise), step forward and continue, but reducing the number of forward steps to 4, turn and make 4 steps backward. Repeat the 4 forward and 4 backward (to complete the fourth count of eight).

---

1. See Page 48 for a description of the **Lunges**.

Repeat the whole sequence from the first 8 walks forward.

This game is good for getting people to move together as a team, develop a rhythmic sense, and to introduce *'Numerical Reduction'* which we call upon later.

Game 8   Walking and Clapping

Walking in a circle as in the previous game; and again counting inwardly in 'eights'. After establishing the rhythm the students are asked to clap their hands on the first of the 8 steps. On the second count of 8 they clap hands on the second step. On the third count of 8, they clap on the third step, and so on until the clap comes on the 8. After that, start again on the first beat:

CLAP/ 2, 3, 4, 5, 6, 7, 8.   2/ CLAP, 3, 4, 5, 6, 7, 8.
3/ 2, CLAP, 4, 5, 6, 7, 8.   **4**/ 2, 3, CLAP, 5, 6, 7, 8.
5/ 2, 3, 4, CLAP, 6, 7, 8.   **6**/ 2, 3, 4, 5, CLAP, 7, 8.
7/ 2, 3, 4, 5, 6, CLAP, 8.   8/ 2, 3, 4, 5, 6, 7, CLAP.

Start again: **CLAP**/ 2, 3, 4, 5, 6, 7, 8. etc.

Game 9a   Put on a Happy Face

Again the inward-facing circle: the right hand, fingers together, thumb proud, palm inwards, is passed slowly over the face upwards from below the chin to just above the forehead, and as it passes a broad exaggerated smile is brought to the face. The player has put on a 'happy' face and until he removes it the facial expression remains fixed like a mask. All movements, sounds, words will be joyful. He then wipes it off with a downward hand movement, from above the forehead to below the chin, culminating in a 'sad' face: corners of the mouth down etc. He now fixes a 'sad' face and behaves 'miserably'. Changes from one to the other may be slow or rapid.

Practise it also with the left hand.

Game 9b   Happy Face Duo

The action can be extended by working in pairs, with the players altering their own *or* their partner's expression, by reaching out and 'wiping' the other's face into 'happy' or 'sad'.

In the 'happy' or 'sad' fixed face we have the first approach to the nature of a mask, and the making of the body movements, sounds or words fit the assumed 'mask'. It is a valuable introduction to the mastering of the facemask technique.

Game 10a   Oppo and Appo

A game to develop physical dexterity, before we get to the more directly related Commedia challenges.

The class face into the centre of the circle. The footwork is simple enough, and should be done in a gentle and relaxed style.

Count 1. Step on the right foot (on place, i.e. on the spot).

Count 2. Low kick with the left foot.

Count 3. Step on the left foot (on place).

Count 4. Low kick with the right foot.

Repeat ad lib. *The whole movement remains on place without travelling.*

Version (a)
As you do this swing the arms in **opposition** – that is:

> **Right** arm forward as you kick the **left** foot.
> **Left** arm forward as you kick the **right** foot.

Do this until everyone finds it really easy.

Version (b)
Start again, but now swing the arms in **apposition** – that is:

> **Left** arm forward as you kick the **left** foot.
> **Right** arm forward as you kick the **right** foot.

Do this until everyone finds it really easy.

Version (c) – the tricky one!

> While keeping the alternating step/kicks going, perform four with the arms in **opposition** and four with the arms in **apposition**.
>
> Repeat ad lib. It helps to give a verbal command for the *arms:* '*Right*, left, right, left – *left*, right, left, right – *right*, left, right, left, *left*,' etc.

Repeat ad lib.

Game 10b   Oppo and Appo Duet

Instead of everyone working together in the circle and remaining on place, this is done in pairs, using the step/kicks to travel in a diagonal line across the studio. All three versions (a) Opposition, (b) Apposition and (c) Mixed can be tried, and once the mechanics are mastered, characterisation can be added with:

(1) Mime: one partner is in a hurry to get somewhere and is being delayed by the other for example, or

(2) Dialogue: while keeping the step going they improvise a spoken conversation on any given subject: say 'money', 'food', or even the weather! (Choose a 'modern' subject before attempting anything on a *Commedia dell'Arte* theme.)

> The purpose here is to provide a preliminary exercise in using movement and speech together. Movement on the whole needs to be 'on the automatic', so that the conscious mind can concentrate on the dialogue improvisation.

Game 11a   The Sad to Happy Scale

All stand in the inward-facing circle. The students are asked to make the most miserable facial and body expression they can; then the most outrageously happy one they can find. The instructor now gives a steady eight counts, and the students, starting with 'extremely sad', progress in sharp stages up to 'extraordinarily happy'. The instructor then counts downwards and they drop in stages to 'extremely sad'.

Example: *allow about 5 seconds for each 'emotion'.*

1. Abject misery! 2. Exceedingly sad. 3. Pity me! 4. A ray of hope. 5. Things are not so bad. 6. No, they're good. 7. Very good! 8. Ecstasy! and similar, coming back down to abject misery.

Game 11b   Jumping the Scale

Once the students have the steps of the scale clearly in mind, the instructor calls out random numbers (1 to 8) the class assuming the appropriate emotion signified by the number.

Note 1: *These are games! The emotions employed are applied externally, and are intended to extend the performer's range and flexibility. It does not mean that in performance, when there is a script or scenario, the actor doesn't need to fully motivate his every move and emotion.*

Note 2 (in reference to Game 10b): *The timing relationship between movement and word is complicated and in performance has to be judged exactly (see page 154), but at this stage we concentrate on trying to do them both at the same time.*

Before we go on to the next game:

A Little Theory: a Language of Movement?

I remember reading in one of those vast Victorian ethnological volumes that of all the primitive tribes across the (then less Westernised) world, only two had been found that didn't agree on the meaning intended by pointing one's finger.[2] The author also cited a few cultures where a shake of the head meant, 'Yes' and a nod meant 'No', but on the whole there seems to be a large number of mimed signals that are part of a universal and inherited language of movement.

For example: Lift the shoulders, and also raise the forearms slightly, turning the palms of the hands upward. Hold the position a moment, then lower. Even without any facial expression, I think you will find this conveys: 'I don't know'. Repeat the action more rapidly and without

---

2. On the other hand if you try to indicate something to a dog by pointing, he'll most likely come and lick your finger.

holding the position, and it will almost certainly communicate, 'I don't know and I don't care'.

It is useful to understand something of this vocabulary of movement for *Commedia* studies. In order to analyse and use it we employ *'Isolation'*, a method borrowed from modern dance; that is, we look at a specific part of the body (and it is surprising how many parts of the body can move independently) to see what signal it can be made to convey by movement or posture. We often combine this with another useful 'tool' – *'Rotation'*. That is, the rotating of the 'isolated' part.

We can now introduce games and drills that employ these principles.

Practice Drill: Hand Movements

a) Raise the right forearm to a comfortable position and rotate the right hand from the wrist:

8 times in a clockwise direction: short pause, then:

8 times in an anticlockwise direction.

b) Repeat with the left hand:

8 times in an anticlockwise direction: pause, then:

8 times in a clockwise direction.

c) Now work with both hands at the same time:

Right hand revolves clockwise, left hand anticlockwise – which may be said to be **'outward'**.

Then, right hand anticlockwise, left hand clockwise – which may be said to be **'inward'**.

This can help us to understand something of this language of movement. If you take the **'outward'** rotations at not more than a second per revolve, with the merest pause at the high point, it will be easily demonstrated that, independent of any facial expression, the signal given is a **positive** one (happy, pleasant, welcoming) while the **'inward'**, with slight pause on the lowest part of the circle, will give a **negative** signal (unhappy, rejective, dismissive).

Game 12a   Happy Hands, Sad Hands

We introduce into this drill the 'numerical reduction' formula mentioned earlier (see Game 7, p. 24). Here it works like this:

7 outward revolutions of the wrists (with both hands) ending with the palms uppermost (See Fig. 1 'A', opposite).

A
OUTWARD ROTATIONS

7 and a half inward revolutions of the wrists ending with the hands in palms down and in towards the chest ('B').

3 and a half outward ending in position ('A').

3 and a half inward ending in position ('B').

1 and a half outward ('A').

1 and a half inward ('B').

Half circle out ('A'). Half circle in ('B').

B
INWARD ROTATIONS

Figure 1. Hand Rotations

As we make the **'outward'** rotation we support the 'signal' by expressing 'happy' – facially, vocally, getting 'happier' on each rotation, and on the **'inward'** rotations 'sad', getting 'sadder' and 'sadder'.

Game 12b   Hands – Delayed

This is the same as Game 12a, but this time start with neutral emotion. Only gradually, as the hand signals give the 'happy' outward rotations, does the rest of the body expression follow suit. On the return eight inward rotations, the face and other body parts try to keep 'happy' as the hands express 'sad' succumbing to an expression of 'misery' only on the last few inward revolves.

The above is an example of the *'movement language'*[3] betraying the true feelings of the person, before they are openly acknowledged by him. Just to labour this point: in the above example, at the start of, say, the inward rotations, the character is really feeling miserable, but tries to put a brave face on it, until it all gets too much for him and he gives in on the final inward rotation.

This introduces an interesting *Commedia* skill, the ability to communicate more than one signal at the same time, expressing different, even conflicting, emotions – so that a character smiling courteously and speaking words of welcome lets us know by *movement language* that he is furiously angry with an unexpected guest.

The difficulty of doing this can be demonstrated by asking any question that would normally elicit a 'Yes' or 'No' answer. The person replying tries to give the opposing *movement language* signal, with his answer.

Example: 'A' asks a question 'Did you have a good lunch?'. If the answer would be in the affirmative, 'B' says 'Yes – yes, very good – yes' but at the same time shakes his head giving the 'No' signal. Conversely if the answer were 'No, it was very poor', 'B' gives the affirmative signal by nodding his head.

Game 13   Pierrot Rotations

Stand with the feet together, toes turned out (see Fig. 2, page 32).

The formula is the same as for Game 12b, but instead of the rotations being made at the wrists they are made at the elbows. The arms are raised to the sides – parallel with the floor. The forearms are first dropped down vertically, then brought upwards, the hands near the chest. They continue moving upwards to form right angles to the upper arms, and finally return to the starting position. Keep the upper arms horizontal and as still as possible throughout. This is the *positive* or **'outward '** rotation. For the *negative* or **'inward'** rotation, the direction is reversed.

---

3. I prefer this to 'body language', which implies an unconscious signal, whereas 'movement language' is under the actor's control.

OUTWARD (POSITIVE)   ENDING POSITION   INWARD (NEGATIVE)   ENDING POSITION

Figure 2. The Pierrot Rotations

Use the **numerical reduction** as before, but in addition bend the knees out (heels down, ballet *demi plié*) on the end of the *positive* rotations and turn them in (knock knees) on the end of the *negative*. In addition at this moment of dejection, the body can slump to either side, giving a further negative signal (see Figure 2, above).

> This game is a useful point of reference for students as it brings to life the familiar 'Poor Pierrot' of popular imagination. The routine should be done fairly slowly and with loads of 'moonlit' emotion!

Game 14a   Yes, Yes – No, No

(We return to the wrist rotations for these next few games.)

For this we make the 8 hand rotations, but gradually raise the arm from low to high as you do the outward positive rotations, and lower the arm on the 8 inward negative ones. The signal may be supported by saying 'Yes' on each of the positive and 'No' on the negative. The exercise can be done with first the right then the left arm and then with both together. A little sway of the body and the head will prevent the movement becoming too mechanical.

Game 14b   Welcome

In *Commedia* there are two kinds of timing, both important: the *dancer/ musician's rhythm* and the *actor/comedian's timing*. The first basically keeps to a repetitive and continuous beat. The *actor's timing* is more flexible and, although still rhythmic, follows the emotional or comic requirements of the scene, rather than a musical tempo. In the next game we can use *actor's timing* to make the rotations freer and more natural.

One at a time the class improvise a welcoming speech, using the outward rotations.

Example: the movements (all outward rotations) are made simultaneously with the words):

'My dear	(both hands outward rotate)
Ladies	(right hand)
and Gentlemen	(left hand)
May I say	(left hand)
how utterly	(both hands)
delighted I am	(both hands high)
to see you	(right hand, then left)
all!'	(both hands, opening the arms apart)

Game 14c Dismiss

As an alternative, each person can improvise a short speech using the inward 'negative' movement. It can be done with either arm, or both.

Example: in this case using one arm only. To increase the idea of 'dismissal' the arm, held at about chest height, starts close to the body extending outward on each of the hand rotations, which also get smaller and smaller.

'Go away,	(large rotation close to chest)
I said, **Go a . . . way**	(2 smaller/quicker twists extending arm)
and don't come . . .	(large slow rotation)
. . . **back**	(quick, arm now straight)
. . . **ever!'**	(merest flick of the fingers)

This last is an example of the rule that once the actor gains the audience's attention by a broad gesture, they will follow even the smallest and most subtle of gestures.

Practice Drill: Shoulder Movements

1. Raise and lower both shoulders. (Arms hang down loosely.) Do this 4 times.
    (Count: **Raise**/ 2 3 4. **Lower**/ 2 3 4. **Raise**/ 2 3 4. **Lower**/ 2 3 4 etc.)

2. Move both shoulders forward, and return to the neutral position. 4 times. (Count: as above.)

3. Pull the shoulders down as much as possible, then return to neutral. 4 times. (Same count.)

4. Pull the shoulders as far back as possible, then return to neutral. 4 times. (Same count.)

Make sure that in each action the movement is as isolated as possible. Arms will naturally rise with the shoulders, and should be kept relaxed, but when you do 'pulling shoulders back', for example, check to see that you are not also thrusting the chest forward.

5. Now repeat the sequence with the right shoulder alone (the left remaining still). Then with the left shoulder alone.

6. For this movement raise the **left** shoulder up, and at the same time bring the **right** into the forward position.

    Alternate with **right** shoulder up and the **left** shoulder forward.

7. Now we can relate this movement to a traditional Harlequin *'attitude'* (see page 147). The right shoulder thrusts forward, and the left raises up (as before, arms still loosely by the sides). As you do this you bend the knees suddenly, one foot crossed in front of the other, its toe touching the ground). The head juts forward and the mouth gapes wide in a rather ape-like expression of astonishment!

The next shoulder drill uses rotation.

8. Raise shoulders and rotate them forward through each of the positions (forward, down, back, and up again).

    After a few circles, rotate them backwards (from up, to back, down and forward).

9. Repeat with one shoulder at a time.

10. Now rotate the shoulders in opposition; the **right** going forward and up, as the **left** goes back and down.

11. Next we get half circles: **'Over'** (that is from back to front via up, or from front to back via up) and **'Under'** (from back to front via down, or from front to back via down).

That completes the drills; now we can use them more interestingly in a game.

Game 15   Shift the Shoulders

This is played in 'mirror position'. Pairs facing each other a few feet apart. Partner 'A' selects moves from the shoulder drill adding an appropriate emotional tone. Partner 'B' mirrors the move and reacts to the emotional stimulus.

An example might be (the words are sub-text and needn't be articulated):

'A' slowly raises both shoulders threateningly.
'B' responds with the same movement but apprehensively.
'A' drops right shoulder suddenly. Mimes: 'I'll get you!'
'B' drops left shoulder: 'Who, me?'
'A' slowly takes both shoulders over and back. 'Yes, you.'
'B' duplicates the move but expressing – 'Oh, no'.
'A' sudden over and forward – 'Oh, yes'.
'B' duplicates the move but expressing – 'Help!'

Partner 'B' is then given a chance to initiate the moves. The scenario could equally well be 'seductive' or one of building up laughter. A more advanced version may be played by the *'initiation'* being alternated. 'A' starts ,'B' copies. Then 'B' initiates and 'A' copies.

Now we are ready for a demonstration of commedia acting.

What is Meant by Commedia Acting?

If you have followed this far, a pattern should be emerging; however, it might be a good time to give a demonstration of just what distinguishes *Commedia* from other forms of acting.

Commedia is exaggerated acting, but it should be the exaggeration of a truth. Its parallel in illustration is caricature, which takes a politician's bulbous nose, or a royal prince's large ears (facts, truths) and 'exaggerates' them for our amusement. Its target is often the same as that of *Commedia* – an attack on the foibles of human vanity and pomposity.

The following is to contrast the difference in the style, goal and purpose of *Commedia* with the extreme naturalism of a TV soap opera. It is an example that has proved workable in the classroom, but other scenarios could, and should, be experimented with.

Game 16   Soap to Commedia

Let us imagine a typical TV soap opera scenario. Carol X is alone on screen for a few moments; she has an important decision to make. She has been left a small legacy from Aunt Y. Should she spend it on that holiday to Majorca she's always wanted or invest it in Brian Z's plans for an electrical repair firm? She must make that phone call to tell him yes or no. She deliberates.

Mime this out in a style low key and naturalistic enough to be acceptable to the TV cameras, but still communicating her indecision. Perhaps she puts her hand to her mouth. Taps her teeth twice with her finger nail, scratches her ear and takes a big breath. Walks towards the phone; hesitates and walks away, takes a breath, walks back to the phone and picks it up.

Now we 'Commedia–ise' it!

Retain the same motivation, and the same basic moves but broaden and exaggerate them by setting them to a rhythm:

1/ 2, 3, 4.   The foot starts tapping in rhythm as the hand goes to the mouth.

2/ 2, 3, 4.   The finger taps the teeth 4 times, the foot still tapping.

3/ 2, 3, 4.   The hand scratches the ear. The foot movement continues.

4/ 2, 3, 4.   Foot movement stops. The arms drop to the sides and the shoulders shrug followed by a big release of breath.

Repeat from the top, this time accenting the first beat of each bar, bending and stretching the knees: **5**/ 2. 3. 4. **6**/ 2. 3. 4. **7**/ 2. 3. 4. **8**/ 2. 3. 4.

1/ 2, 3, 4.	Pause to deliberate!
2/ 2, 3, 4.	A decisive walk to the phone.
3/ 2, 3, 4.	Freeze for 2 beats, shake head: 'No, no, no.'
4/ 2, 3, 4.	Walk away, on the rhythm.
5/ 2, 3, 4.	Freeze for 2 beats. Nod head: 'Yes, yes, yes!'
6/ 2, 3, 4.	Walk to phone on the rhythm.
7/ 2, 3, 4.	Freeze, shake head frantically: 'No, no, no, no.'
8/ 2, 3, 4.	*Run* away. Double rhythm.
1/ 2, 3, 4.	Big breath, Clench fist across the body: 'Yes!'
	Break rhythm: casual walk to phone, pick it up non-chalantly.

Practice Drill: Foot Rotations

Stand on the left foot, raise the right foot just above the ground and rotate it at the ankle 8 times in an outward circle (clockwise) and 8 times in an inward circle (anticlockwise). Repeat with other foot.

Game 17   Bold and Shy

Stand with the weight on the left foot, right foot just off the floor, the leg extended to the side.

Count:**1**/ 2, 3, 4.	The right foot makes 4 outward rotations. End with flexed heel touching the floor.
Count:**2**/ 2, 3, 4.	Arms starting close in and extend outward as you make 4 outward *hand* rotations (foot remains still).

That's the BOLD bit: head held high, chest expanded.

Count:**3**/ 2, 3, 4.	*Hands* make 4 inward rotations as arms are brought gradually close in.

Count:4/ 2, 3, 4.   Foot makes the 4 inward rotations coming closer in on each. The 4th ends with the foot and knee turned in, toe touching the floor; the body shrinks and turns bashfully away to the left.

Yes, that's the SHY bit!

Head Movements

We use four types of head movement:

1.   Turning.
2.   Tipping (see page 39).
3.   Rotating.
4.   Lateral 'translating' (see page 77).

Game 18   Eyes Right, Eyes Left

This demonstrates head *turning*: unlike the owl, we humans are limited to a quarter turn of the head to either side (without moving shoulders, trunk or feet).

Stand straight, arms at the side, head facing front.

Count 1. Turn head smartly to right, chin over right shoulder.

Count 2. Return head to front.

Count 3. Turn head smartly to left, chin over left shoulder.

Count 4. Return head to front.

Count 5. Repeat to right.

Count 6. Return to front.

Count 7. Repeat to left.

Count 8. Return head to front.

Continue by repeating from the top, *but* reverse the head directions by making Count 1 to the *left* instead of to the right, and Count 3 to the right, and so on.

When you've got the above (so it can be done without thinking) do it again *but* as you do the first '8', take 8 small steps forward R, L, R, etc., and as you do the second '8', take 8 small steps back R, L, R, etc.

Game 19   *Jaunty Walks*

This introduces head *tipping*, or inclining. It is also a 'contrary vector' exercise, a sort of movement equivalent of the tongue twister, and serves a similar purpose. It helps increase physical, rather than vocal, dexterity.

Turn feet outward. Starting with the right foot, take seven rhythmic walks forward.

Hold the eighth count.

Starting with the left foot take seven walks back.

Hold still the eighth count.

On each step incline the head from one side to the other. On the first step on the right foot incline the head to the right (over the right shoulder) and on the second step tip it over to the left (over left shoulder) and so on. Hold it over on the right on the eighth count. Keep it there (inclined to the right) as you make your first step backwards and tip it to the left on the second step backward. Again hold it to the right after you've completed the 7 steps back. And you're ready to start again. (Are you?)

> The inclining of the head is a very typical nineteenth-century Harlequin gesture, which will be included in a later section.

We'll end the warm-ups with an energetic jumping sequence.

Drill for Jumps

Stand with the feet together.

Count 1. Jump in the air landing with the legs apart, knees bent.

Count 2. Draw the legs back together again by sliding the feet along the floor. Repeat ad lib.

Game 20a Quarter Jumps

Count **1/** As you make the first jump turn a quarter turn to the right.

Count 2. Stay facing the right side as you draw the legs together.

Count 3. Jump to face the back (feet apart).

Count 4. Stay facing the back as you again draw feet together.

Count 5. Jump a quarter turn clockwise to face left (stage-left).

Count 6. Stay facing there as you close feet.

Count 7. Complete the circle by jumping to face front again.

Count 8. Stay facing front as you draw legs together.

Count **2/** Again jump to face right side.

Count 2. Make quarter turn to the back as you draw feet together.

Count 3. Jump feet out to face left (stage-left).

Count 4. Draw feet together to face front.

Count 5. Jump a *half* circle to face back (landing feet apart).

Count 6. Draw feet together turning half circle to front.

Count 7. Jump a *full* turn in the air to land feet apart, facing front.

Count 8. Keep knees bent and hold position.

Applause!

A Note on Masks

The above sequence is an opportunity to introduce masks for the first time. The routine should be learned before putting on the masks. Use **practice profile** masks, as described in the Appendix. Make sure that the nose of the mask points precisely to the direction faced, and that the eye level is straight forward, neither up nor down. It is a good idea to divide into two groups, so you observe each other, in turn. Errors will be apparent which are not so obvious to you when you are working in the mask.

Game 20b   Opposing Quarter Jumps

This can be done in two groups. The first group does the routine as before in a *clockwise* direction, making their first quarter jump to the right, while the second group does the routine at the same time but turning in an *anticlockwise* direction, making their first quarter jump to the left.

Game 20c   Free Quarter Jumps

Divide into small groups, and give each a theme. For example, Group 'A' might pretend they are in a haunted house, and each jump is made in reaction to a 'spooky noise' made by one or more fellow students. This is a good development because it frees the players from a rigid rhythmic beat. The set routine is adhered to, but the timing of the movements depends on noises made by their colleagues.

Game 20d   Random Quarter Jumps

This works best with a small group who must know their 'directions' well. Here a random element is introduced into the directions instead of, as in Game 20c, the timing. A steady beat of 16 slow counts is maintained and the players select at random any one of the movements – quarter, half, and whole turns in *any* direction. This works particularly well with a scenario such as being 'lost in an alien environment'.

6

7

MIME AND MOVEMENT GAMES

Introduction

It is a basic tenet of stagecraft that the actor must know his **'Front'**; it is an ancient part of his art. Long ago it was perhaps the sacred totem, the ark of the covenant, the altar, the kingly presence, and always of course the audience; one turns one's back on it only in defiance. This awareness of 'Front' is perhaps more important in *Commedia* than in other theatre forms; as we will discuss later it is essential for the proper use of the masks. Here we are concerned with its application to stage 'orientation' – the eight directions. To this sense of 'Front', which still applies, even in the open air, in theatre in the round, in any performing situation, the actor must anchor all other positions and directions. Many of the games which follow only work if the directions are precisely made.

The Eight Directions

In the jumping sequence with which we ended the Warm-up section you will have noticed that we introduced four of the directions: front, side right, back, and side left (stage left, which is not always your left) They form an 'addition' cross (see Fig. 3a, below). Now we add four more, i. e., right diagonal front, right diagonal back, left diagonal back, and left diagonal front. These form a multiplication cross (Fig. 3b). If we superimpose one on the other we get a compass of 8 points (Fig. 3c). Now we number them in clockwise order starting with 'Front' ((Fig. 3d)).

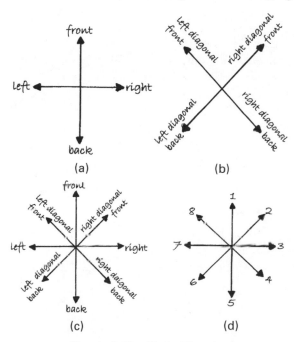

Figure 3. The Eight Directions

1/   **Front,**
2/   **Right diagonal front,**
3/   **Side right,**
4/   **Right diagonal back,**
5/   **Back,**
6/   **Left diagonal back,**
7/   **Side left,**
8/   **Left diagonal front.**

This directional numbering can be useful in rehearsal and also in performance improvisation.[1]

Directional Lunging Drill

A simple exercise for identifying and using the directions.

Stand straight, facing front, feet together, and arms by the sides. Head, shoulders, torso remain facing **front** throughout, no matter in which direction the leg moves. The basic 'Lunge' is a sudden forward movement ending with the advancing leg supporting the weight of the body on a bent knee, the other leg remaining straight as in the fencer's movement. We extend this to mean a similar move in any direction.

The count should be slow and deliberate. The '**&**' (and), is another borrowing from dancers, and is used so that there no is confusion between the counts and the directions. See Fig. 4, opposite.

Count 1/ Lunge with the right leg directly forward to direction 1 [dir. 1].
Count &/ Return to starting position.

Count 2/ Lunge to right diagonal front with the right leg [dir. 2].
Count &/ Return to starting position.

Count 3/ Lunge to side with the right leg (torso still front) [dir. 3].
Count &/ Return to starting position.

Count 4/ Lunge to right diagonal back with the right leg [dir. 4] (torso front).
Count &/ Return to starting position.

Count 5/ Lunge back [dir. 5] with left leg! (but still facing front).
Count &/ Return to starting position.

Count 6/ Lunge to left diagonal back with the left leg [dir. 6].
Count &/ Return to starting position.

Count 7/ Lunge to left side [dir. 7] (with the left leg, of course).
Count &/ Return to starting position.

---

1. A similar idea is used in Italian ballet (Cecchetti). I was coached in the Harlequin role in 'Carnaval' by Idzikowski who had performed the role in the Diaghilev Company. He told me that the *Commedia* companies had also used the system. Unfortunately I have not found any documentary evidence. It is in any case a valuable instrument for modern *Commedia*.

DIR 1:FRONT   DIR 2:R.DIAG FRONT

DIR 3: SIDE RIGHT   DIR 4: R.DIAG BACK

DIR 5: BACK   DIR 6: L. DIAG BACK

DIR 7: SIDE LEFT   DIR 8: L. DIAG FRONT

Figure 4. Directional Lunging

Count 8/ Lunge to left diagonal front [dir. 8] (left leg).
Count &/ Return to starting position.

Also practise in an anticlockwise circle, which will give:
Lunge to: [dir. 1, 8, 7, 6, 5, 4, 3, 2.]

From now on we will often use the shorthand **[dir. 1–8]** to indicate direction, which can refer to general body direction, or the direction of any body part. For example, in the above sequence on count 3/ we have the lunge made to [dir. 3] with the head and torso still facing [dir. 1] but one could make the lunge to [dir. 3] with the torso and shoulders also facing [dir. 3] and perhaps just the head facing [dir. 1]. One can also travel towards any of the eight directions. So if you had the instruction: move towards [dir. 7] while facing [dir. 5] you would have your back to the audience moving to *your* right, or stage left. This may seem at first a little over-complicated, but it is very useful and worth spending some time on.

Game 21a   The Harmonic Lunges

This is worked in pairs, who face front standing about 4 feet apart. Partner 'A', who is to the right of 'B', does the lunging drill in a clockwise circle; partner 'B' in an anticlockwise circle. The instructor gives the count as before. The students are to be encouraged to express their reactions to one another as the spatial relationship varies (on count 3 they are trying to get away from each other; on count 7 they are coming together). Repeat with each going the other way round.

Game 21b   Random Lunges
[Masks: practice profile][2]

The instructor still gives the count – or a clap or drumbeat can be used. The players now have eight lunges in directions of their own choosing. They can use *any* one of the 8 lunges in *any* order, reacting and relating

---

2. Suggestions for appropriate masks are given in square brackets (see Appendix for profile mask). Their use is not essential at this stage.

to each other as they wish. If they are careful to maintain the accuracy of the positions, no matter which ones they strike, a kind of 'harmonic picture' is preserved. As the musician uses harmony to please the ear, and the painter uses composition to satisfy the eye, the performer uses both to create a sense of well-being in his audience which is, perhaps surprisingly, a helpful condition for laughter.

Game 22a   The Lantern
[Masks: practice profile]

Stand with the feet apart and turned out (ballet 2nd position). Hold a mimed or prop lantern in the right hand, prepare to bend the knees and sway, while 'searching' with the lantern.

1.   Sway to right [dir. 3].
2.   Sway to left [dir. 7].
3.   Sway diagonal forward [dir. 2] stepping onto the right foot.
4.   Sway diagonal back [dir. 6] stepping back onto the left foot.
5.   Step back with right foot to diagonal right and sway diagonal back [dir. 4].
6.   Sway diagonal forward onto the left foot [dir. 8].
7.   Sway to the side right onto the right foot [dir. 3].
8.   Sway to the side left onto the left foot [dir. 7].

Game 22b   The Lantern Figure 8
[Masks: practice profile]

Still miming the lantern.

Count:

1/ 2, 3,   Take 3 furtive steps turning in a circle on yourself (clockwise): right, left, right.
4.   Close the left foot to the right foot *without* putting weight on it.

2/ 2, 3,   Take 3 furtive steps turning in a circle on yourself (anti-clockwise): left, right, left.
4.   Close the right foot to the left foot to complete a figure '8' floor pattern.

Next run 22a followed immediately by 22b to form a short routine, and practise it until it can be performed with ease.

Game 22c   The Lantern Impro
[Masks: practice profile or Zanni]

The routine of Games 22a and 22b should be tried in pairs, side by side. It can then be varied with the couple starting on opposite feet, swaying in against each other. There are a half dozen or so such variations, e.g., back-to-back, facing each other, one behind the other, etc. Working in pairs and trios the students are given time to develop the idea. They are then asked to perform the set routine and extend it with a further sequence of their own devising, in the same style, and remembering that the only light is from the dim lanterns.

> This is part of the tradition of the *'night scene'* found in all early theatre. Most performances would have been in daylight so the lantern became the symbol for 'night'. The goals in these games are to create an air of menace, the steps creeping and cautious. Here we explore a feature of *Commedia*, which is that the feet and legs maintain a continuous rhythm (almost dance) while the upper part of the body explores the greater freedom of the actor.

> In the final improvised part, the couples usually lose one another; walk backward and bump into each other (pantomime); freeze and then break the rhythm by running off in fear, etc., but this is up to the performers themselves.

Ribcage Drills

Ribcage drill: side-to-side

In modern dance this is usually called 'translation' (non-dancers often find it difficult but amusing to learn). Stand upright and slide the ribcage gently first to the right and then slowly to the left. The difficulty is that the movement must be isolated so that other parts of the body do not move, paying particular attention to the hips, which must remain immobile. The shoulders naturally move laterally with the ribcage but must remain level, with the arms hanging relaxed by the sides.

Ribcage drill: forward and back

This is even trickier! Here the ribcage 'floats' forward and through the central normal position to as far back as it can. Again the ribcage is isolated from other movement. The pelvis must remain static, and the shoulders must remain relaxed and make no independent movement of their own.

Ribcage drill: rotations

When the above has been mastered, we do a ribcage rotation by making the forward move, followed by a quarter of a circle (clockwise) to the right side, continue a quarter to the back, a quarter to the left, and a final quarter to the front. The circle can then be repeated in an anticlockwise direction: side left, back, side right and front, stopping briefly in each position.

Game 23   Focusing Mime, Using the Ribcage
[Masks: *Commedia dell'Arte* as named]

Partners stand as far apart as possible across the available space. They take a few small steps towards each other. Then stop; they are trying to identify the figure approaching them. They add suitable gestures (shading the eyes, rubbing the chin, scratching the head) as they do the ribcage movement focusing on the distant person.

Example:
Pantalone and The Doctor perceive each other at a distance.

Mime: Subtext[3]	*Ribcage Movement*
'There's someone coming!'	Side right, side left, side right.
'Who can it be?'	Circle of clockwise quarters.

Both take a few more steps towards each other.

'I do believe it's . . . '	Anticlockwise rotation.
'Can't be, he's got a limp!'	Back, forward, back.
'It is him! Damn nuisance!'	Side to side.
(*Aloud.*) 'Ah, hello my friend.'	Waving and coming together, etc, etc.

---

3. Subtext: the actor's silent inner monologue, which helps clarify the actions and emotions to be expressed.

Hip Isolation Drills

These are more easily achieved than the ribcage movements, but I have found it better to do them after trying the ribcage exercises, as any little reluctance or embarrassment felt by students should have evaporated by then.

Side-to-side

Stand upright but this time, with the knees slightly bent, swing the hips to the right and then to the left. Again, make no extraneous movements, paying particular attention to the torso, and also to the shoulders, which mustn't 'tip', but remain horizontal. (There will be a natural movement of the knees from side to side.)

Note: *These moves can be done 'academically' – just as movement – but it is usually a good idea to introduce a comic or character element in their execution from the beginning.*

Forward and back

This is simple, and just consists of thrusting the pelvis forward, and back (sticking the bottom well out). Just check for isolation: that there are no unnecessary movements.

Hip rotations

Hips thrust forward, then –

1. A *quarter* circle (clockwise) to the right, hip extended.
2. Quarter circle to the back, bottom stuck out.
3. Quarter circle to the left, hip out.
4. Quarter circle to the front, bottom tucked under.

Repeat the drill in an anticlockwise direction. Also perform the movement using the numerical reduction, i. e., four quarter circles clockwise. Four quarter circles anticlockwise. Two *half* circles clockwise (from front to back, and from back to front). Two half circles anticlockwise. One *complete* rotation clockwise. One complete rotation anticlockwise.

Game 24   Happy Hips
[Masks: Pantalone and The Doctor]

Couples face each other a few feet apart – mirroring each other's movements. For partner 'A' the routine is:

> Clockwise rotation of 4 quarter circles, of *ribcage*.
> Clockwise rotation of 4 quarter circles, of *hips*.
> Repeat the above.

> *Partner 'B's rotations, being a mirror of 'A's, will be in an anticlockwise direction.*

Now we add the 'emotional' content, expressed with face and hand gestures, in the following sequence:

> 'Happy Ribs' as you do the 1st circle.
> 'Happy Hips' as you do the 2nd circle.
> 'Angry Ribs' as you do the 3rd circle.
> 'Angry Hips' as you do the 4th circle.

Drill: the Leans

'To lean', for our purposes, means to incline the upper body from the waist, and it can be done in each of the directions. Practise them through in order; clockwise [dirs. 1, 2, 3, 4, 5, 6, 7, 8], and anticlockwise [1, 8, 7, 6, 5, 4, 3, 2], then do them in random order such as that below (note: you're facing [dir. 1] throughout):

Example only: Lean: [dir. 1], then [dir. 5] [dir. 3] [dir. 7] [dir. 1] [dir. 2] [dir. 6] [dir. 8] [dir. 4] [dir. 1] [dir. 5].

Figure 5. Lean to Dir. 7

Game 25   Zanni Prologue
[Masks: Zanni, none for Zanne]

One of the servant Masks of the *Commedia dell'Arte*, a *zanni* (male) or *zanne* (female) welcomes the audience and sets the scene. He or she stands centre stage and improvises a speech using the leans, with appropriate arm and hand gestures. The servant Masks tend to use movements with the hands flat, fingers together, palms up, alternated with clenched fists going to the waist.

An Example (Zan Padella)

'Well, well, well.	Leans back [dirs. 6, then 4, then 6]. Hands on hips.
Good folk of Torino	Lean back [dir. 5]. Arms wide, palms up.
Welcome	Lean forward [dir. 1]. Arms still out.
You remember me,	Lean [dir. 2].
Zan Padella, your servant	Lean [dir. 8].
Pantalone's servant,	Lean back [dir. 5].
Everybody's servant.	Increase lean [dir. 5].
You remem . . . No that wasn't my fault. How was I to know she	[Dir 8] pointing at member of the audience. Then stand straight.
was the Mayor's wife?	Turn back on audience and pause.
Anyway welcome and let	Return to facing front.
me fill you in.	Lean back [dir. 5].
There's just been an	Well forward [dir. 1] confidential.
awful row . . .	Twist upper body and look [dir 4].
Pantalone and The Captain.	
	Return to [dir. 1] whisper.
You don't believe me? Well, there has . . . '	

And so on, and so on . . .

Here we have introduced a bit of word improvisation. The player can use a Cockney or other regional accent. It is included here and not in the Word Games section because the stylised movement is the more important factor. In any case there is no real division of skills in performance, and they are separated in this book only for convenience in learning.

In the example above you will notice that the *zanni* breaks the routine, making a completely unrelated movement by turning his back on the spectators. This is an important moment, which we call the *'break'*, where the actor escapes from the formula and stylisation, relaxes and waits for the audience to catch up. It should come at a dramatic or emotional climax. It can be a real 'moment of theatre'. To achieve it, the performer has to withdraw from the role. It is a moment of stillness and silence. There is an opposite mechanism where the tension is held – this is a *'hold'* or *'freeze'*.

Drill: the Sways

As the servants tend to express themselves with *'Leans'*, the masters prefer to employ the *'Sways'*. The **Sway** is a gentle curving movement, again possible in each of the directions. The hips lead, but instead of being isolated as in the 'Hip' movements (page 52) they are part of an arc made by the whole torso. The feet and legs are kept close together while the head remains on a plumb-line over the feet.

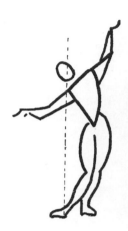

N. B. It is the hips that lead and give the direction, so that a move like **Sway [dir. 1]** (a move frequently used by Pantalone to express surprise), might seem to be a backward **Lean** not a forward **Sway**. The rule is that in **Leans** the shoulders lead, and in **Sways** the hips lead!

Figure 6. Sway to Dir. 7

Unlike those of the Servants, hand gestures tend to be flowery, relaxed, the fingers separating from each other in rolling and unrolling movements (these are explained further on pages 65 and 67). Those with ballet training have the advantage of experience in the right type of flowing *'port de bras'*, but there is a major difference: the Baroque *Commedia* (seventeenth century) encouraged a break in the line at elbow and wrist (see page 70), which has performance values as well as purely stylistic ones (see Fig. 13 and the picture on page 72).

Game 26   A Lover Confides in the Audience

The Lovers are among the Masters and here he/she addresses the audience.

'As you will no doubt have gleaned,   Hip curve (sway) to [dir. 7].

I am on the horns of a dilemma;   Hip sways over to [dir. 3].

an uncomfortable position at the best of times . . .   Hip sways to [dir. 6].

And alas, for me, these are not the best of times.   Slow deep movement to [dir. 2].

Falsely accused . . .   Quick transfer to [dir. 3].

denied access to the object of my adoration . . .   Huge sigh and transfer to [dir. 7].

Scorned . . .   Quick to [dir. 3].

. . . Shunned . . .   Quick back to [dir. 7].

Without a friend in the world . . .

Break: TURNS AND STARTS TO WALK TOWARDS [dir. 4] THEN RETURNS

. . . Or are you my friends?'   Deep and elegant sway to [dir. 8].

Tapis Walks

The following series of games are based on a mime movement, which we call **tapis walks**. *Tapis*, French for carpet, also referred to a 'moving

carpet' – a device, resembling the moving walkways of airports, which was installed in the more affluent Paris theatres of the early 1800's and in conjunction with the 'panorama' rolling backcloth, gave an illusion of movement. For those who couldn't afford to install one (and for us), **tapis walks** provide a cheap alternative. They are usually seen in profile, so we'll start the walk on, say, the left side of the stage facing right [dir. 3], legs together, feet turned straight. Imagine that the knees are tied together and then take small rhythmic walks (made with heels first and toes turned up. See picture on left). You

8

are travelling very gradually towards stage right. For the moment head and shoulders are also facing the way you're going.

Game 27a *Tapis Front Cloth*
[Masks: practice profile or frontal]

In a conventional theatre this would be done down-stage, before the front cloth, entering from the wing nearest the audience on either side. We will do it from stage left (as above). Here is a good example of using the **Numerical Reduction** to theatrical effect.

Counts **1**/ to 8.   Eight *tapis walks* with the head facing the way you're going [dir. 3]

Counts **2**/ 2, 3, 4.   Continue with four more *tapis walks*, but with the head facing the audience! [body dir. 3, head dir. 1]

Counts 5, 6, 7, 8.   Four *tapis walks* with head facing the way you are going [dir. 3]

Counts **3**/ 2, 3, 4.   Two *tapis walks* with head facing audience [dir. 1]

Two *tapis walks* with head facing the way you're going [dir. 3]

Counts 5, 6, 7, 8.   One *tapis walk* with head facing audience [dir. 1]

One *tapis walk* with head facing the way you're going [dir. 3]

One *tapis walk* with head facing [dir. 1]

One *tapis walk* with head facing [dir. 3]

Counts **4**/ to 8.   Eight *tapis walks* exiting right wing, head [dir. 3].

Divide the class into threes or fours. The above movement is performed in file, one closely behind the other. While preserving the routine each group can devise their own variation, e. g. (a) smile and wave with the right hand when facing the audience, and deadpan when facing the way you are going, or (b) slouch miserably when facing [dir. 3] and cry when facing the front [dir. 1]. The head movements must always be done very sharply and any emotional change must be equally abrupt.

Game 27b   Tapis Animation (One)
[Masks: none]

This is worked by one person at a time, using the basic continuous *tapis walks* with the head facing front [dir. 1] throughout. Each performer has to assume an expression, which reveals an emotion or thought, and maintain that expression without it dimming, altering or flickering on and off. The actor can use the face, arms and any upper part of the body, but the pose adopted must not move or vary throughout the crossing. We call this *tapis 'animation'* because it echoes the economy used by cartoon animators wherein the upper part of a figure makes no change while the legs move.

> It is quite a difficult acting exercise. Here we are looking for truth; that is, theatrical truth. The starting expression must be pure, and absolutely unquavering, and the actor behind the character must not be intrusive.

Game 27c   Tapis Cross-Fades

This, as before, crosses from one wing to the other. The aim now is to start with one expression (that is, one thought), and imperceptibly change it to another. It is not a rule, but the face normally starts in the direction you're going and turns very slowly towards the audience, and away again.

Example

Character 'A' might enter and gradually become aware of the audience, head turning slowly to front, register surprise or embarrassment and slowly turn shyly away.

Or Character 'B' enters in deep thought, becomes aware of the audience, scowls at them and exits in high dudgeon.

Character 'C' might enter with deadpan expression, spot the audience and greet them with a gradually expanding manic smile. Continue to look front and so bump into the wing at the other side of the stage as he exits.

Game 27d   Tapis Animation (Two)

Here we take the 'animation' connection a step further. We count the **tapis walks** in fours.

Count **1**/ 2 3 4 animation X (1st set of face/upper body movements)

Count **2**/ 2 3 4 animation Y (2nd set of face/upper body movements)

Example

On the first 4 walks make four hand movements with right hand pointing to [dir. 3], with head also to [dir. 3]. Then four fist-shaking movements with right hand, head turned to [dir. 1]. Repeat first four finger points, but head still [dir. 1]. Last four fist-shakes while exiting, head [dir. 3].

Game 28a   Pierrot Passes By
[No mask: Pierrot white face]

This is the first of two similar stage crossings across the front of the stage, but for Commedia dell'Arte Masks. Both are nineteenth century in style, but show a difference between Pierrot (French) and Harlequin (Italian) that had long existed.

Instead of **tapis walks**, Pierrot has his own step, which is done like this:

Face [dir. 3] feet together, raise right leg, lifting it as high as you can, but with a slight bend at the knee, toe well pointed. The knee of the left (supporting) leg also bends, and the heel comes off the floor (sorry, ballet dancers). The next step is made by stepping onto the ball of the right foot, and swishing the left through, till it is raised in front, as you did with the right.

Progress across the stage slowly, stepping right, left, right, left and so on. Don't stop!

The arms are very specific; a little difficult and awkward at first. Your head, feet

Figure 7. Pierrot Passes By

and your hips face the direction in which you're going [dir. 3], but your shoulders face front [dir. 1], like in an Egyptian painting. You must also lean back from the hips throughout! Now raise your arms with the elbows uppermost, to shoulder level. The hands (in costume, hidden by the long Pierrot sleeves) hang down, the arms forming the arc of a circle (see Fig. 7, page 59).

This is the traditional *lazzo*: as Pierrot walks, the head turns slowly towards the audience. Very gradually a look of horror spreads over the white face. Very slowly he turns his upper body away. The back arm circles round to the front to hide his face. The body leans forward and he sneaks off (without changing the step). The student can improvise any other reaction to the audience, but whatever it is it must be slow and continuous. Compare with further information on the character in Part Two.

Game 28b Harlequin Hurtles Past
[Masks: Harlequin or black domino]

The *Harlequin 'trot'* – this is a sort of 'knees up' movement. The right leg is raised with the knee well bent, and the foot pointed, and then

exchanged for the left in the same position, The best effect is if the supporting leg is slightly bent, and the landings are made on the *ball* of the foot. (Note: *this can be quite a strain on the calf muscles so only do it when you are fully warmed up.*) The torso is facing [dir. 3] with shoulders facing [dir. 1]. The curve of the arms is the reverse of Pierrot's, a curve raised to a mid position with the elbow's lowest, hands raised, with the palm of the right hand facing [dir. 3] and the palm of

Figure 8. Harlequin Hurtles Past

the left hand well behind you, facing [dir. 7]. As you trot don't let the back hand jog about.

The traditional *lazzo* is: 4 very quick trots on, 4 very quick trots with the head sharply turned to the audience. On the first of the next 4 trots, the right hand changes into a point, indicating [dir. 3] 'I'm going that way', and the left arm comes instantly into the waist. After 4 trots like this, the original position is resumed as he exits at speed. In executing this, the students are required to use the trot, and they must not stop, but otherwise they can act out any theme.

> Pierrot is timid about going anywhere, so he tends to lean back on entering, and forward as he leaves. His reactions are nearly always slow. Harlequin/Arlecchino, on the other hand, although he can have bouts of laziness, is usually restless, always wanting to get to somewhere else.

Game 29   Tweedling
[Masks: Zanni]

'Tweedling' is moving in pairs close together, shoulder-to-shoulder, like Tweedledum and Tweedledee. The game is improvised but a little preliminary practice of *'the creep'* makes it easier. That is: feet together, bend the knees. 'A' raises a bent left leg, toe turned up; puts it down making a pace forward, both knees bent. Repeat with other foot. 'B' does the same on the *opposite* leg.

Now the couple clasp hands tightly: 'A's right in 'B's left, arms straight down by the sides. 'A' pushes downwards, and 'B' pulls upwards, to create a firm tension between them; necessary so that 'B' can feel 'A's intentions. They must start side by side in very close contact. Very slowly 'A' improvises a forward creep, and 'B' moves with him. 'A' is giving the speed and direction. 'A' can draw feet together, pause a moment, and then walk backwards.

By pulling back the right arm (with the clasped hand), 'A' can bring the partners to face each other – or by pushing forward with the right arm the partners come back-to-back. In either of these last positions it is possible to change hands and move in a new direction. Using the joined arm 'A' can push 'B' into a side lunge, etc. By gradual acceleration the partners can keep together in a run or other fast movement. An experienced leader can 'control' a partner who has never done the exercise before. After a little practice a couple will be able to add a mime theme or dialogue.

Game 30a   Rhythm Afoot

This is a sequence where a basic rhythm made by walking, tapping or other movements made with the feet, is varied to communicate an idea or emotion. The steps are meant to be heard – sound being an important part of the impro. One of the most useful rhythms is called *'triplets'* from the musical term for three notes tied together. It in fact consists of four counts: (1) step (2) step (3) step (4) hold. This is repeated ad lib. There is no restriction on tempo or the type of step. The students are presented with this (or any other repeated rhythm) and asked to improvise a scene in which the rhythm is introduced and then altered to make a dramatic point. The examples should make it clear. The impros can be solo, in pairs, or small groups.

Solo Example: The Missing Purse
[Masks: Pantalone or other 'old' mask]

An elderly person is walking along the street, their mind on other things; expressed by *triplets* of small steps at a fairly rapid pace: right, left, right, pause – left, right, left, pause – right, left, right, pause – etc. As they reach centre we get: right, left, right, pause – left, right, left, pause – right, left, right – STOP (long pause), right, left, right STOP (long pause). Then only two steps: left, right STOP. Two more steps: left, right *STOP*. Thought: 'My purse! Did I leave it at the butcher's?' A series of steps, or stamps on place, as the person searches about his person for the purse. The stamps get faster as panic sets in. At last he finds it (big sigh of relief), right, left (starting to move off), STOP (gasp to get breath), left, right, STOP (gasp). Change to a fast continuous rhythm – left, right, left, right, left, right – etc. for exit.

Game 30b   Causerie
[Two or three persons. Masks: none or domino]

The basis for this is also *triplets* but in a rather 'dancy' form which needs to be practised first. It is a very feminine movement, and originates with the nineteenth-century Columbine and a girl friend. The step sequence is: two steps of the *triplet* made high up on the balls of the feet – right, left. On the third step, right (also on the toes), the stepping leg bends, giving a slight dip. The knees are kept together as the foot of the working leg (left), turned in, kicks up to the side, sole of the foot upwards, rather like a 1920's Charleston movement. The torso bends strongly towards the raised foot. Repeat the step starting on the other foot.

9

Two young ladies at a ball: as they do the triplets they flutter their fans in their right hands, and chat to each other ceaselessly (in mime, or actuality). They should start on opposite feet and advance from up-stage towards the audience. The tempo is really fast.

1/ 2, 3 – **2**/ 2, 3, – **3**/ 2, 3 – **4**/ 2, 3, triplets.

Pause for a bit of scandal, behind the fans.

1/ 2, 3 – **2**/ 2, 3, triplets.

Pause as Young Lady 'A' imparts a bit of scandal.

3/ 2, 3, – **4**/ 2, 3, triplets.

Pause for Friend 'B' to register incredulity!

1/ 2, 3, – **2**/ 2, 3 – **3**/ 2, 3 – **4**/ 2, 3, Demurely they face front.

Pause for whisper, crouching low. End with a shriek.

Change rhythm to fast tip-toe run 1, 2, 1, 2, 1, 2, 1, 2 . . .

As they do this they swing round to face wing [dir. 3].

Return to original triplets as they exit with barely contained laughter.

This can be done with three players, and is amusing if one is a man in the female character of the chaperone.

Game 30c   The Haunted House

[Masks: Callot or other 'Stupid Zanni']

This involves two players, one of them off-stage. The basic rhythm is a slow even beat as the on-stage performer enters the Haunted House. The off-stage player (who although not seen is clearly heard) starts with his partner and both give a clearly audible tread.

Player 'A' on-stage	Player 'B' off-stage
7 slow treads R. L. R. L. R. L. R.	7 treads (synchronized with 'A').
Pause to listen!	Silence!
4 slow treads R L, R, L. Stop.	Wait for 'A', then echo 'A's treads.
Trembles. Then 4 more steps.	
He listens for the echo. None.	
Sigh of relief till . . .	4 loud echoes.
Change of rhythm: in terror,	
runs towards exit, but can't	
get out. Return to first beat.	
3 treads and pause.	Silence.
3 treads and pause.	Echo, but 4 treads.
Puzzled 'A' tries 2 treads.	Echo 3.
He tries 3 treads again quicker.	Pause then lots of stamps.
Horrified; little runs on place.	Silence.
Then very slowly lifts leg and	
makes a very quiet step.	Silence.
Just raising other leg when . . .	Great clatter of noise.
Pause, then does rhythmic step:	
Da – da da – da – da . . .	*Da! Da!* [4]
Panic. Running all over.	
Goes to exit. Pause.	Hollow laugh.
Exit in terror.	

Finger Drills (*Inward*)

This is a fairly advanced but important element in *Commedia* style, particularly that wishing to duplicate the power, elegance, and exuberance of

---

4. The tap-dancing rhythm known as 'shave and a haircut – three bits'.

the seventeenth century. It is also one of the more difficult to describe or to pick up from the printed page. So give yourself a little time to understand it.

Drill 1

A beckoning movement: raise your right forearm towards [dir. 2], the hand, palm up, at about chest height, the elbow separated a little from the body. Starting with the little finger, draw the fingers towards you with a beckoning movement (see Fig. 9).

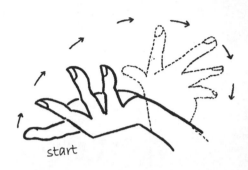

start

Note: *this should be a powerful or commanding gesture. The hand is tense; the fingers separated as much as possible. The hand also twists at*

Figure 9.
Beckoning movement (right hand)

the wrist so that the palm faces not upwards, but as much to the right as you can. There is a slight emphasis with the index finger, the thumb then closing quickly, ending with the hand clenched.

Alternate right and left hands, as if gathering people round you.

Drill 2

Now lift the right hand to eye level, and use it directly in front of you. Alternate hands in an almost hypnotic 'Come to me'.

Drill 3

This displays a bit of **movement language** – if, as above, you beckon towards the eyes it means 'Come to me'. Now use almost the same movement at waist level, drawing the hand towards the stomach and the meaning becomes 'Give it to me'.

Alternate 4 to the eyes: right, left, right, left, with 4 to the stomach, right, left, right, left.

Drill 4: Beckoning and Lunging

Start down-stage, and travel up-stage in a series of lunges.

Lunge up-stage with the right leg [dir. 5] shoulders and torso [dir. 3] but head stays facing front [dir. 1] as with the left hand you make the beckoning movement (in apposition) as if luring the audience to follow. Repeat with the left leg (towards [dir. 5] shoulders [dir. 7] head [dir. 1] and beckon with the right hand.

Two variations can be introduced as you travel up-stage: (a) as you lunge back with the right leg, bring your right arm across the body making the beckon in opposition; (b) instead of changing lunges by continuing to face front make a swift turn via [dir. 5]: that is, if you are lunging on the right leg continue clockwise and then lunge on the left leg.

Game 31   Said the Spider to the Fly
[Masks: sinister exotic [5] and Stupid Zanni]

There are two players. 'A's movement is based on the above drill, but with the orientation changed to one of crossing the stage (or any performance area) from one side to the other.

The goal is to lure performer 'B' across the stage from left to right and into the 'parlour' just off-stage. His movement is based on the lunge and beckon, but he is free to add any other movement (without touching) to cajole 'B' to follow (mesmerism, rope mime, pointing). The approach can also vary – angry, seductive, friendly – but whichever, it should be highly stylised, physically low (deep *plié*) and sensuous. 'B's moves, in contrast, are naturalistic, remaining upright, casual. A simpleton, he tries to resist but is intrigued. As the actor, he must in the end give in, so as not to **'block'** the impro, but as a Mask he refuses the invitation, for as long as he can. 'A's attention is entirely on her/his victim. 'B' can if he wishes communicate with the audience. 'Shall I? Yes? No?'

> We have met a few circumstances where the highly formal stylised movement is suddenly changed by the artist into a more natural one. In the above, one actor exaggerates the stylisation while the other plays in casual manner, acting as a foil – it is a known mechanism for creating comedy. A good workshop formula after the first impro is for 'B' to enact the 'A' role to a third person's 'B', and so on, till all have tried each character.

---

5. Any suitable non-*Commedia* mask.

Finger Drills (Politesse)

Drill 5

Unlike 'beckoning', there doesn't seem to be any word in common use for the outward movement. It is usually a movement denoting politeness or courtesy, hence the title. It is a reversal of the beckoning, with the thumb leading, followed by the index and then each of the other fingers. Again the wrist is twisted, and there should be a nice rolling rhythm as each finger is released from the clenched fist. Use the routine as in Drill 1, right and left hands alternating (see Fig. 10).

Figure 10.
Politesse movement (right hand)

Drill 6

This movement is a traditional one frequently seen in balletic mime.

Start with the hand near the mouth, making the finger movements as in Drill 5 – right hand, left hand, right hand, and right again 3 or 4 times getting smaller and more relaxed; the mouth opening and shutting to represent song, or speech.

The 'politesse' gesture is taken up again, after discussing the 5 positions of the feet.

Drills – the Positions and Stances

The five positions of the feet, established around the time of the founding of Louis XIV's Academy of Dancing in 1661, were undoubtedly known to many of the *Commedia* players. It is true that many of them were dancers, but one must also remember that dancing was not only a pastime but considered to be a training in refined movement, as important in distinguishing the *gentilhomme* from the *bourgeoisie* as the manner of his speech. The players, particularly on their sojourns in the French capital, would have wished to ape their betters if only to parody their affectations. In any case, the five positions are useful to us now, both as starting points for many movements and also if we wish to recreate the *Commedia* style at its apogee during the seventeenth century. Many will be familiar with them, but for those who aren't . . .

Of the five positions, three are closed, that is feet together, and two open, that is feet apart.

1st Position: Heels together, toes turned out (the turn out need be no more than '10 minutes to two' – not the ballet '15 mins to three').

2nd Position: An 'open' position, turned out as in 1st Position but with the feet about one foot apart.

3rd Position: Toes turned out and feet together as in 1st Position but with one foot in front of the other, the heel of the front foot against the arch of the back foot.

4th Position: This can be either made by separating and advancing either foot forward from 1st position – in which case it is called 'open' 4th position . . .

. . . or advanced from 5th position – in which case it is called 'crossed' 4th position.

5th Position: Like 3rd, but with the front foot crossed further, with the heel of the front foot touching the big toe joint of the other foot.

Figure 11.
Positions of the feet

All positions may be held with either the legs straight, a medium bend called *demi-plié*, or a full or *grand plié*. Many of the engravings of the period show the actors in one or other of these positions. The knees, more than often, are bent. A major difference from modern balletic practice is that one heel is often raised from the ground, thereby increasing the bend in that knee (see picture p. 72).

Figure 12. The *Commedia* Stance

This is seen in all the positions, and with either foot. In 3rd and 4th Positions it is often the back heel that is raised. There is a special position, almost a 'second' but the foot with the raised heel is brought some few inches forward. This is so typical that I call it the *'The Commedia Stance'* (see Figure 12, above).

Game 32a Courtesies

This explores the use of the *'Commedia Stance'*. It is called *'Courtesies'* because it involves a period movement of exaggerated politeness.

1/   Face [dir. 1]. Stand in 2nd Position slide the right foot forward 3 or 4 inches and raise the heel of the right foot (into the *Commedia Stance*). Make the *Politesse* movement with the right hand at chest height to [dir. 3]. As you do it, the torso turns to face [dir. 2].

2/   Press the heel of the right foot down, and raise the heel of the left, at the same time turning the torso to [dir. 8] and make the *Politesse* hand movement to the left [dir. 7].

Repeat on each side ad lib.

LOW   MIDDLE   HIGH

Figure 13a. The Eleven Little Courtesies, 1-6

Game 32b   The Eleven Little Courtesies

Counts

1/   Starting in the **Commedia Stance**, the foot movement stays the same as in Game 32a, alternately raising the right and left heel. On the first movement to the right make the **Politesse** hand movement as before but *lower* – at about your own hip level (see Figures 13a and 13b, above).

2/   And the same to the left.

3/   Repeat to the right taking the *middle* level (as in Game 32a).

4/   And the same to the left.

5/   On the third one to the right side, raise the hand *high* at about eye level.

6/   Repeat to the left.

7/   On the fourth movement to the right take both hands to the low position.

8/   On the movement to the left take both hands to the middle position.

9/   On the next to the right take both hands to the high position.

10/   On the following left move the left hand is placed in the high position and at the same time the right is held in the low position.

11/   Finally raise the right arm and lower the left as you do the last movement to the right.

70

Figure 13b. The Eleven Little Courtesies, 7-11

As you will have changed 'heels' on each move you should end with the right heel up.

Game 32c   The Eleven Alternated

[Masks: any profile mask]

Repeat Game 32b, but this time work in the inward-facing circle, with each *alternate* person in the circle starting to the left (left heel raised). This means that they will face one partner on Count 1/ and another partner on Count 2/ changing from one to another throughout the routine.

> Acting-wise try to relate to each partner in a different way. This is a good introduction to the axiom: 'in improvisation your attention is directed to your fellow actor (or actors), and not on yourself nor anyone watching'. So in this game make eye contact and let a rapport – friendly or otherwise – develop as the moves are made. 'Let' is the operative word; you don't have to strive for anything.

Game 32d   The Courtesy Harmonics

10

The same as Game 32c, but performed in pairs. Firstly go through the routine to check that both are familiar with the 11 arm positions, starting on opposite feet to each other, facing and turning away from each other as they continue. Then the players are asked to perform the 11 arm positions, but in a random order of their own choice, as they keep the legs and feet alternating. This is similar to the Harmonic Lunges (Game 21a, page 48). Although the partners are doing different arm movements from each other, a clearly 'harmonic' picture will be created on each move. Comedy can then more easily succeed when its anarchy shatters a formal condition.

Note on the Baroque *Commedia dell'Arte*

If we take '**new *Commedia***' in its broadest sense, there is no limitation to one style; any cultural source can be used as inspiration, from medieval mummers' plays to pop art and disco dancing. The only requirement is that enlargement, exaggeration and stylisation are used to relate a story or dramatic situation. However as the *Commedia dell'Arte* is the only Western form of theatre to truly develop this genre it is helpful to keep referring back to it, to establish our parameters. The last two games and drills we have just examined are very much of that pure seventeenth-century *Commedia dell'Arte* tradition, and before we open out again to more generalised applications, we will look at it in a little more detail.

The Baroque style in *Commedia dell'Arte* is flamboyant and curvilinear, as in other Baroque art. It is shown in nearly all *Commedia dell'Arte* representations prior to the early 1800's, at which date a very abrupt change occurs: the lines elongate, limbs become straight, the poses simplified and broader. The main reason is most likely the change from small intimate aristocratic theatres to vast public ones, so the more subtle gestures that had worked well until then, even in the open air where the audience tended to be small and gathered closely round the trestle stages, were replaced with a style that could more easily be 'read' at a distance. An example follows from each of the periods to illustrate this change.

Arlecchino (1690)
is asked where Pantalone may be found

He replies:	*He is in Commedia stance, right heel raised.*
'Err . . . did he go to market?	Right arm raised, elbow bent, hand prone, index finger points [dir. 3].
Or . . . was it to the Rialto?	Changes to left stance, points [dir. 7].
Market? Rialto? Market?	Changes as above on each word [dir. 3, 7, 3,].
No, no , no . . . I forgot,	Faces front. Closes feet to 1st Position. Shakes head.
he's at home, counting money.	Points over his shoulder.
You've already tried there?	Scratches head.
Well, if he's not at the Market . . .	Points to right (very quick move).
and not at the Rialto . . .	Points to left (very quick).
and not at home . . .	Points behind himself.
He's *not* up there!	Opens feet to **Commedia stance** to right. Arm bent, elbow raised, points up to heaven!
So he must be down there!	**Commedia stance** left. Points down between legs to hell!
And he can stay there for all I care . . . '	He walks away.

Harlequin (1830)
is asked where Pantaloon can be found

Harlequin D. S. L.[6] stands upright with one foot crossed in front of the other, his head resting in the palm of his right hand, his left hand on his hip. He ignores the question completely!

The visitor repeats his request and Harlequin replies:

'You want to find Pantaloon?	Right arm goes to his hip.
That's odd, very odd . . .	Feet change to 1st Position. Head tips from side-to-side.
Everyone I know, is trying to lose him!	(After line) step left [dir. 7] and cross right foot over. Hands turn palms up.
If you must find him! Let me see . . .	Finger of right hand taps teeth.
He went to the butcher's to buy some fish.	Full side lunge to [dir. 3] (see Fig. 4). Points to [dir. 3] with straight arm.
No . . . wrong . . .	Straightens up from lunge, finger goes to mouth.
He went to the fishmonger to to buy some meat.	Lunges and points [dir. 7].
No, wrong . . .	Stands straight, finger to mouth.
He went to the baker to buy some apples!!	Lunges and points to [dir. 2].
No he didn't . . .	Stands straight.
He went to market to sell some apples.	Lunges and points to [dir. 6].
But he hasn't got any apples.	Slumps, hands hang by his sides.
So I should sit down and wait for him here'.	Harlequin's legs sink under him, ending with him sitting crossed legged on the floor, head resting in the palm of his right hand.

---

6. Down stage left – see Appendix.

Game 33   Ornamentations

There are a number of ways to draw attention to a movement (which in turn is most likely drawing attention to a spoken word). One of these is to *'ornament'* the gesture with a rotation of the wrist. Decide on an action (it can be mimed or actual) such as tying a shoelace, shaking hands, scratching oneself, picking up a knife and fork. Carry out the action – making it very precise. Then repeat with the mime movement or series of movements, preceded by a single, or more turns of the wrist (see **Hand Drill** figures, page 67).

Example One – Picking up a knife and fork

You are seated for a meal; your place set before you.

1/   Two hand rotations inwards – pick up the knife and fork.

2/   One rotation outward holding the knife and fork.

3/   One slow rotation inward bending over the plate to smell the food.

4/   Three happy rotations outward, raising hands: 'Delicious'.

5/   Two fast inward rotations getting down to the meal.

6/   Left hand (or right if you're left-handed) inwards rotation and plunge fork in the steak.

7/   Right hand inward rotation and knife cuts into the steak.

Example Two – Traditional *Commedia Dell' Arte*

Point the finger of the right hand to [dir. 2] in prone position (the ultra polite point, palm up) make a 'hip sway' to [dir. 6], which has the effect of a gentle bow towards [dir. 2]. Reverse the sway to [dir. 2], and point at yourself the finger touching the chest. Repeat the two movements, adding two clockwise rotations of the hand before the first point and two anticlockwise rotations before the point to yourself. Use convention as throughout for counts.

Count   **1**/ 2, clockwise rotations,
         3, point
         4, pause – 'You'
         5, 6, anticlockwise rotations
         7, point at self
         8, pause – 'Me'

This is an exaggeratedly affected movement used by an aristocratic Mask wishing to ingratiate a superior, or a servant Mask making fun of a master.

Game 34   Retraction Accents

Retraction is another way of giving emphasis to an action; a movement is made, then relaxed or withdrawn and repeated with greater force. The bend at the elbow, so frequently shown in early illustrations, means that there is still scope to extend the meaning of a movement 'signal' (see Fig. 12).

We will use the pointed finger again as an example:

Example (still a favourite of politicians)

   Sub-text: 'Freedom, we demand, freedom!'

   1 Raise the hand to about head
     level, finger pointed to heaven,   *'Freedom . . .*
     medium bend at the elbow.

   2 Lower hand several inches.   *. . . we demand*

   3 Thrust arm higher than in 1.   *. . . freedom!'*

Invent a sentence supported by the triple move of action, retraction, and restatement.

Game 35a   The Accusing Finger
[Simple version]

Point an accusing finger at someone – real or imagined. Hold the hand at about chest height, finger horizontal (parallel with the floor); a medium bend at the elbow. Use a phrase, such as 'YOU, YES, YOU!' aloud or to oneself to motivate the action.

1 Point on	'YOU . . .
2 Retract the hand towards yourself along a parallel line by moving at the elbow joint only.	. . . YES . . .
3 Thrust the finger forward until the arm is almost straight.	. . . YOU!'

Game 35b   The Friendly Warning
[Masks: Captains]

1 The first movement is the same as above (Game 35a).	'YOU . . .
2 Instead of retracting, raise the finger to the vertical.	. . . YES.
3 Lower the finger extending the arm but less rigidly.	. . . YOU!'

The first version (Game 35a) gives a very aggressive signal. Version 'b' still accuses but is more tolerant, even affectionate – as one might use to a child. Support the action with appropriate expression and tone.

The action can now be played again, but with a *conflicting* emotion. Try to convey affection and toleration on the aggressive movement (35a) and aggression on the second less emphatic gesture (35b).

This is simple enough to be given at a first session and works well with children who get a chance to express aggression without actual bodily harm to anyone. We will return to the moves in an advanced exercise shortly.

Game 36a   Lateral Head Movements

On page 38 we referred to the use of 'lateral' head movements, without describing them. These are horizontal 'translations' of the head, which, although a very limited movement, can be done in each of the directions [dir. 1-8]. If we alternate between [dir. 3] and [dir. 7] we get the motion famous in classical Indian dancing. The most useful for *Commedia* is forward and back.

If we take the sequence from Game 35a – 'The Accusing Finger' – we can *augment* it with other isolated movements like the following head movement:

Two players confront each other *Commedia Stance,* their bodies face front [dir. 1]; 'A' has the left heel raised in the *Commedia Stance,* and 'B' the right heel. 'A's left hand points at his partner. 'B' points at 'A' with right hand. Heads are turned to face each other. They jut the head forward to each other as they move the finger on the first 'YOU . . .', slide it back as they retract the hand on ' . . . YES . . . ' and thrust it forward again, almost nose to nose, on the last point ' . . . YOU!'

Game 36b   Elaborations
[Masks: any of the profile]

The head movement can also be in the opposite direction to the finger. The head *'translates' back* on the first point, and *forward* as the finger is drawn back, and back again on the final finger accusation: 'YOU!'

These last games are examples of advanced experimental *Commedia.* The idea is to extend the player's vocabulary of movement. It can be developed with hip and rib translations, and the complicated body directions one sees in the Callot engravings of Captains and Zanni. The effects can be startling, dynamic and oddly contemporary.

The Mélanges

We will complete the Mime and Movement section with a couple of examples of *'Grands Mélanges'* (some of the nomenclature of the late *Commedia* has acquired French form).

These are large set pieces or group *lazzi* in which the whole cast is involved, and demand a large stage or performing area, rather than the small trestle platforms of sixteenth-century *Commedia dell'Arte.* They might show a *'General fight mêlée'*, a *'Hide and seek scena'*, involving trap doors and 'bungees' ,[7] or the two we'll now examine: *'The Banquet'* and *'The Chase'.*

Game 37   The Banquet

This, for safety reasons, demands some set choreography and rehearsal. The theme is the preparation of a Banquet, usually to celebrate the wedding that ends the performance. Servettas and Zanni dash about carrying plates, food, table ornaments (mimed or prop). A Master of Ceremonies (Burattino) directs and misdirects the proceedings. I will not attempt to give the whole production, but just indicate some of the more colourful and traditional moves.

The basic movement is a run; and it is just that – not a trot or prance but a full-out run.

a) Run and Split Jump
Enter up-stage corner (U. S. L) carrying a large dish. Exit opposite corner down-stage (D. S. R) .[8]

Counts		
1/ 2, 3, 4, 5, 6	Six Runs [dir. 2] R, L, R, L, R, L.	
7,	Small preparatory jump bringing feet together.	
8.	Big jump, legs in the air in splits: right leg forward, left leg back. Both straight or nearly so.	
2/ 2	Land both feet together.	
3, 4, 5, 6, 7, 8.	Run R, L, R, L, etc. to make the exit.	

b) Split Jumps and Direction Change
Enter up-stage corner (U. S. R.) and exit same side (D. S. R.).

Counts **1**/ 2, 3, 4, 5, 6,	Six runs L, R, L, R, L, R.
7,	Preparatory jump.
8.	Split jump: left leg forward, right leg back.

---

7. The elaborate eighteenth–nineteenth century system of trapdoors included 'elasticated' shoots which could throw a performer 20 or more feet into the air.

8. For anyone not familiar with these stage directions they are given in the Appendix.

2/		Preparatory jump feet together.
2,		Make a second split jump but with right leg forward.
3,		Land feet together.
4,		Split jump left leg forward.
5,		Land feet together.
6,		Split jump right leg forward.
7,		Land feet together, but exaggerate knee bend.
8.		Swivel to face [dir. 8] miming loss of balance.
3/ 2, 3, 4, 5, 6, 7, 8.		Run off in a new direction [dir. 2].

c) The Promenade Spin

This needs a fair deal of practice, and is easier for trained dancers. Two characters (Zanni or Servettas) enter from the corners, one up-stage and one down-stage. Partner 'A' starts D. S. R, a plate (mimed, at least to begin with) in the left hand, and 'B' starts U. S. L. with the plate in the left hand.

Counts	**1/** 2, 3, 4, 5, 6,	Six runs (more if needed) to meet centre stage. 'A's right shoulder to 'B's right shoulder.
	7, 8. **2/** 2, 3, 4,	'A' raises left leg in front and balances on the ball of the right foot and is spun round by 'B' as he/she makes a series of *small* runs round 'A'. 'A' places her/his right arm across 'B's chest and holds onto 'B's shoulder with right arm for support,while 'B' holds onto 'A's waist (this is a fast and comic version of the male dancer 'promenading' round the ballerina!)
	5, 6, 7, 8.	Exit runs 'A' – U. S. L. 'B' – D. S. R.

d) Which-Way What-Way

Note: *This is another alternating split jump, which can be done in a workshop, and is a good one to give a class of energetic children towards the end of the session.*

Practice Drill

Face sideways on [dir. 3]. Stand straight, feet together, jump in the air separating the legs into the split jump. The right leg goes forward, and the left leg back; legs straight or nearly so. Land with feet together, knees well bent. Practise the same on the left [dir. 7]. Left leg will separate forward, the right leg back. Now stand facing front [dir. 1]. As you do the split jump with the right leg forward, turn the body to face right side [dir. 3] as before, but land facing *front* [dir. 1]. Alternate left and right but facing front on each landing (feet together).

e) Which-Way What-Way Sequence for Banquet

A Zanni enters from C. S. L. (the middle wing) holding a dish in each hand.

Counts	
1/ 2, 3, 4, 5, 6,	Make six runs towards [dir. 3] starting on the right foot. Stop centre.
7, 8.	Preparatory jump facing front [dir. 1].
2/ 2, 3, 4, 5, 6, 7, 8.	Split jumps: right, left, right, left (on the odd counts) land front on even counts. Look at the right dish on the right jump, look at the left dish as you do left jump.
3/ 2, 3, 4, 5, 6, 7, 8.	Run off [dir. 3].

f) Belly Bumps

Follow the drill carefully to avoid accidents!!!

Drill: First Stage

Partners start about 4ft apart, facing each other. Legs separated (2nd Position, feet straight forward). Bend knees and jump, legs remaining apart. As you jump curve the legs and also the head and upper part of the body back, sticking the tummy right out! Arms **must** also be held back out of the way. Land back in the starting position bending the knees for a soft landing.

Drill: Second Stage

Start 15 or more feet apart (in performance you'll both be off-stage in opposite wings). Run towards each other until you reach the distance apart already rehearsed. Make a small preparatory jump into 2nd Position, and then make the curving jump and land holding the position. It is essential to practise this until the preparatory jump and the curved jump are both exactly timed with one another.

Drill: Third Stage

Now make the run and relocate the preparatory jump closer together; about 2ft apart. Don't do the big jump yet.

Drill: Final Stage

Now make the run, the preparation 2ft apart, and the curved jump, bumping bellies. This causes one to stagger back . . . Then the run and bump can be repeated before running past each other and off.

To these sequences any number of acrobatic tricks that are within the capabilities of the performers can be added.

Game 38   The Chase

This is one of the simplest but most effective of the **'Grands Mélanges'** dating perhaps from the time of the **Tapis** and Panorama, c. 1800 (see page 56). A *Commedia* theme would be the climax of an elopement. The Lover, while rescuing the heroine from an upper window, is surprised by a Zanni who raises the alarm. Pantalone is woken and the entire cast gives chase.

As an alternative, it presents a very good chase to evoke the era of the Keystone Cops and the silent movies, when strobe lighting can be added.

The only movement to be learned is a version of the tap dancer's step known as '**Trenches**'. For **The Chase** it has to be done sideways-on to the audience. So turn the body to face [dir. 3]. Place the feet together (turned straight forward to the direction you're going). Lean forward [dir. 3] from the hips, start by sliding the left foot along the floor until you raise the leg as high as you can behind you (almost straight, but not rigid). Then start to slide the right foot back, delaying the transfer of weight and landing on the left foot till the last moment. Repeat right, left, right, etc. so you have a running motion on place, in which the leg action is all behind you. Legs and feet remain turned straight throughout.

Next practise the sequence travelling:

> 8 '**Trenches**' on place.
>
> 16 '**Trenches**' gradually moving forward towards [dir. 3].
>
> 8 '**Trenches**' on place.
>
> 16 '**Trenches**' gradually moving backwards *away* from [dir. 3].
>
> 8 '**Trenches**' on place.

Note: *when you travel backwards away from [dir. 3] the movement of the 'Trenches' remains exactly the same.*

Repeat the sequence in pairs. Partner 'A', after the initial movement 'on place', travels forward as above. Partner 'B' starts in front of 'A', about 3 metres towards [dir. 3], and a few paces further up-stage, and does the routine in reverse order travelling backwards after the first 8 on place. They should become level with each other at the half-way point. The step keeps going, as they mime the actions of a chase.

To produce the **Grand Mélange**, on the *Commedia dell'Arte* theme: start with the fleeing Lovers and the chasing Zanni. The choice of **Trenches** (forward, backward, or on place) can be freely improvised, the Zanni gaining on the Lovers but never quite catching up. Add a character at a time – Pantalone shaking his fist, an elderly fiancé of the Heroine (The

Doctor) puffing and blowing, a Servetta waving arms in dismay, etc, etc. The majority of the cast should be limited to the **Trenches** movement, but it is possible to replace the Heroine's movement with tiny little running steps on the balls of the feet. The Servetta can do the same.

11

WORD GAMES

12

Introduction

There are two things that many fear when coming to improvisation. They are usually expressed as:

(1) *I won't know where to start!* This we solve by limiting the students' 'freedom' to the extent that there is very little choice in the way they start. It should be stressed that any improvisation flourishes best where some form of restriction, barrier or formal requirement is involved. The worst thing a novice can be told is: 'Go ahead, improvise'. All the *Commedia* impro games impose a formal framework, some quite complicated but which are well worth taking time to establish.

(2) *I won't know what to say!* The solution here is to convince everyone that it matters not a jot *what* they say, but only *how* they say it. To demonstrate this, the first few Word Game impros use no words at all.

Game 39a   Alphabeta

Each student is asked to address the group on a subject dear to his/her heart. (Animal Welfare – Equal Opportunity – Third World Debt). However they are allowed no words, but merely to recite the alphabet through. They are asked to add as much expression and gesture as they can and, of course, vary the grouping of the letters as they wish.

Example

'a, b . . . c . . . d, e . . . f, g, h . . . i . . . j . . . k, l, m, n . . . o . . . p, q . . . r . . . s, t, u, v, w . . . x, y . . . Z! . . . '

This can be used in conjunction with *Commedia* Mime and Movement Games like the **Courtesies** (page 70), **Sways** (page 55), **Leans** (page 53), **Hip Movements** (page 52).

Even if the aim is a Commedia dell'Arte production, it is as well not to limit the games solely to the traditional Masks at this stage. Allow contemporary and mundane subjects for the impros as well.

Game 39b   Alphabeta Two

Work in twos, each pair being set a theme, e. g. husband and wife arguing; customer and shop assistant; a Victorian proposal; or a *Commedia dell'Arte* theme like Pantalone and The Captain discussing a dowry. In this version, the alphabet need not be used in sequence; it can jump about to odd letters or groups of letters.

In both Games 39a and 39b, **numbers** can replace the letters.

Game 40   Gibberish

As a third choice, both Games 39a and 39b (above) can be improvised with **'Gibberish'** instead of letters or numbers. **Gibberish** (sometimes known as Grummelot) has a long pedigree in the *Commedia dell'Arte* and was often used in performance. It is also helpful as a gradient between those Mime and Movement Games which use gesture alone, and those in which improvised dialogue is added.

Game 41   Double Talk

This is played in pairs: couples face each other, sitting or standing about a foot apart. Partner 'A' leads the improvisation by speaking slowly and enunciating very deliberately. Partner 'B' must duplicate what is being said, pronouncing the words at the *same* time by watching the lips closely and anticipating. To begin with, 'A' aims to make it easy for his partner, but should not let the pace become fixed, speaking more rapidly on simple and more easily guessed phrases.

A good workshop formula, if the group is not too large, is to sit on the floor in a circle. The first student takes on the role of 'A' working with the person next to them as 'B'. When they have completed the exercise, student 'B' becomes an 'A', who turns to face the next person, who acts as 'B' and so on round the circle, so that all get a chance in both capacities. After quite a lot of practice 'A' can try and catch 'B' with non-sequiturs, and 'B' can try to alter his responses, adding his own originations to the scene, so as to improve the sense as in the following example:

Example

A: W-e-ll, F-a-n-c-y seeing you here! H-o-w have you
B: W-e-ll, f-a-n-c-y seeing you here! H-o-w have you

A: been, Eh? It's been such a long, l-o-n-g time. How's
B: been, Eh? – It's been such a long, l-o-n-g time. How's

A: your father? Gone? alas! Yes, all alone now. Sad, very
B: your . . . wife? Gone! alas! Yes, all alone now . . . Sad,

A: Sad. Sometimes I think I'll get a . . .
B: Yes. Sometimes . . . Do you really? Another wife?

A: No, a pet. A dog . . . A cat . . . A bud-geri-gar . . . a **duck**
B: . . . Yes. A dog . . . A cat . . . A bud-geri-gar . . . A **duck**

A: **billed plat – ee – puss!!**
B: . . . Eh? – **ee-pussy cat** . . . That's what I'd get.

A: . . . a sweet little pussycat.
B: . . . a sweet little pussycat.[1]

The purpose of the exercise is to force the actors to really concentrate attention on their partners. It also encourages partner 'A' to find new and unusual word connections. See the Face Mask section (page 113) for an advanced version of the game.

Game 42   Parroting

For this the players sit or stand side by side. It is easier than **Double Talk** because player 'B' repeats the sentences *after* 'A' says them. 'A' plays most of his lines to the front. 'B' plays most of his lines to his partner! To begin with, the words are duplicated precisely but soon 'B' should be able to introduce some flexibility, so as to be in agreement with 'A', but not saying exactly the same words. Usually this will develop to a point where 'B' frees himself/herself from the formula:

Example

A: Oh, it's a lovely day today!

B: Yes, it's a lovely day . . . today.

A: It's too hot though . . .

B: Yes it's too hot. I'm too hot.

A: It would be nice to go for a swim.

B: Yes, it would be nice to go for a swim . . . But I can't go for a swim.

A: Why not

B: I haven't got a bathing costume.

A: That doesn't matter. You can swim in the nude!

B: I can't swim in the nude!

A: Of course you can. People don't worry about a little thing like that.

---

1. From an audio recording taken during a workshop session.

B: A little thing like what?

A: Nowadays people don't worry about a little thing like swimming in the nude.

B: I – can't – swim – in – the – nude – because I *can't swim!*

Note: 'A's originations must refer to present time and locality, or to some future action to be shared with 'B'.

Game 43a   Little Lies

Students are seated in a circle, in the centre of which three or four everyday objects are placed – e. g., a chair, a coffee cup, a bag, a coat – anything that's to hand. The leader points to one of the items and says, 'Tell a lie about that chair'. The students each in turn invent a lie about the object. As with all exercises of this type, it must be done at speed and without hesitation. This is repeated round the circle several times before starting again with another of the objects.

> In this version of the game the participants should 'originate' the lie without being influenced by the previous player. At first they tend to be very conservative – 'That chair is blue' (it's actually red) – but the aim is to encourage imagination. Soon we get things like, 'It is made of solid gold!' and later the real freedom of an outlandish lie: 'It's a large jar of marmalade'. Justified lies are a bonus: 'It may look like a chair to you, but it is in truth Sherlock Holmes in one of his many disguises'.

Game 43b   More Lies

This version can be done in teams of three or four, who perform for the rest of the class. The objects are again used and can now be handled. Team member 'A' chooses one. He sets up a scene and introduces the object without identifying it. He then 'passes the impro' to another team member who creates the lie about the object. Other members of the team can introduce the remaining items, which must fit in with the general theme and location of the scene. This should be clearer with the following example:

Example

A: You are very lucky to have visited us today at our dig on this ancient burial mound, for after months of fruitless search we have found (*showing coffee cup*) this fantastic . . . (*passes impro to Team Member 'B'*) . . .

B: . . . skull of a Saxon warrior, etc. There must be further remains . . .

C: I'll fetch the echo-sounder . . .

He brings on a hat stand. Etc, etc . . .

Game 44a   Noun Play (*No Nouns*)

This is an improvised duologue in which both players are required to avoid the use of *nouns*. It is performed in pairs to the rest of the class. Student 'A' starts to relate an incident, in intimate conversation with student 'B' who responds with suitable (noun-less) interjections. When 'A' reaches a point where a noun seems unavoidable, 'B' must come to the rescue, and in turn 'A' must 'rescue' 'B' when required. 'A' however retains the initiative throughout, 'B' agreeing, supporting, encouraging.

Example

A: I say . . .

B: Yes . . .

A: Come close . . .

B: Yes.

A: Still closer. I don't want to speak too loud

B: I understand . . .

A: You see I trust you . . .

B: That's nice . . .

A: I can trust you?

B: Implicitly . . .

A: Then I shall tell you what has happened.

B: . . . Yes. What?

A: But you must not repeat it to . . . (*potential noun*) . . .

B: I wouldn't . . . not even to my . . . (*another potential noun*)

A: Not even to her! Well, I got up early.

B: You always do . . .

A: It was very cold so I put on my . . .

B: Yes, you must keep yourself warm . . .

A: . . . and went across the . . .

B: . . . I bet that was cold too . . .

A: . . . so that I could milk the . . .

B: . . . it would be unkind not to . . .

A: I was sitting there milking when I heard . . .

B: Go on . . .

A: . . . very quiet at first . . . then getting louder.

B: What did it sound like?

A: Scraping . . . filing, as if . . .

B: . . . as if?

A: They were trying to cut through the . . .

B: . . . and did they succeed?

A: No, I stopped them. I raised my . . .

B: . . . that was brave of you!

   Etc, etc . . .

The goal of this game is again to increase the attention level given to each partner by the other, and to train the actor in the very rapid exchanges essential in *Commedia* impro.

Game 44b   'B' Supplies the Nouns

In this variation, 'B' is permitted the nouns, which he supplies, where needed, to 'A's narrative. In this way, 'B' is largely controlling the direction of the impro. In order to give an idea of 'A's line of thought, his 'intended' noun is given in brackets in the following example. After 'B's interjection he is forced into a change of direction in which he still tries to make sense.

Example

A: I was wondering if you know how very fond I am of . . . (*'A' is going to say 'summer'*).

B: . . . Cockroaches.

A: Yes. I consider them the most delightful of . . . (*creatures*).

B: . . . Snacks!

A: I prefer them sautéd with a little (*butter*).

B: . . . Butter (*'B' thinks alike this time*).

A: And a glass of white (*wine*).

B: – wash.

A: Then I'm ready to go to (*bed*).

B: . . . The Himalayas.

A: To hunt for the fabulous (*Yeti*).

B: Haggis!

A: Eaten only by the monks of Sh . . .

(*To make a neat ending they both say*) Shangri-La!

Note: these examples of impros are just that, and not intended as scripts of any kind.

Game 44c   'A' Rejects the Nouns

A further variation is made by 'A' rejecting several nouns and finally getting out his noun so as to persist in his narrative direction. The example below has a *Commedia dell'Arte* setting: a dialogue between two Zanni – 'A', the stupid Mortadella, and 'B', the quick-witted Zan Padella.

Example

B: What on earth is the matter? Is your tail on fire?

A: (*breathing heavily*) Just . . . just a . . .

B: (*prompting with a nounal phrase*) Just a matter of . . .?

A: No . . . no . . . just . . .

B: . . . just one of those things . . .?

A: No . . . just . . .

B: . . . just a song at twilight?

A: No . . . just a minute!! I'm all out of . . . of . . .

B: . . . sorts?

A: Sorts? No I'm just out of . . . of . . .

B: Luck? Out of money? Ah, out of condition!

A: No, out of breath!! Well, I went out early this m . . . m . . .

B: . . . Morning . . .

A: . . . this morning to see if I could buy something for . . .

B: . . . sixpence . . .

A: . . . no, supper. So I was walking round the m . . . m . . .

B: . . . mulberry bush? Merry-go-round?

A: Market!!! When I bumped right into . . . er P . . . er . . .

B: A policeman?

A: No . . . no . . . er . . . you know . . . er . . .

B: A penguin? . . .

A: No . . . Pulcinella!! He set about abusing me. Hitting me about . . .

B: The place?

A: No about the . . .

B: Head?

A: No about the other end. Yes with his great big . . . (*pause*) stick . . . and calling me a th . . . th . . .

B: Theologian? A thing-ami-jig . . .

A: A thieving Bu . . . Bugg . . .

Both: . . . Blighter!!!!!

Game 44d   *Alternative Nouns*

Here the orientation is changed from one of conversation between the two characters to one in which 'A' addresses the audience. (Each of the preceding versions can also be used in this form.)

Example

A: My most noble and distinguished g . . . g . . .
B: . . . geese . . .

A: g . . . guests. Welcome to the p . . . p . . . p . . .
B: . . . pigsty.

A: P. Palazzo Bisognoso. Home of my dear master and . . . f . . .
B: . . . fiend . . .

A: f-friend, Signor Pantalone de' Bisognosi. He apologises for not greeting you himself but he is at the moment in . . . in . . .

B: . . . incontinent . . .

A: in conference, s-s-itting . . .
B: . . . on the bog . . .

A: in the council chamber . . .
B: . . . on the chamber pot . . .

A: . . . passing . . . a . . .

B: . . . load of sh . . .

A: passing a law on, I believe, the trade of glass-making in our great city of V . . . v . . .

B: . . . very stinking canals . . .

A: Venice.

Often while running the games, a characterisation will develop that can easily be adapted to the tradition of the *Commedia dell'Arte* Masks. In this last example, we have the stuttering Tartaglia and a villainous and resentful Brighella.

Game 45a   Misemotion

This is a game in which any statement made is met with an inappropriate response. There are numerous potential versions. In a workshop situation an actor could be asked to face the rest of the group and relate a very sad story. Gradually they begin to laugh, at first the merest giggle, but as his tale gets more tragic the laughs grow till they greet the end with a burst of happy applause as if the actor had performed a successful comic routine.

Although this is a simple routine, it is best *not* to try it with new students or those who are not used to working together, as it can be upsetting for the fledgling student. If you do want a really 'cruel' version, prime the rest of the class without warning the solo performer what is going to happen. The purpose of the **Misemotion** games is to encourage the player to find unusual responses to another's communication, or to the situation.

Game 45b   Misemotion Two

A version for two players, who sit side by side. Both 'misemote' with the subject of the conversation, but they *agree* with each other in their response.

Example

> A: I've not been feeling well!
>
> B: That's good. (*Smiling*) I've been sick myself.
>
> A: Ah, really? Anything serious?
>
> B: I should think so.
>
> A: Oh, that's good. I've got this pain in the head.
>
> B: You lucky devil. Where?
>
> A: Just here. Do you think it's terminal?
>
> B: Oh, I'm sure it is! Congratulations!

This too can be quite uncomfortable! Of course the misemotion doesn't have to be either of the above. A happy statement can be greeted with tears, threats with affectionate amusement, etc.

Game 46a Advanced Gibberish (The Turk)

As we mentioned, gibberish was used by *Commedia dell'Arte* companies, and is often found in the scenarios when a foreigner, often a real or a false Turk (*Il Finto Torco*) makes an appearance.

The following is for three players. Player 'T' (The Turk) talks in gibberish, and has a definite idea or goal in mind; he uses mime and the repetition of certain words of gibberish in the attempt to make it 'translatable'. 'B' and 'C' try to understand him.

'B' and 'C' walk on from stage right. 'T' (The Turk) enters from stage left and stops them in their path.

> T: Gwata Galumpus! (*Bowing politely.*)
>
> B: Ignore him – he probably wants money.
>
> *They try to pass but he bars their way.*
>
> T: Gwata Galumpus! Ig skalo melemka.
>
> C: Melemka?
>
> T: . . . Melemka.

C: Sorry, haven't any 'melemka' on us.

B: No. In fact we're short on 'melemka' ourselves.

T: Ig skalo Melemka . . . (*The Turk becomes aggressive.*)

B: You'd better give him some. He's the sort who'll draw a knife.

     'C' gives a small coin to 'T'.

T: Micanooooga?? (*He throws it aside contemptuously.*) Yag meg
     Micanooooga? Ig – mog – Torco! (*Proudly.*)

B: There you are; Torco . . . he's a Turk, I thought he was.
Salaam, Salaam.

     All start bowing.

T: Gwata Galumpus!

B and C: Gwata Galumpus! Gwata Galumpus!

T: Nig . . . Nig. Ig Galum*pam* (*Points to himself.*) . . . Yog
     Galum*pam* (*Points to the two of them.*) Galum*pam* (*Points to self.*)
     Galum*pam* (*Points to 'B', then comes between them, drawing them*
     close to him.) Galumpus!!!

     Much ad libbing until they are made to understand the difference
     between the singular and the plural.

T: Ig skolo Melemka . . . Galum*pam* (*Points to self.*) Melemka.
     (*Mimes woman.*)

B: Sorry old chap, we don't go in for that sort of thing!

T: Nag! Melemka dag Pantalonag.

B: Pantalonag . . . ? Can he mean Pantalone?

T: Yag . . . Yag Pantalone, Melemka dag Pantal*one*!

B: Pantalone's not a Malemka .

C: No . . . don't think he's ever been a Malemka . . .

T: Nag . . . Malemka (*Mimes girl.*) dag Pantalone (*Mimes*
     old man.)

B and C: Pantalone's daughter! He must be the rich suitor the old
     devil's been boasting about . . . This way Galumpam . . .

     They exit together.

Game 46b   Gibberish (*The Interpreter*)

This version, involves two players: 'A' speaks in gibberish, 'B' translates for the audience. The most successful situation seems to be 'The Guest Speaker'.

Example: The Guest Speaker

Player 'A' addresses the audience and explains that the distinguished speaker who is to talk to them tonight doesn't know any English, so he/she will translate. He/she introduces 'B' (The Guest Speaker) who greets them with gibberish, pausing to allow 'A' to translate. 'A' will occasionally consult 'B' also using the gibberish to clarify a point.

A: We have been looking forward to the talk being given tonight; Professor Ohoni Ahioba, who holds the chair of Zoology at the renowned university of Ahogiweegee. Professor Ahioba . . .

B: Osgoo lahi hajia c hoonee.

A: 'Good evening ladies and gentlemen.'

B: Ajjejo mandoi zin parho kakiki zodlarbi e gozoolo.

A: 'I propose to talk on my work in the crossbreeding of silk worms with fountain pens . . . ?' (*He speaks to 'B' in gibberish.*) Eeholas ni zodlarbi e geezarlo??

B: Geezarlo? Geezarlo? Kis eeholas geezarlo kik gozoolo.

A: Ah of course . . . zodlarbi e gozoolo . . . Sorry ladies and gentlemen. 'Silk worms with glow worms . . . '

B: Parho glotee ganzo ipscula!

A: 'In order to get a silk fabric that glows in the dark!'

   And so on . . .

Game 47   Rhythm and Space

This is a drill in which a *preset rhythm and space* pattern is used as a basis for the spoken impro. The counting pattern differs slightly from our usual one, having four counts instead of eight, and the 'bars', as you will see, are counted right to the end (i.e: Bar 20). The sequence, which should be learned ahead, is as follows. The two players face each other about 10 paces apart. They count to themselves – **1**/ 2, 3, 4. **2**/ 2, 3, 4. **3**/ 2, 3, 4. etc. 'A' and 'B' are allocated certain beats on which they will later improvise dialogue. To make sure they know where they occur, they are asked to count those beats out aloud.

Counts: **1**/ 2, 3, 4,   Stand still.

2/ 2, 3, 4,   Walk 4 paces towards each other.

3 /2, 3, 4,   'B' freezes. **'A'** turns to face **front** and *counts out aloud:*
'. . . **3**/ 2, 3, 4.'

4/ 2, 3, 4,   'A' turns back. **'B'** faces **front** and *counts aloud:* '. . . **4**/ 2, 3, 4.'

5/ 2, 3, 4,   'B' turns back and both walk towards each other

6/ 2, 3, 4,   They stay facing **each other**, *'A' counts aloud:* '. . . **6**/ 2, 3, 4.'

7/ 2, 3, 4.   Still facing **each other**, *'B' counts aloud:*   '. . . **7**/ 2, 3, 4.'

8/ 2, 3, 4,   They walk towards each other for 4 steps.

9/ 2, 3, 4,   They face **each other**, *'A' counts aloud:*   '. . . **9**/ 2, 3, 4.'

10/ 2, 3, 4, Continue facing **each other**, *'B' counts aloud:* '. . . **10**/ 2, 3, 4.'

11/ 2, 3, 4,   *'A' counts aloud:*   '. . . **11**/ 2, 3, 4.'

12/ 2, 3, 4,   *'B' counts aloud:*   '. . . **12**/ 2, 3, 4.'

13/ 2, 3, 4,   'A' walks down-stage, 'B' walks up-stage.

14/ 2, 3, 4,   *'A' counts aloud:*   '. . . **14**/ 2, 3, 4.'

15/ 2, 3, 4,   They make a circle clockwise round each other.

16/ 2, 3, 4,   **'B'**, now down-stage, *counts aloud:*   '. . . **16**/ 2, 3, 4.'

17/ 2, 3, 4,   They walk in opposite directions.

18/ 2, 3, 4,   They turn to each other and both count aloud:
'. . . **18**/ 2, 3, 4.'

19/ 2, 3, 4,   They walk away from each other.

20/ 2, 3, 4.   They face the **audience** and *both* count aloud:
'. . . **20**/ 2, 3, 4.'

A little time should be spent on this, so that the routine becomes almost automatic. Then the players should be ready to improvise the dialogue within the movement framework.

Example

1/ 2, 3, 4.   *(They look at each other across the distance.)*

2/ 2, 3, 4.   *(They walk towards each other hesitatingly.)*

3/ 2, 3, 4.   'A': There's that woman who borrowed my book. *(Aside – to the audience)*[2]

4/ 2, 3, 4.   'B': Oh that's the person whose book I've lost! *(Aside.)*

5/ 2, 3, 4.   *(They walk to meet each other.)*

6/ 2, 3, 4.   A: I was hoping to meet you.

7/ 2, 3, 4.   B: Yes, it's always nice to meet a friend.

8/ 2, 3, 4.   *(They come close together.)*

9/ 2, 3, 4.   A: I was wondering about that book I lent you.

10/ 2, 3, 4. B: Book? Ah yes I . . . I haven't finished it yet.

11/ 2, 3, 4. A: It was three years ago!

12/ 2, 3, 4. B: Ah well, I'm a very slow reader!

13/ 2, 3, 4. *(A walks down-stage, 'B' up-stage.)*

14/ 2, 3, 4. A: I bet she's spoilt it or lost it. *(Aside.)*

15/ 2, 3, 4. *(They circle each other.)*

16/ 2, 3, 4. B: I'll avoid her next time. *(Aside.)*

17/ 2, 3, 4. *(They walk away from each other.)*

18/ 2, 3, 4. *(Turn to each other.)*

           A: Don't forget the book.

           B: No, I won't!

19/ 2, 3, 4. *(Continue the walk away.)*

20/ 2, 3, 4. *(To audience)*

           A: Damn woman!

           B: Damn book!

This is less difficult than it might appear on the page. Any movement and counting pattern may be devised and learnt and, of course, any dialogue can be improvised to it.

---

2. See page 130.

Game 48   Sausages

This is a typical bit of traditional *Commedia dell'Arte*. It involves two Zanni; the capable major-domo, Burattino, and a stupid greedy fellow – the early Arlecchino. Burattino tells the audience of the sumptuous feast he is preparing for the nuptials of Isabella and Lelio. He lists the items on the menu. Arlecchino interrupts with the single suggestion 'Sausages' and minor variations on that commodity.

Example

Burattino:	First as an antipasto, I think quail's eggs in aspic.
Arlecchino:	. . . Yes . . . with a few sausages.
Burattino:	Nightingale's tongues on thin slices of . . .
Arlecchino:	. . . Sausage . . .
Burattino:	Sturgeon stuffed with . . .
Arlecchino:	. . . Sausages.
Burattino:	I'll stuff you with . . .
Arlecchino:	. . . Sausages . . . please!!
	Etc, etc . . .

Game 49   The Two Suitors

This involves three players, using a movement pattern of three steps and a pause. The routine faces [dir. 1] throughout.

1/	Step with the right foot toward [dir. 2].
2,	Step across with the left foot, still toward [dir. 2].
3,	A large step or lunge with the right foot [dir. 2].
4, 5, 6, 7, 8.	*Hold* a position for word impro.

Repeat sequence starting with the left foot travelling to [dir. 8].

Example: The Old and the Young Suitor (The Doctor and The Innamorato)

The two suitors stand some six feet apart: the object of their desires is between them. All three do the steps, but in their own character. The movement can get stronger and faster, with the suitors ending on their knees. The Young Suitor advances on the lady; she retreats, and the Old

102

Suitor is also forced back. During the first pause, the young man says his line of improvised dialogue. It is then the Old Suitor who approaches, with the girl and younger man retreating, and so on.

Example of improvised dialogue

Young Man: I offer you my undying love.

Old Man: I offer you a carriage and pair.

Young Man: I can offer only my heart.

Old Man: I can offer a town house in the heart of Padua.

Young Man: Can this old fool bring you love?

Old Man: I'll bring you days of sunshine and leisure.

Young Man: I'll bring you nights of moonshine and passion.

(*Unobserved by the men the damsel slips from between them.*)

Young Man: I'll give you my lips . . .

(*The young man mistakenly flings his arms around his rival.*)

Old Man: I'll give you a good clip round the ear hole!

The above mechanism can be used in other contexts: a simpleton between two brigands, a patient between rival doctors, etc.

Game 50   Split Personality

This is where the role, in a moment of indecision, talks to him/herself, urging the respective pros and cons of alternative courses of action. It is very typical of Arlecchino/Harlequin from any period, so we'll give the example to Harlequin; but of course it can be done by any character, ancient or modern. The character becomes, as it were, two people, debating with each other (see also Colombina, page 229).

The audience partially identifies the character by the space it is occupying, so it is important to step into the same spot on each '*change-over*'. The basic '*change-over*' to the right is:

Take a large step onto the heel with the right foot towards and facing the right side [dir. 3]. Then make a swivel round to face left [dir. 7] by drawing the left leg to join the right. The left '*change-over*' is the same reversed.

There will be slight variations in the way the *'change-overs'* are made in order to fit the scenario. The first move is unusual here, in that Harlequin says his first whispered line facing front, and there are different moves for the 'run' and the 'fisticuffs'.

Example

HT: *Harlequin Tempted*
HC: *Harlequin's Conscience*

Harlequin enters from U. S. L, looking back and down into the wings. He stops D. S. C. He takes a small step to his left side and beckons surreptitiously with his right hand, as if asking someone to come close. He whispers out of the corner of his mouth.

HT: Did you see what I saw?

        (*He makes a change-over to his right, and talks as if to someone on his left.*)

HC: What of it? The man's just having a sleep.

        (*Left change-over. He talks to someone as if on his right.*)

HT: His moneybag is hanging from his belt.

HC: (*right change-over*) Where else would it be?

HT: (*left change-over*) Hanging from my belt!

HC: (*right change-over*) You mean you'd steal it?

HT: (*quick left change-over*) Just a swift slash with my knife.

HC: (*right change-over*) What if he woke?

HT: (*quick left change-over*) I'd run . . . (*Turn away to left [dir. 7] and mime running on the spot.*)

HC: (*right change-over*) Suppose he could run faster than you?

HT: (*left change-over*) I'd fight him! (*Mimes fisticuffs; ends by getting the worst of it.*)

HC: (*right change-over*) There! Aren't you glad I persuaded you against it?

Though both the identities are Harlequin, a distinction would be made between the two 'selves' – HC being upright and dignified, HT furtive, posture crouching, voice scheming.

Game 51   That Tree

This game exploits a couple of early *Commedia dell'Arte* traditions.

1) The most interesting perhaps: the setting up of imaginary objects (and people) by one actor, that must be accepted by the rest of the cast and eventually the audience. Here we touch on something very fundamental in the art of theatre and the nature of reality!

2) The partnership of the 'Crafty' and the 'Stupid' Zanni. An early pairing, to last to our own times as British panto's Broker's Men. Here too, we get the beginnings of the Comic and his straight man.

Set up an impro, using these elements. Choose a 'Crafty Zanni' – who leads the impro – and a 'Stupid Zanni' – who follows his partner, reacting to his lines and coping with the imaginary objects the 'Crafty Zanni' introduces to the scene.

The example is of a really advanced nature but the idea of illusory objects could be introduced at a more elementary level.

Crafty Z: Come here.

Stupid Z: Here? I am here.

Crafty Z: No – you're there. I need you here.

Stupid Z: (*comes close*) There! I'm here.

Crafty Z: Now listen here. No, listen. Do you hear?

Stupid Z: No.

Crafty Z: Well, be quiet, and listen. (*He makes clicking sound, like horse's hooves. Both put hands to their ears.*)

Stupid Z: Yes! Is it a horse?

Crafty Z: Yes a man on a horse. He's a traveller and he's got a lot of money.

Stupid Z: How do you know he's got a lot of money?

Crafty Z: Listen. Can you hear that? (*Like a ventriloquist.*) Chink . . . chink chink . . .

Stupid Z:	You're saying 'Chink . . . chink chink'.
Crafty Z:	No, *I'm* not saying it. That's his money. Listen . . . chink . . . chink. (*Less than before.*)
Stupid Z:	He's not got as much as he had a moment ago! Perhaps he's lost some. Or he's stopped for a drink.
Crafty Z:	Of course he's not stopped for a drink. He'll be here in a moment.
Stupid Z:	Shall I give him a drink?
Crafty Z:	No, no, we're going to take his money.
Stupid Z:	Take his money? That's not nice.
Crafty Z:	Of course it's not nice. *We* are not nice.
Stupid Z:	Aren't we? I think you're nice!
Crafty Z:	I – am – not – nice. You – are – not – nice. We're brigands.
Stupid Z:	Oh! Am I a brigand?
Crafty Z:	Yes, you're a little brigand, and I'm a big brigand. Now be quiet because we must hide.
Stupid Z:	Where shall we hide?
Crafty Z:	I'll hide behind this tree and you hide behind that tree. (*He points to empty space.*) That one, that one (*The Stupid Zanni moves about, utterly confused.*) No, no, not that tree. That one.
Stupid Z:	(*going where he's told, but suddenly runing out*) I'm not going behind that tree; it's full of nettles.
Crafty Z:	Get back, get back. (*He does.*) Keep behind it – I can still see you. (*Crafty Zanni mimes carrying large hammer and goes towards Stupid Zanni.*)
	Now take this hammer. (*Stupid Zanni takes hammer and drops it.*) Ow! You've dropped it on my fooooot!!!
	(*Stupid Zanni picks up the 'hammer'.*) Now when he comes by . . . I'll knock him off his horse with this rake. (*Mimes holding rake.*)
Stupid Z:	Is that a rake? Oh, I thought it was a hoe!

Crafty Z: Now once I've knocked him off his horse, you hit him on the head with the hammer. Have you got the hammer? (*Stupid Zanni mimes holding the hammer.*) Right. Well, show me how you're going to hit him on the head. Go on, show me.

(*The Stupid Zanni raises the illusory hammer and fells the Crafty Zanni with a mighty blow.*)

Stupid Z: (*standing over the senseless body*) Sorry.

Game 52   *A Proposal Scorned*

Soggetto[3] for a *Commedia dell'Arte* improvisation.

> Pantalone – *an impoverished merchant.*
> Captain Spavento – *an elderly suitor of imagined means.*
> Flaminia – *Pantalone's daughter.*
> Spinetta – *her maid.*

Three-quarters of the performing space (from stage-right) is considered to be **Flaminia's** boudoir; an imaginary wall separating it from the last quarter (stage-left) which represents an ante-room. An equally imaginary door provides an entrance through the 'wall'. **Flaminia** is seated on a chair, placed D. S. R., her back to the rest of the stage, looking into a fictional dressing mirror.

> **Spinetta** attends her mistress, putting the final touches to her toilet. She tells her mistress: 'You want to look your best when The Captain proposes'. **Flaminia**: 'No I don't . . . I refuse to marry the old goat.' She appeals to **Spinetta** for help. They whisper and continue the dressing.

> **Pantalone** and **The Captain** enter into the ante-room, Pantalone very propitiatory, anxious to gain The Captain, whom he believes to be wealthy, for a son-in-law. He tells The Captain that Flaminia will be delighted to marry him, but she being a flighty young thing, he must be firm and not take no for an answer. He goes to open the door, and, finding it locked, demands entrance. **Spinetta** opens it and **Pantalone** enters the boudoir. He insists that Flaminia should

---

3. An alternative to 'Scenario'; useful where a shorter item is intended.

accept The Captain. She refuses – tears from her; threats from him. **Spinetta**: 'Leave her to me for a few minutes – I'll persuade her.'

Pantalone quits the boudoir. Tells **The Captain** that he must be patient a little longer – she is making herself pretty for him. He exits, leaving **The Captain** to cool his heels in the ante-room.

Attention returns to **Flaminia** and her maid, who suggests that they change places. They have a short rehearsal in which **Spinetta** coaches **Flaminia** in how to be a servant, and **Flaminia** coaches **Spinetta** in how to be a Lady! Both overdo it.

The Captain is getting impatient and knocks at the door. **Flaminia** answers it (in the character of a servant) and makes every excuse to delay **The Captain's** entrance. 'I'll see if she's in; who did you say it was?' etc.

Eventually **The Captain** rudely brushes aside the true **Flaminia** and makes a very formal proposal to **Spinetta**, who is hiding her face behind a fan. She leads him a dance, never being there when he gets down on his knees, etc. Eventually **Spinetta** says: 'Are you sure it's little **me** you want? Wouldn't you rather have my maid?' **The Captain**: 'No you, no one but you.' She accepts him.

Enter **Pantalone**: 'That's not my daughter – that's her maid. You'll have to marry her. Breach of promise, you know!!!!' **The Captain** makes a very hasty retreat.

Game 53   The Rival Captains

Finally, an example of a large-scale word and action impro, involving a fixed structure, but giving plenty of opportunity for invention. It involves two rival gangs and their champions and can be set in any period or locality (*Romeo and Juliet*, *West Side Story*, a scene from a martial arts film, or a school playground).

We'll use a *Commedia dell'Arte* **soggetto** as the example.

Example: The Rival Captains

The two champions are Captain Spavento and his arch-enemy Captain Matamoros. Each has his band of supporters. Imagine the stage divided into three:

(1) Spavento's realm stage-right; (2) stage-left: that of Matamoros; (3) 'no man's land', lying between them. The supporters of each captain do not stray out of their champion's territory.

Fixed Movement Routine to be Learnt

Spavento and gang start U. S. R. facing downstage [dir. 1]
Matamoros and gang start D. S. L. facing upstage [dir. 5]

Counts 1/ to 8.   Spavento and gang take 8 walks D. S. [dir. 1]
                     Matamoros and gang take 8 steps U. S. facing [dir. 5]

Counts 2/ to 8.   Spavento and gang turn and take 8 walks U. S. [dir. 5]
                     Matamoros and gang turn and take 8 walks D. S. [dir. 1]

Counts 3/ to 8.   Repeat First '**8**'

Counts 4/ to 8.   Repeat Second '**8**'

Counts 5/ to 8.   Spavento and gang take 4 steps D. S. [dir. 1]
                     Matamoros and gang take 4 steps U. S. [dir. 5]
                     Spavento and gang stop and turn to face rivals [dir. 7]
                     Matamoros and gang stop and turn to face rivals [dir. 3]

As Spavento walks down-stage the gang move with him encouraging him to pick a quarrel with Matamoros: 'You said you'd kill him if you ever saw him on the streets of Modena'; 'Go on, show him who's boss', etc. The walk downstage is quite slow, and exactly balanced by the up-stage walk of the rivals. The members of the gang vary their movements; some come very close, others walk backwards, etc. and all speak together. On the turn up-stage, they continue the business, but in *mime* or with very quiet mutterings, so that Matamoros' group gets the chance to gain the audience's attention as they walk down-stage.

After the 'walking routine' and the confrontation, the insults start. Spavento, somewhat reluctantly, is pushed forward into 'no man's land'. Matamoros comes in a little way to meet him. Spavento improvises an insult: 'You, Sir, are nothing but a piece of dog shit.' Pleased with himself he retreats to the congratulations of his supporters.

Matamoros goes to his fellows and says: 'Did you hear what he called me? I won't stand for that.' It is then his turn to throw the insult and meet Spavento in 'no man's land'. The insults can be physical (but no contact) as well as verbal.

This is repeated until the Captains are obliged to draw swords. They are both very reluctant to actually fight and are dragged and pushed by the gangs into the centre of no man's land. (see The Captains, page 173, for movements)

The scene usually needs to be brought to an end by the intervention of another character, who might well be one of the female roles, from whom both Captains and their followers fly in ignominy.

13

FACE MASKS

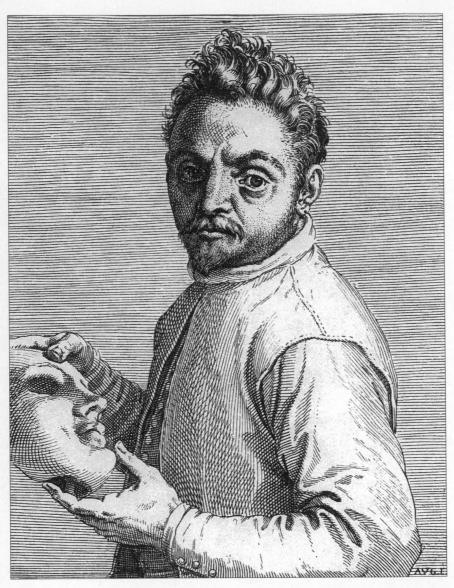

14

Commedia and the Mask

Before examining the nature and techniques involved when using the *Commedia* masks, we should perhaps consider some of the limitations and disadvantages they present. In electing to cover the major part of the face with a rigid appendage, the actor denies himself his most expressive feature. He is rather like a boxer who chooses to fight with one hand tied behind his back, and unless he can overcome and turn to his advantage the restrictions he has imposed on himself he will not survive the challenge.

And let it be said that, however important masks may be to its origins and however valuable to us as part of an actor/performer's armoury, *Commedia* can exist without them; neither masks nor the traditional characters should restrict creativity.

The history of the *Commedia dell'Arte* has been an almost continuous battle between pro-mask and anti-mask factions. Goldoni, the author of perhaps the most famous written *Commedia* play 'The Servant of Two Masters', was anti-mask, and there have been many others. Early pictures all seem to show masks, but by the middle of the seventeenth century they were often dispensed with. One problem with the traditional masks is that they tend to limit the roles to stereotypes originating in sixteenth and seventeenth-century Italy, which are not entirely relevant today, dealing largely with master/servant relationships, and the male/female divide.

I am far from advocating that masks should be abandoned, only that they should be used skilfully, adapted to the requirement of the production and the place in which it is played, that new characters should be created and that different techniques should be explored both in performing and in mask-making.

Another problem stems from the work of a highly skilled and creative craftsman, Donato Sartori, who virtually re-invented the leather mask in the 1950's. The difficulty is that mask-makers now are inclined to merely copy him, adding nothing new and perpetuating some of the disadvantages of his admittedly beautiful work. A beautifully made mask, which might look superb on the studio wall, is not necessarily the best one for performance. These masks are frequently too dark: dark browns and blacks may be suitable for the bright Italian sun but are rarely satisfactory under stage lighting.[1] They are generally too shiny, causing another lighting difficulty. They also tend to a smoothness and regularity that counts against character. The highly polished surface in no way duplicates the texture of skin, and the colour range is extremely limited.

That having been said, to be true to *Commedia*, the masks must be half-masks; the full-mask is a different creature altogether. *Commedia* is a theatre of direct communication, of intense give and take between the actor and his fellows, between the actor and his audience. It is not that the full-mask is something less. It is in fact something grander, but more remote; a thing for gods, heroes, demons, sprites. It can include fools, old men, saints and beggars, but they are archetypes, not humans. The half-mask is human, expressing humanity's frailties, greeds, ambitions, pretensions and loves.

Working in a Mask

Now to the practicalities of working in a mask, so that it enhances the performance, rather than restricting it. Occasionally someone will put a mask on for the first time and do everything right, but this rarely happens; even a most experienced and talented actor will usually need some training or guidance. From the beginning the games and drills we have been looking at will have been guiding the performer towards good mask technique, as well as to general *Commedia* skills.

Let us consider things you can't do when you wear a mask:

- You can't act 'naturally'.

- You can't expect the dialogue, written or improvised, to carry you: by this I mean that the 'manner' of performance, unlike in a well-made play, is more important than the 'content'.

- You can't stand stiffly, like a pole. The posture and restricted movement of many a straight actor is not suitable for work in a mask.

---

1. Arlecchino and The Doctor are special cases. See the section on the individual Masks.

- You can't fidget – every move you make is magnified.

- You can't let your head loll about.

- You can't move in an indecisive or slovenly way.

- You can't speak indistinctly or sloppily. You need to enunciate extra clearly in a mask.

What should you do, then?

- You must cultivate stillness. You should be able to take a pose, not only holding it physically, but holding and maintaining an emotion, thought, or intention.

- You must cultivate 'communication' with your fellow performers. You must know what they are saying, how they are breathing, what they are feeling, where their weight is placed, so that you know what their next move is likely to be. Further, you must know it all at two levels. You must know what the *actor* is doing and also what the *role* is doing.

- You must also be in communication with the audience. Not as a mass but as individuals. You must know where the good-looking man/woman is sitting, where the old woman, where the child. When you address the audience you must address your lines to them. Not at 'Them' – the great amorphous mass of an audience – but to the old woman, the child, the handsome creature in the third row.[2] That is why *Commedia* cannot readily be played in a darkened proscenium-type theatre.

- You must be able to express emotions and thoughts through the body. Unlike the mime, you are without the full potential of the most flexible instrument of expression, the face. So it is helpful to know **movement language**: the style, moves and stances of *Commedia* we have been examining.

---

2. This is explored and explained more fully in 'The Player and the Audience', to follow.

The Types of Mask

The *Commedia* mask is known as the half-mask. It covers the face from the hairline to the upper lip, dipping at the sides to cover the cheeks, and leaving the mouth, chin and jaw free, so as not to prohibit speech.

The half-mask comes in two main types, which are important for the performer to distinguish between, although the difference isn't greatly obvious to the spectators. They are the *'profile mask'* and the *'frontal mask'*. The *'profile mask'* has strongly marked features, especially a prominent nose, and is best seen 'sideways on'. The *'frontal mask'* on the other hand has flat features and is best seen when the actor faces front. Pantalone, Pulcinella and The Captain are examples of the *profile,* Arlecchino and Brighella of the *frontal*. The Zanni generally are something between the two and demand a mixture of both techniques.

There are also exaggerated *profile* masks, like certain *Callot*[3] Captains and Zanni, each with a startling proboscis. These demand special care: for example, you need to tilt the head down when you face front. The Doctor is more or less unique, with a quarter-mask covering only his forehead and nose. There are other oddities like that of Tartaglia, which has large spectacles forming part of the mask.

There remains the *bauta*, with its rather sinister white face and outward sloping lower edge usually held on a handle and often seen in the Venetian paintings by Guardi; and the flat *domino* mask without moulding (also known as a *loup*), only covering the area around the eyes (often just made from cut-out paper). Traditionally black, it originated in eighteenth-century Venice, and was worn at Carnival and other times by ladies of quality when they ventured beyond the walls of their palazzo. In the early nineteenth century it became the mask of the dancing Harlequin.

With the exception of these last two, the *bauta* and the *domino*, the *Commedia* masks represent the character's face, so we might well get an occasion when a character puts on a *domino* over his *Commedia* mask.

---

3. Jacques Callot – the engraver of 'Balli di Sfessania'; the inspiration for much of present-day *Commedia* and for the masks taken from his engravings.

Game 54   The Ritual

This is a private moment, rare in *Commedia*, when you put on a mask (especially when you do so for the first time). If you can be alone, all the better; if not, try and mentally isolate yourself. If you are in a studio or workshop turn your back on the rest of the group, if only for a couple of minutes.

Take the mask and hold it at arm's length with the 'face' towards you. Imagine the Mask, alive, animated. Put it on slowly, almost reverently; it's a bit like a matador dressing. Don't look in the mirror – yet! Don't talk to anyone! Look at your surroundings through the mask. See them as the mask's character would see them. Make a few small movements, which you know to be in character: sit down, stand up, yawn, stretch, cough, hum or sing a phrase. If the Mask (i.e. character) is 'doing it', risk bigger movements. Go over a few lines of dialogue or bits of business. If *you* are doing it – reduce, do less. Even take the mask off and have another good look at it. This feeling that the mask has an identity, a force of its own, that *it* is dictating the character's behaviour and not you, the actor, is shared by most performers experienced in mask-work, and whatever the psychological reasons for the phenomenon its theatrical value is considerable.

When you are really secure in 'being' the Mask (one might almost say when the Mask takes over) consult a mirror. Don't do anything, just stand there until the Mask wants to do or say something. As in all acting, you are being two people at once – what is sometimes referred to as being both 'puppet' and 'puppet master'. The puppet master will be able to remain detached while checking to see if the puppet in the mirror is reacting correctly when he pulls the strings.

Do's and Don'ts

- Do choose masks lighter in colour than the seventeenth-century originals; they were designed for Italy's blazing sun.

- Don't be frightened to use elastic but make sure it is hidden by wig or hat; if the seventeenth-century Italians had had it, they'd have used it. The ribbons on most commercial masks are a nuisance in performance.

- Don't expect to see perfectly!

- Don't cut the eye openings too big. Not only will you spoil the look of the mask, you will destroy the desirable effect that the mask's restricted vision imposes on the style of the performer: a sort of peering look that seems to give intensity to the proceedings.

- Do know if your mask is basically *profile* or *frontal*.

- Do stick sponge pads to the inside of the mask to keep it from putting pressure on the eyelids and anywhere else that is uncomfortable.

- Do touch the mask in moves where you would touch the face, but don't adjust it during performance; you must see that it's comfortable and secure before you start.

- Do remember the adage: 'Stillness is golden. Slow movement is silver. Quick movement is mercury.'

- Because the *Commedia* half-mask is the face of the character, it is generally speaking a good idea to try to blend in the mask to the actor's face and to the costume worn, using make-up, beards, moustaches, hats, bonnets and wigs, to draw attention from the mask edge. But this is a matter of taste and proportion; the mask is not meant to be like the elaborate latex make-ups for horror and sci-fi films. The old engravings seem to get it exactly right. If you look closely you can tell 'yes, it is a mask', but not so that you are more aware of the actor beneath than the role he's playing. Few photos of recent *Commedia dell'Arte* performances, on the other hand, show that this balance has been achieved. For some roles, such as Harlequin/Arlecchino, the convention of the mask is so familiar that to try to blend it in would be counter-productive.

Establishing the Mask

This is a 'ruse', doubtless of great antiquity but surviving until the matinée idol of only a few decades ago. The star actor (yes, in a straight play) makes his first entrance from the wings. He takes a few paces until he is sure he is seen by all, and then pauses with his face in profile ('That's what I look like side view on'), turns his head to the audience, pauses ('That's me, full face'), and after the expected applause, turns profile again, continues his entrance and on with the play.

This practice has thankfully all but disappeared, with our more ensemble philosophy, but it is an excellent and acceptable practice for the Masks. It should be done in character of course, and for the **profile masks** the routine is the same as the matinée idol's. Enter a few paces. Show the profile: if you are The Captain, the nose tilted up; if you are Pantalone, level or down. Then briefly present a front view, making sure that you're not looking up on this. Return to profile and continue the entrance. For the **frontal mask**, enter a few paces. Immediately present a 'front' view; pause there, and continue with the entrance.

In a mask, this ruse is not a selfish one. It helps the audience familiarise itself with the Mask's identity, and come to terms with its strangeness.

With a few exceptions, all the games and drills from both the Mime and Movement and the Word Games sections can profitably be repeated with the masks, and suggestions for appropriate ones are given with the Game titles.

There follow a few more games and drills specifically for mask training. The first drill uses **head rotations**, and is for developing the movement potential of **profile masks**.

Head Rotation Drill

'Under and Over'

Figure 14. Under and over

Face [dir. 1].

Count **1/** Turn the head sharply to the right to face [dir. 3].

Counts 2, 3, 4, 5, 6, 7. Make a complete rotation of the head by dropping the nose downwards, passing through the lowest point (looking down) then raising the head till you are looking towards the left [dir. 7]. Continue the clockwise circle looking up and ending by looking in the original direction [dir. 3].

Count 8 Hold position.

Repeat from Count 1/ looking left [dir. 7] then making an anticlockwise circle. ending looking towards [dir. 7].

119

'Under' (Half-Circles)

Count 1/	Look right (as before) to face [dir. 3].
Counts 2, 3, 4,	Complete the half circle, down and to the left [dir. 7].
Counts 5, 6, 7,	Return, down and back to right [dir. 3].
Count 8.	Hold position looking right.

Repeat from count 1/ starting looking left [dir. 7].

'Over and Under'

Count 1/	Look right as before [dir. 3].
Counts 2 to 7,	Slowly rotate the head, but this time anticlockwise, so you look up first, then to left, then down, and finally back to the right [dir. 3].
Count 8.	Hold position.

Repeat in clockwise direction starting looking left [dir. 7].

'Over' (Half-Circle)

Count 1/	Look to right [dir. 3].
Counts 2, 3, 4,	Half anticlockwise circle, up and to left [dir. 7].
Counts 5, 6, 7,	Return by half clockwise circle, up and to right [dir. 3].
Count 8.	Hold position.

Repeat from count 1/ starting looking left [dir. 7].

Game 55a   Profile Mask: Looking

The Routine

Facing [dir. 1] take the **Commedia Stance** (see page 69) right heel up.

Count **1**/	Look to right [dir. 3].
Count 2, 3, 4,	'Scoop' under. End looking left [dir. 7].
Count 5,	Hold position.
Count 6, 7, 8.	'Scoop' under. End looking right [dir. 3].
Count **2**/	Hold position – looking right.
Counts 2, 3, 4, 5, 6, 7,	Scoop 'under and over' (down, left, up, right).
Count 8.	Hold right.
Count **3**/	Look left. [dir. 7].
Counts 2, 3, 4,	Scoop over (up and to right) [dir. 3].
Counts 5,	Hold position.
Counts 6, 7, 8.	Scoop over (up and to left) [dir. 7].
Count **4**/	Hold position (looking left) [dir. 7].
Counts 2, 3, 4, 5, 6, 7,	Scoop over and under (up, right, down, left) [dir. 7].
Count 8.	Hold left position.

There are three ways of making the above moves, which demonstrate the three principal ways of moving the head in a profile mask.

1) Very quickly and suddenly, the position arrived at being held very still, and often lengthily.

2) In slow motion, very smooth and controlled.

3) Also slow, but with a rhythmic nodding of the head up and down; a move which can vary from mere vibrations to a shake, or an undulation, depending on the character required.

The game can be played in pairs or small groups. Possible variations are similar to those introduced in 'The Lantern' (Game 22, page 49).

1) Side by side, working in the same or opposite directions.

2) One behind the other (if working in the same direction, the back partner must make bigger moves – and there is an opportunity here to exploit differences in size and build).

3) Trio: 'A' and 'B' work in the same direction; 'C' makes the same moves but very slowly. 'A' and 'B' hold the position until 'C' has completed the move, and so on. (*'C's moves belong to the tradition of the slow-witted Zanni.*)

Game 55b   Look Again

An advanced version introducing '***timing impro***'. The original routine is used so that both 'A' and 'B' start with a look to the right. 'A' on stage-right cannot now see partner 'B' on his left. 'B' *can* see 'A', so is able to follow 'A's lead. 'A' can make any of the moves, in any style and at *any speed* of his choosing, which 'B' duplicates. If the move ends with the head facing left, 'B' must take over the initiation of the next movement (so that 'A' is able to follow 'B's lead).

The Use of 'Frontal' Masks

The accepted rule is that, as the *frontal* mask is not at its best seen from the side, you face front wherever possible. So [dir. 1] is best – [dir. 2 and 8] acceptable, [dir. 3 and 7] to be avoided. Remember though, the restrictions needn't apply to the rest of the body.

If two *profile Masks* (Pantalone and The Captain) meet centre-stage and talk, one would be likely to face [dir. 3] and one [dir. 7]. If it were two *frontal Masks* then the heads might face [dir. 2 and 8] though their bodies from the shoulders might be facing each other squarely [dir. 3 and 7].

The 'standard' meeting of two *frontal Masks* is however side by side, facing front, [dir. 1] and turning the head [dir. 2, 1, 8]. This stage relationship may well seem odd if you are not familiar with the conventions found in music hall, opera, and pre-1900 theatre.

Example

Here is the sort of thing you might have seen in a music hall some years ago.

The 'Straight Man' enters and comes D. S. C. and addresses the audience.

Straight Man: Ladies and Gentlemen. For my first number I would like to sing the ever-popular 'Song of the Flea'. Thank you Maestro . . .

Comic enters and stands very close to Straight Man.

Comic: Is this where I catch the 74 bus?

Straight Man: The 74 bus?

Comic: Yes . . . well you see if I take the 187, I have quite a long walk when I get there.

Straight Man: Would you please go; I'm just about to sing for the ladies and gentlemen. (*Points to the audience.*)

Comic: (*seeing the audience for the first time*) Oh are they all waiting for the 74 bus?

Straight Man: Can't you understand I'm going to sing for them?

Comic: That'll be nice . . . Especially if we have to wait a long time for the 74 bus.

Straight Man: This is not a bus stop. This is the stage of the Metropolitan Music Hall and I am about to sing for the ladies and gentlemen.

Comic: (*noticing the band in the pit*) Are they ladies and gentlemen?

Straight Man: Of course not – they're the orchestra. (*Rude noise from a trombone.*)

Comic: What's that?

Straight Man: It's the trombone.

Comic: Oh, I thought it was the 74 bus.

Game 56a   Playing Front

Run the above sketch through, or improvise a vaudeville double-act. Use any gestures and body directions (don't forget the leans which are useful here), but limit the entire head directions to [dir. 2, 1, and 8].

The purpose of this is to train in the *'frontal'* approach, and if you have no experience in this tradition, it would be as well to also try it first unmasked.

Game 56b   Playing Front (Two)

Repeat the above, but this time the restrictions are limited to the actual speaking of the lines. (The turns into profile should be brief.) For example on the Straight Man's line (from Game 56a):

Straight Man: Can't you understand? (*Turns head directly to comic and scowls. Returns head to front for the remaining line.*) I'm going to sing for them.

Comic: That'll be nice . . . (*Turns head to Straight Man and smiles; then turns to front.*) Especially if we have to wait a long time for the 74 bus!

Note: this is a training drill and the principal would be applied with considerable flexibility during actual performance.

Game 41 (from the Word Game section, page 88) can now be revised using frontal orientation, and masks. (It is tricky to duplicate what your partners are saying without facing them – but it can be done!)

Game 57   The Interview

The Interviewee, wearing his (or her) mask, enters, and is asked to take a seat – a single chair in the middle of the studio. The rest of the group, the Interviewers, sit facing him (located as an audience) and one by one put a question to the Mask. He has come for a job, and one suitable to his status should be selected. Of the *Commedia dell'Arte* characters, Arlecchino would apply for the post of valet; Colombina for lady's maid; Franceschina for cook; and The Doctor for the Chair of Mathematics at a university. The first questions, put by a Chairperson, should establish the Mask's identity.

Example

> *Pedrolino (here a dim-witted fellow) enters.*

Chairperson: Please take a seat (*Pedrolino looks confused*). Yes that one, that one (*Pedrolino picks up the chair and starts to walk off with it*). Where are you going? Put it down. Sit, sit. (*He does so.*) Now what's your name?

Pedrolino: Pedrolino.

1st Question: Where do you live?

Pedrolino: With my brother.

2nd Question: Well, where does he live?

Pedrolino: With me.

3rd Question: Where do you both live???

Pedrolino: Together.

4th Question: Have you worked as a cook before?

Pedrolino: Before what?

4th Question: Before you came here. ★

Pedrolino: No, I've only just had my breakfast.

> *Etc, etc . . .* [4]

★ *Note: if the Mask asks a question back, as here, the same interviewer can answer it. The purpose of the game is for the Mask to find his own identity. The answers don't have to be 'jokey' as above but if they are, all the better.*

---

4. This originates from an Italian book of humorous extracts, part of my L. A. M. (Lazzi Access Memory!)

Game 58   The Interrogation

This version of Game 57 is for an actor who is well established in his Mask to see how he will react under pressure. The set-up is the same. The Interviewers become Interrogators, and after the establishment of name, domicile, age, etc., the Mask is accused of a crime; Arlecchino of stealing a chicken, for example, or The Doctor of being a member of some subversive and forbidden society.

Game 59   Spotting

This is the technique of directly involving the audience, mentioned earlier, in which the actor addresses, or appears to address, those present as individuals. It is particularly effective when wearing a mask and does something to break down the barrier between the actor and the audience that the mask induces. The Mask of Pantalone is particularly good at it, so we'll call on him for an example.

Example

Pantalone enters from up-stage, walking backwards, and talking to someone in the wings.

Pantalone: No, no, no, I repeat, no. I will not give my permission for you to pay your addresses to my daughter!

He faces front and takes a few paces down-stage. Says next line to the audience in general.

Pay? He couldn't pay anything!

Takes a few paces back and delivers next line to off-stage.

This interview, like my patience, is at – an – end!!!

He walks down-stage.

That told him, worthless young blighter!

He comes right down to the edge of the stage.

Noble pedigree and all that . . .

This is said 'to the air', but he then leans forward suddenly, fixes his beady eye on someone in the front row to his right ('X') and says:

But not worth a brass farthing!

He turns his head from 'X', 'spots' 'Y' to the left of the front row, and says very rapidly:

Not a brass farthing!

(Returns his gaze to 'X') I should know . . .

(Looks back at 'Y') I should know,

Straightens up, leans back and speaks to the audience in general.

I ruined his father!

Leans forward again and directs his next line to the second or third row, panning the mask slowly from right to left as he delivers the line:

And – what's – the use – of – going to all the trouble – of ruining a man –

Turns head abruptly back to 'X' and rapidly says:

If the family is going to get half of it back by marrying yer' daughter?

Nods head up and down in laughter spotting 'X' and 'Y' and anyone else whose eye he catches.

'X' is the 'anchor'; someone responsive should be chosen, and ninety per cent of those first selected will prove suitable. If they are *not*, a new 'anchor' should be located. A whole scene could be addressed to the 'anchor' and returned to in later scenes. One might have thought that the rest of the audience would feel neglected, but this doesn't seem to be the case, and the 'anchor' is as important a 'bridge' (mixed metaphor) for them as it is for you.

Note: there are a couple of occasions when the actor must apply the technique with caution. One is when the 'house' is half empty. There is the likelihood that some of the audience will feel self-conscious, and uncomfortable at being 'picked on' – in which case use an imaginary 'anchor'. The other time is at an early point in the performance when the audience is still 'cold', and the same method should be applied. Judging the temper of the audience is one of the more difficult skills required of the player, and you must be careful not to force communication until they are willing to accept it. If you start with a feeling of holding back you will usually feel the audience reaching towards you.

The Game

The formula is for a solo player in a mask of their choosing to work an improvised or learnt speech before the rest of the group. He/she must split up the 'spotting' between an 'X', a 'Y' and a 'Z' if desired, and the rest of the group.

Game 60 *Equivocating*

This is another approach to 'Spotting' but adds a new improvising aid – 'equivocating'. You take some known speech, poem, or nursery rhyme, and at the first opportunity sow the seeds of doubt, offer alternatives, go off on a tangent. Any mask appropriate to the theme could be worn. The 'spotting' should be used, selecting 'X', 'Y' and 'Z' to whom you direct your mistrust of the known version. Equivocating can, of course, be used by an unmasked character like either of the Lovers.

Example: 'Variation on a Cupboard'

Speaker: Old Mother Hubbard went to . . .

Well, I don't like to say old, but she was getting on a bit . . .

Getting on a bit Mother Hubbard . . .

Funny. I'm not sure she was a 'mother'; Never saw any children. I know she had a dog! Before that kept a goat, I think; but children? No, it wasn't her. It was the getting on lady who lived in a shoe who had the children!

Getting on dog lover Mrs Hubbard? Miss Hubbard? Ms Hubbard?

I think her name was Hubbard? Yes, yes, it has to be Hubbard, to rhyme with cupboard, I suppose. It could have been . . .

Getting on dog lover Ms Bridge went to the fridge . . .

Etc, etc . . .

THE PLAYER
AND THE AUDIENCE

15

I have stressed the *Commedia* player's links with the audience. He/she never severs the link, but there are differences in the degree of contact, from the direct to the oblique, which can be divided into six types:

1) **The Address**

   These are moments when a character directly addresses the audience to set the scene, narrate off-stage events, explain relationships: typical examples already shown are the Zanni's speech in Game 25 (page 53) and that of the Lover in Game 26 (page 55).

2) **The Appeal**

   This is when the audience are called upon to judge on a matter within the play, suggest a solution, offer advice: Harlequin has decided to kill himself and asks the audience for suggestions on how he should do it. Or asked for direct help as in pantomime, when Buttons says to the audience: 'If you see Baron Hardup snooping around, call me and I'll come at once.'

3) The Soliloquy

Here the character is talking to himself, but includes the audience as silent witnesses to his dilemmas or ambitions. He distances himself, so as not to demand response, but still makes them consider themselves involved. A *Commedia* actor performing the Hamlet soliloquy might exaggerate, using prolonged pauses to draw the audience in:

> 'To be or not to be,
>
> *Freeze in 'thinking' attitude for 5 seconds.*
>
> That is the question!
>
> *Pace about in deliberation for at least 10 seconds.*
>
> Whether 'tis nobler in the mind to suffer . . .
>
> *Another long pause for the actor to register suffering.*
>
> . . . the slings and arrows of outrageous fortune . . .
>
> *Spoken at great speed.*
>
> Or to take arms against a sea of troubles, and by opposing
>
> (*Long pause*) end them?' *Etc, etc . . .*

4) The Aside

This is a comment on a scene in progress directed at the public **'behind the hand'**. There is the use of the brief **'aside'** typical of Restoration drama;

> She: Pray Sir, is this the house of Lady Tweezle?
>
> He: I fear she is away. (*Aside.*) This is a monstrous fine filly, I would fain seduce her!
>
> She: Away? (*Aside.*) Here's a likely dupe; should be rich pickings here!

He:	She has gone to Bath.
She:	To Bath?
He:	Yes, to Bath to bathe. *Etc, etc . . .*

There is always the difficulty of what the other characters in the scene are doing during the *'aside'* – so it usually has to be brief.

In *Commedia* we have a solution in the *'freeze'*, which means the *'aside'* can be as long as required. Anyone else on-stage freezes for its duration and the more frozen-like movement the characters assume (the mouth open to speak, a limb ready to move) the more acceptable will be the break. The actor making the *'aside'* can even walk around among the 'statues' and make comments about the situation in hand.

5)   The Action Shared

This is the permanent condition the actor adopts when not using one of the foregoing direct approaches to the audience. It is a state of heightened awareness of the public's presence, in which the actor is mindful of communicating the **intention** of his actions or spoken words to them, at the same time, or even before the on-stage recipient. Often there are also actions, which the on-stage characters are not supposed to see: the Lover hides a letter from Pantalone, for example, but he makes sure the audience sees the move. Every line is pitched to the audience; if the actor speaks in a whisper it is a stage-whisper; if he raises his hand to strike an opponent, he makes sure that it is the down-stage hand and he will raise it higher and pause longer than required by the natural action, signalling to the spectators: 'Look now, don't miss, I'm going to strike the scoundrel'. This is necessary, to some degree, in all stage performance, but *Commedia* takes it further, so that the audience will take pleasure in their advance knowledge of the coming action; before kicking Arlecchino on the behind, The Doctor exaggerates the preparatory back swing of the attacking leg.

6)   The Reaction Shared

This is where the actor, being on the receiving end of an action or a line of dialogue, shares his feelings with the spectators. It is a silent form of the *'aside'* using expression or gesture. A comic possibility is the use of a misemotional reaction: after a threat of violence, the recipient turns to the front with pursed lips – 'Ooh!' – or a silly smile. A deadpan turn of the head to the audience and back, called *'clocking'*, is often used in this context.

16

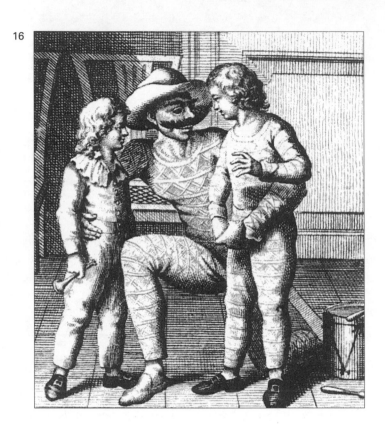

PART TWO
THE LEGACY

17

A BRIEF HISTORY OF
COMMEDIA DELL'ARTE

I would really like to start this short historical survey with: 'To begin at the beginning . . . ' but unfortunately this is very nearly impossible. Not only do we not have the moment when someone got some actors together, clapped his hands and said: 'Look here guys, we are going to start a new form of theatre called the *Commedia dell'Arte*. Hands up all who'd like to have a go' – but the *Commedia dell'Arte*, when we get the first evidence of its existence, was, if not fully grown, at least no longer in its infancy. So I'll start with some relevant facts and see where it gets us.

Angelo Beolco (1502–1542)

Maurice Sand[1] thought that he had identified 'the man who clapped his hands' as Angelo Beolco, an actor and dramatist who delighted Venetian audiences at Carnival time under the name of '*Ruzzante*' (the Gossip); he was a shrewd peasant type, given to long but amusing chitchats in the dialect of Padua, and Sand named him as the father of the *Commedia dell'Arte*. Beolco did indeed gather round him a small company of excellent amateur actors, who performed his plays to much acclaim. They were in dialect, and may have used masks, but they used little or no improvisation, and didn't present any characters recognisable as *Commedia dell'Arte* Masks, nor introduce their names. Although Beolco may have been a contributing influence, it is doubtful if he can claim a relationship as close as paternity.

Andrea Calmo (1509–1561)

Another contender was Andrea Calmo, also a writer/actor, whose principal creation was an elderly Venetian with some affinity to Pantalone, but again not using the name. He too must be rejected for anything

---

1. Maurice Sand: 'History of the Harlequinade' 1915 (probably basing his conclusions on the authority of Riccoboni (see page 145).

more than a contribution to the general conditions in which the infant *Commedia dell'Arte* found nourishment. The works of both Beolco and Calmo are worth study, providing glimpses of the type of farcical material, based on the caricature of local types, which would have gained a ready audience among the crowds at the Venetian Carnival.

The Market

Though we are unable to find a father for the *Commedia dell'Arte*, we can say with certainty that its mother was necessity – necessity stimulated by hunger and want, and something of that hunger, that urgency, needs to be simulated even today if we want to capture the atmosphere and vitality of those early performances.

Let us consider that it is market day – anywhere. In the cold and early light you stand before a small pile of cabbages, carrots and onions, on which you have placed your hopes. You leave at home a weeping wife, a squalling baby and a threat of eviction. Your heart drops when you realise that directly opposite you, there is a man who has for sale a similar pile of cabbages, carrots, onions and leeks! The crowds arrive and you call out as loudly as you can, 'Best cabbages in the market, best cabbages, only three pence, cabbages.' You start to draw some customers, but your rival has brought out a drum, and the punters are drawn to see what he has to offer. Not to be outdone, you bang two pans together, and do a cartwheel and then call out:

> Gather round Zan Padella,
> Acrobat and cabbage seller
> Sommersaults I do for free
> And carrots are five pence for three.

You start to sell some of your vegetables. Your rival has noted your success and you are alarmed to see him, a burly fellow of ferocious appearance, approaching you; but he has come not with a threat, but with the suggestion of an alliance. He is a musician and plays the pipe as well as the drum. 'You,' he says, 'are quite a tumbler, and not bad with the repartee.' For the rest of the day, you pool the resources of your talents and merchandise, and at the end of the day your share of the takings is enough to keep you out of difficulties, at least until next market day.

This little fiction introduces two elements which would have been needed at the inception of the *Commedia dell'Arte*: the need to draw a crowd and the idea of co-operation. If our two greengrocers continued their partnership, they could have developed a humorous cross-patter which would help to put the crowd in an easygoing and hopefully spending mood. A possibility was the building of a double-act, in which one partner plays the slick, quick-witted salesman (to be known as 1st Zanni) and the other a dimwitted assistant, or a supposed customer (2nd Zanni), who could play it straight, pretending to offer his money and take the product – or sometimes letting the crowd into the scam.

2nd Zanni: (*as country yokel*) I'll take me a poun' of they cabbages. I bought um last week an t'were best cabbage I ere tasted.

1st Zanni: Pound of cabbage, there you are young man. Anyone else? (*2nd Zanni just stays there.*) Is there something else you want? What are you waiting for?'

2nd Zanni   I'm waiting for the sixpence you promised I, if I said they were the best I ever tasted!

To the delight of the crowd he would get a mock thrashing.

The Mountebanks

As confirmation of this close link between the performer and the salesman, we have accounts of the Venetian 'mountebanks' who were each day to be found drawing large crowds in St Mark's Square. These purveyors of quack medicines, oils and unguents, cure-alls and love potions called upon the help of actors and acrobats as aids to their sales pitches and were soon to draw on the Masks of Pantalone, Zanni, The Captain, and others, to promote their wares.

A free performance of a play involving the, by then popular, masked characters of the *Commedia dell'Arte*, would be announced, and after a noisy display of acrobatic skill, juggling, dancing and music, the mountebank himself would appear; the word 'mountebank' denotes one who 'mounts' a 'banco' or platform. From a large trunk he would draw the mysterious items he offered for sale. That he could be no mean performer himself is borne out by the account given by a Sir Thomas Coryat, an English visitor who witnessed the mountebanks in 1608:

> . . . Truely I wondered at many of these natural orators. For they
> would tell their tales with such admirable volubility and plausible
> grace, even extempore, and seasoned with that singular variety of
> elegant jest and witty conceits, that they did often strike admiration
> into strangers that never heard them before. The head Mountebank
> at every time that he delivereth out anything, maketh out an
> extemporal speech, which he doth efstoones intermingle with such
> savoury jests (but spiced now and then with singular scurrility) that
> they minister passing mirth and laughter to the whole company,
> which perhaps may consist of a thousand people that flock together
> about one of the stages.

That the Mountebank could also be a conjuror is made apparent.

> Also I have seen a Mountebank hackle and gash his naked arm with
> a knife most pitifully to beholde, so that the blood hath streamed
> out in great abundance, and by and by after he hath applied a certain
> oyle unto it, wherewith he hath incontinent both staunched the
> blood and so thoroughly healed the woundes and gashes, that when
> he hath afterward shewed us his arme againe, we would not possibly
> perceive the least token of a gash.[2]

After nearly an hour of such salesmanship, in which the masked actors
played their part in collecting money and distributing the merchandise,
the promised play would be given.

My account so far has not given any indication of how the street
performers came to give 'plays' rather than mere exhibitions of
performing skills, or how the Masks of Pantalone, Arlecchino or The
Doctor were adopted. The origins of the different characters will be
taken up when we look at the individual Masks, but as an example of
how easy it is to leap to erroneous or partly true conclusions, we should
perhaps consider The Doctor, who has many similarities to the mountebanks just discussed; he makes the same attempts to bamboozle with
rhetoric and apparent erudition, and he was often called upon to offer
quack remedies and apply enemas (a favourite source of humour,
no longer to our tastes). However, in the early days he is a Doctor of
Law not of medicine, so he cannot have developed directly from the
mountebank.

---

2. 'Coryats Crudities' – T. Coryat, London, 1611, quoted by Winifred Smith,
op. cit.

18

The question of how and why street and carnival entertainers started presenting the particular type of plays they did is also difficult to answer categorically. It was at the beginning of the sixteenth century that an interest in classical plays was being fostered both in the learned academics and in royal and ducal courts. Plays, particularly by Roman authors, were revived and performed by aristocratic amateurs, and used as models for new plays, which were also presented.

By the 1540's, groups of actors had established themselves as professionals, and as such were sometimes invited to play alongside the amateurs in the new plays and classical revivals, taking on the comic and character roles. These players were, of course, also engaged to entertain at courtly functions, weddings and feast days, and, having been familiarised with the new fashion, presented pieces that would appeal to the tastes of their clients. Having an oral rather than a literary education, they would have been more likely to reproduce the dramas by improvisation than by memorising a written script. What had started as a necessity became an asset. Even when they performed in less exalted surroundings, they found the plays popular, and when broadened with plenty of comic action entirely suited to the crowds in the piazza.

The Great Companies

The era of the great companies followed. They were soon travelling widely throughout Italy, and extending their public to France, Germany, Spain, and to a lesser degree England. The companies were under royal or noble patronage, thus gaining some protection from the threat of expulsion, persecution, imprisonment and even death which was meted out to common rogues, vagabonds and players.

Such were the *'Confidenti'* under the patronage of the Medici, the *'Accesi'* in the employ of the Duke of Mantua, and a group belonging to the Duke of Modena. The story of these troupes is beyond our scope here, and we'll just outline some of the characteristics they had in common. They numbered ten to fifteen players, which would be likely to include the following: a Pantalone, a Doctor, two pairs of Lovers, a Captain, a maid-servant such as Colombina, an Arlecchino and a Brighella. The company was completed by a couple of other Zanni, a character actor or two to take on the odd roles, plus perhaps musicians and singers. The director, quite frequently a woman, would also be one of the leading players.

The company was often run as a co-operative, the majority of the cast being shareholders. After travel and living expenses had been deducted, all profits were kept in a locked chest until the end of the season, when a share-out would take place. Younger members would be considered apprentices and would only get their keep, and non-performers and utility actors paid a wage instead of taking a share. There were fines for unpunctuality, drunkenness, and even swearing. There were often conditions imposed on the company by the elders of the towns they played in, or by the wealthy client who employed them. Their patron would also exact a certain behaviour, which could include a promise to attend confession, to refrain from profanity, and to limit indecent dialogue or action in performance. The amount they were permitted to charge for admission to public performances was regulated, and the times of performances were not permitted to interfere with church services.

In 1571 the Ganassa Company, then under the direction of Flaminio Scala (who was to publish a book of scenarios in 1611), made a first visit to Paris, and returned in 1577 under the directorship of Francesco Andreini whose beautiful wife was the first and most accomplished of all Isabellas. For the next hundred years one or more companies found a second home in Paris, and an appreciation of their art, if not greater than in Italy, was at least more fully documented there.

Not that all was a bed of roses; though the Gelosi company, for example, had the support of King Henri IV, many of his subjects looked on the Italian invasion less kindly. He had married Marie de Medici, who had brought her favourites with her; many felt that her influence on the King was too prevalent and to also introduce Italian actors was going a step too far. French actors of the Hôtel de Bourgogne, the first regular theatre in Paris and the cradle of the Comédie Française, were hardly welcoming. They had inherited a monopoly from the Confrérie de la Passion, originally a body of non-professionals entrusted with the mounting of passion plays; no one else was permitted to present spoken plays in the capital without their permission and a hefty payment. They were often to make life difficult for the Italians in spite of the royal support they enjoyed.

The date 1658 is of interest in that Molière paid a rental to the Italians in that year to share the Petit-Bourbon Theatre where they were ensconced. The *Commedia dell'Arte* company played on Tuesdays and Sundays, Molière and his company on each other day of the week. He had to work in the *'three-house-set'* [3] favoured by the Italians. Some few years later Molière was in the dominant position, and it was the *Commedia dell'Arte* who paid him rent. Molière was undoubtedly influenced by the *Commedia dell'Arte*, but probably from earlier contact during his youthful years of touring.

It was around this date that all things Italian, including the Italian language, lost some of their popularity. Besides this, many of the actors of the *Commedia dell'Arte* had absorbed much of French culture, some having actually been naturalised, and so it was that a good admixture of French was included in the performances. This trend reached its zenith when the brilliant Evaristo Gherardi (1663-1700) joined the company. He was the son of Giovanni Gherardi, known as Flautino, a Zanni of Brighella appearance, who specialised in whistling and making bird noises. In spite of this, Flautino was a man of some cultivation who had given his son a classical education along French rather than Italian lines. The Company at the Hôtel de Bourgogne, in which Evaristo took over the role of Arlecchino in 1689, was by then greatly 'Frenchified'. Gherardi went on to publish a book of French language scenes which were not improvised, but written by French authors and used by the *Commedians* between his joining the company and its disbanding in 1697.

---

3. See footnote 3, page 6.

Throughout all this period, the *Commedia dell'Arte* players back in Italy, who continued to perform on their trestle stages in the town squares, were by then such a common occurrence that they would be no more remarked on than a ballad singer and pianist would have been in a Victorian pub, and only seem to have invited anyone to put pen to paper when they were exceptionally good or more frequently bad. Then we get complaints of:

> Scenery chalked out with charcoal in the vilest taste, an overture of braying asses and buzzing bees, a prologue fit for nothing, intermedi bad enough to send the actors to the gallows, a Manifico (Pantalone) not worth a farthing, a Graziano (The Doctor) who mumbles his words, a Lover who torments his arms at every speech, a Burattino who has no other gesture but that of putting his hat upon his head, a Signora with a voice like a ghost, and the gestures of a sleep walker . . . [4]

It was only when the players left their native land that the genre was considered unusual enough to be written about, and depicted in paintings and engravings. This gives the erroneous impression that Arlecchino, Pantalone and the rest suddenly left their native Italy and took up residence in Paris, and would do a similar 'flit' to England in the eighteenth century. But while larger companies would appear in Paris and other major cities in France, Germany and England, less affluent troupes, ranging from one man and a boy to those with eight to twelve players, would be seen at fairs and carnivals, and now and then in ducal palaces, and as Cole Porter's song reminds us, trudged their way 'around the map of little Italy', doing so for another 200 years. We should remember this when we are studying the literature on the *Commedia dell'Arte*, the bulk of which refers, after 1600, to the visits of the major companies and artistes to Paris.

1697 is one of *Commedia dell'Arte*'s few dates that stick in the memory. It marks not so much an event as a non-event. Not a moment when some great thing happened but when something great stopped happening, for it marked the date when perhaps the greatest of all the companies at the Hôtel de Bourgogne was forced to disband. At this time a book called '*La Fausse Prude*' was causing much gossip around Paris. It had been published in Holland, a centre of illicit printing, and was said to be an attack on Mme de Maintenon, the powerful mistress of Louis XIV.

---

4. Garzoni, 1587, quoted by A. Nicoll, 'Masks and Miracles', 1931.

19

We are told that the troupe had a play called '*La Finta Matrigna*' in preparation (as we've seen, the days of near complete improvisation had passed) by De Fatouville, and some bright spark within the company thought it a good idea to cash in on the attendant scandal and advertise the production as '*La Fausse Prude*'. Although there wasn't any intention of including anything from the book, the performance was never permitted to take place. Madame put her dainty foot firmly down, and crushed the *Commedians* beneath it. On May 13th (unlucky for some) the chief of police received instruction from the palace: 'The King has dismissed his Italian actors: His Majesty commands me to write to you, ordering you to shut up their theatre for good.' When the *Commedians* went to the theatre the next day they found the doors locked against them. They were not permitted to work elsewhere in the capital and the great company dispersed. A regular company was not to be seen there again for nearly 20 years. A continuity was, however, maintained: not by the Italian actors, who dispersed far and wide, but by the Masks themselves, or rather by the public's desire to see them endure.

Since medieval times the great fairs of Saint Germain and Saint Laurent had included all manner of entertainments, and by the seventeenth century assorted tightrope walkers, acrobats, sword-swallowers and jugglers had borrowed the apparel, if not the personas, of the *Commedia dell'Arte*, and the marionettes presenting truncated scenarios purloined from the Italian actors were proving popular. On the suppression of the King's players, several of these puppet masters, realising a gap in the market, gathered together small groups of live actors for performances at first in makeshift booths, and later, as their popularity grew, in purpose-built theatres of some size and permanence.

So strong is our concept of the Masks themselves, and their survival, there is a tendency to think that the royal players set up and started performing in the fairground booths. But, in the main, this was not so. Some of them returned to Italy, some found work in other countries, and the rest joined the small companies that were still permitted to perform around France provided they didn't come within thirty miles of the capital. There are those who would not admit that these new companies of the fairs were *Commedia dell'Arte* at all. They were made up with perhaps a few old hands from touring companies, but most were either amateurs, or performers without experience of acting in plays, and they were predominantly French! But in many ways this was a return to the earlier style of instant creation, of performing to a restless, demanding and less cultivated public, adapting to ever changing demands.

In any case their success was prodigious, enough to dent the egos of the actors of the Comédie Française; and worse, to make a hole in their box office receipts. The theatres of the fairs were infringing the monopoly they still held, allowing only them, the legitimate actors of the Comédie Française, to present dialogue plays within the environs of Paris. The *forains*, the players of the fairs, admitted that this was so; but how about monologues? They contrived performances in which the Arlecchino spoke all the lines, or one in which each actor would be alone on the stage when he spoke, hopping quickly into the wings to make place for another. Printed leaflets were handed out, giving songs which the audience were encouraged to sing and which substituted for the dialogue of the actors, or the players held up scrolls, like the captions of the silent films; at first transferring them from one pocket to the other, giving immense scope for comic by-play, but later lowering them from above, like a song sheet. The public would have been aware of the embargo and took pleasure in the antics with which the *forains* attempted to circumnavigate it.

These tactics kept the theatres of the fairs going for over ten years, but when the audiences tired of these capers the players slipped back to the forbidden dialogue, and the legitimate actors were not slow to declare war in earnest. On the night of February 21, 1709, with a posse of forty archers, and as many carpenters and labourers, they attacked the fair's principal theatre, smashing the seating of the auditorium and the scenery and machinery of the stage. But by the following evening the *forains* had made good the damage and were open for business. The Comédie Française returned a few days later and, again at night, attacked the building, this time razing it to the ground. For once the law favoured the *forains*, for their adversaries had acted illegally in demolishing the theatre at night, and they were obliged to pay enough compensation for the theatre to be rebuilt. The conflict continued for nearly a hundred years with gains and losses on both sides.

By the 1800's the fairs had made a virtue of silent pantomime and it was from this fertile ground that Deburau arose to establish the great French mask of Pierrot (see page 203). It also proved an inspiration to the largely silent Harlequins that became popular in England in the early eighteenth century. Before discussing that, we should return to 1716 and the recall of an Italian company to Paris.

The Return to Paris

On the death of Louis XIV in 1715, Philip, Duke of Orleans, became Regent to the young Louis XV, and it was he who re-established a *Commedia dell'Arte* company in Paris. The Duke of Palma recommended Luigi Riccoboni,[5] known as Lelio, and he was accordingly invited to form a company. They opened at the Théâtre du Palais-Royal, to great acclaim, largely due to the successful début of Thomassin as Arlecchino. Within six months they were re-established in their old home, the Hôtel de Bourgogne, now luxuriously re-appointed, and there were many triumphs of both new and old scenarios. However gradually there was less enthusiasm for the old ribaldry and greater demand for finesse and the elegant use of the French language. French playwrights were engaged and the graceful plays of Marivaux replaced the vitality of the old *Commedia dell'Arte*.

---

5. Born in 1675. His 'Histoire du Théâtre Italien', from which more recent authors have gathered much of their material, was published in 1727.

Harlequin in England

Not considered by most modern writers to be part of the real *Commedia dell'Arte*, the form taken by the Masks across the Channel was quite distinct from the Italian or even the French. Short visits by *Commedia* troupes, dating from the earliest days, had failed to make the style really take root in England, though English performers and writers, including Shakespeare, were well enough aware of the characters and of the technique of improvising. Will Kempe, the clown of Shakespeare's company, had worked with the Italians and claimed to be proficient in improvisation, but it was never to become part of the English theatre tradition.

In the early eighteenth century, the names of the *Commedia dell'Arte* Masks were often used, but they were very soon anglicised both in character and name. Stemming, it would seem, primarily from the *forains* theatres of Paris, they tended towards silent mime, a style that was to predominate throughout the next two hundred years of pantomimes and Harlequinades[6] in England.

The first English theatre Harlequin was a Joe Haines, who played the part in *Scaramouche a Philosopher, Harlequin a schoolboy, Bravo, Merchant and Magician – a Comedy after the Italian Manner,* 1667. In 1687 Tom Jevon appeared as Harlequin in *The Emperor of the Moon,* Mrs Aphra Behn's adaptation of a French original. John Weaver claims to have devised the first English pantomime: 'carried on by Dancing, Action and Motion only, performed by Grotesque Characters (the Masks) after the manner of the Modern Italians'. It was called *The Tavern Bilkers* and given at Drury Lane Theatre in 1702.

The eighteenth-century concept of pantomime, which had nothing in common with the modern British variety, consisted of a classical story of heroes, or gods, preceded, followed, or interrupted, by the entrance of the anglicised *Commedia* characters, who might present an interlude, later to be known as a Harlequinade, that had little or nothing to do with the serious story. A tradition was soon established of a prologue, in which the Immortals bestowed a magic wand on Harlequin which had the power of initiating the transformation scenes, which were the highlight of the productions. The popularity of these hotchpotch affairs was the despair of theatre managers like David Garrick, who were forced to mount such fare alongside their Shakespearian productions in order

---

6. In the early nineteenth century the flow was in the opposite direction, Deburau coming under the influence of the English clowns.

to keep their houses out of debt. Garrick himself was much admired as a 'speaking' Harlequin, and there is an amusing story of an old actor who, when being asked about Edmund Kean in his great parts of Richard III and Othello, replied: 'Ah, but you should have seen his Harlequin'. As the success of these productions increased, Harlequin became the central character, and there are scores of titles in which he is the eponymous hero.

The most famous of the Harlequins of the time was John Rich who, working under the stage name of Lun, established himself in 1717. He changed the costume to the tight-fitting leotard of diamond patches and encouraged the legacy of silence. Knowing that his voice was not a pleasant one, he concentrated on his undoubted ability as a mime and dancer. Second only to him was his pupil, Henry Woodward, originally billed as Lun Junior, who later joined Garrick and became a rival to his former master. The Harlequins of this time specialised in what they called 'attitudes' – static poses expressive of an appropriate emotion with which to begin or end a scene. They are attractively illustrated in the later 'Penny Plain' prints, but I find it hard to discover anything that I would call 'good theatre'.

Harlequin's dominance was brought to an end by the appearance in the 1800's of Joseph Grimaldi, whose character of 'Clown' drove Harlequin from centre stage, turning him into the rather vapid dancing partner of an equally vapid heroine, Columbine. The surviving scripts of the Harlequinades throughout the nineteenth century are mostly sad affairs of rhymed doggerel, mostly devoid of characterisation or humour. They must have been redeemed by stage tricks like the exploding policeman, inherited from the Grimaldi age. The Harlequinade, which had never been more than a part, or interlude, in a programme, was shortened even further and lingered as the afterpiece of the British pantomime until the early years of the twentieth century.

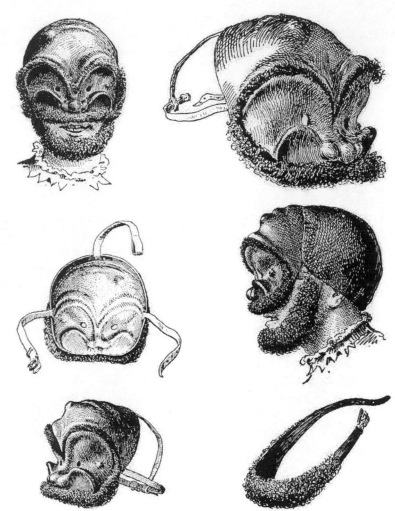

20

PLAYING THE INDIVIDUAL MASKS

Introduction

I hope that I have made it clear that, although we have been working within the framework of a disciplined form and technique, I consider the potential subjects, themes, scenarios – whatever we want to express – as being as open and as diverse as the human condition.

But now we are going to step back firmly into the world of the *Commedia dell'Arte*, and examine its principal characters and how they may be played; stressing again that we study them partly as a guide to mastering/creating a *Commedia* technique, not solely to perform the ancient Masks.

★

Before describing the individual Masks, we should look at the position they occupy in the plot's structure, and their relationship to each other. A *Commedia dell'Arte* scenario from its Baroque golden age invariably centred on what is known as 'the Italianate plot', which also formed the basis of many of Shakespeare's plays. It had derived its composition from the Roman playwright Plautus, and ultimately from the writer of the 'New' Greek comedy, Menander. Whatever its ramifications, it commences with one or more pairs of lovers, being forced into parting and betrothal to others of their parent or guardian's choice: usually it is the female who is to face a forced marriage, her true love being banished from the town. The rest of the play is spent in the efforts of the lovers to be reunited, aided by the exploits of the servants of both households. There are sub-plots dealing with the foolishness and greed of the respective fathers, and the ambitions and amorous adventures of the lower orders.

To fulfil these plot requirements we need:

a) A male and a female lover, known as the Innamorato and Innamorata.

b) A parent (or guardian) for each of them. These two older men are nearly always provided by Pantalone and The Doctor. Sadly a female parent is almost entirely unknown.

c) We now need a rival – the father's choice for his daughter – this function usually being filled by The Captain, a stranger who has gulled the father into the belief that he is a man of wealth and consequence (occasionally The Doctor is the chosen man).

d) . . . And finally, the servants, whose plot function is ostensibly to put things to rights, but whose real purpose is to provide most of the comedy and action of the play. These servants are known collectively as the Zanni. If female, they are referred to as Zanne, or Servette (both plural forms of the word)

The word Zanni, which doesn't alter in the plural, comes from Venice and was applied to a porter, or other casual workman. Zanni is a local variant of Giovanni (John), and is used in much the same way as Jock is (or was) used in Scotland: for example, 'Hey Jock, gi' us a hand wi' this load'; 'Aye, Jock, where d'ye want it put?' So it is a name and a type. In early scenarios they are simply called 'Zanni', or are distinguished from each other by names such as Zan Padella, or Zan Mortadella. Later they developed individual identities, with new names such as Brighella or Arlecchino. They tended to work in pairs, one being the 'crafty' Zanni (Brighella) and the other the 'stupid' Zanni (Arlecchino). This pairing survives in the 'broker's men' of British pantomime, and the countless double-acts of British music hall and American vaudeville.

A cast is completed by two or more male servants and one female servant (a Servetta) who was usually known as Franceschina, Spinetta or Colombina. Additional special characters could be introduced such as Tartaglia, a lawyer; Burattino, who might fulfil the role of innkeeper; or La Ruffiana, an old woman sometimes played by a man in panto dame style; and so on.

In Part One, I have not devoted much space to the concept of **status** in improvisation. This is not because it is not an important element of *Commedia*, or that it is not a useful tool for all types of improvisation, only that since Keith Johnstone's valuable book[1] there has been a tendency, because it works so well, to consider it the only approach rather than one among many. The *Commedia dell'Arte* is interesting in that it has a built-in hierarchy, with Pantalone at the top of the ladder. He will always lead the impro when on-stage. An artiste's popularity and success in no way influenced his *on-stage* status. At a time when Dominique as Arlecchino was the toast of Paris, he still remained almost on the bottom rung. See the **Chain** series of impros (page 201).

---

1. Keith Johnstone, 'Impro: Improvisation in the Theatre', 1979.

When it comes to examining the characteristics of each individual Mask – the way they talk, move, behave, even dress – you may find that the experts (and the sources they interpret) give different, even conflicting indications. This doesn't necessarily mean they are wrong. It would be surprising if, over the five hundred years of its history, at the hands of a multitude of different players, the interpretations had not varied widely.

In suggesting a particular approach to each role, I have followed six guidelines:

1)   To choose the most distinctive form of the Mask; that which makes it most different from the rest. For example: Brighella's facemask is recorded as having been either brown or green. So I would choose green, as he is the only character to appear in that colour.

2)   To choose that which conforms to good theatre practice. As well as describing external traits, I will try to help the actor find himself within the role. In the final performance any eccentricities of voice or movement should represent a true, if exaggerated, portrait of the character's 'internal' emotions and motivations. I am doubtful about the comic walks and movements sometimes attributed to individual Masks. The longer I work in the field, the more I am inclined to let the performer make his own 'informed' choice of the movement, and not impose on him stock comic walks and business, which in any case I am convinced are nineteenth-century or later accretions. Some time spent in *Commedia* training (which uses such business, but only for practice purposes) should prepare a performer, so that he can transform his inner emotions to the expansive *Commedia* style.

3)   To favour, where possible, those aspects that will entertain today's audiences.

4)   Not to settle for the obvious stereotype. It is for this reason that I find the muscular, dynamic Pantalone of the earlier pictures more interesting and worth performing than the old dodderer bent over his cane (see page 157). I think there have also been too many skirt-swishing Servettas, a distinctly nineteenth-century Neapolitan invention (see page 225).

5)   To present as three-dimensional a portrait as possible. With the exception of certain interpretations of Pulcinella, and the nineteenth century Pantaloon, none are completely villainous. I like to think that Pantalone loves his family, The Doctor loves the 'idea' of learning, and The Captain, for all his cowardice, admires valour.

6) For the more famous of the Masks, I have tried to indicate changes that occurred during their long history, and draw distinctions of style between the three or four different periods. For the lesser-known Masks, I show them at the height of the Baroque (seventeenth century), when *Commedia dell'Arte* reached its zenith.

Returning to Guideline 2: although not wishing to fix rigid rules, I would like to discourage performers from going against known theatre practice without a good reason for doing so. One of these rules is: *Don't move on the line*.[2] If you need to run across the stage, and say a line, you can either run first and then say your line, or you can say your line and then run. Don't try and do the two together. This may appear to conflict with one of our very definitions of *Commedia* (see page 9), but even a gesture should be slightly ahead or behind the spoken sentiment. A more important rule is: *Never move on another player's line*. This needs some common sense application, and might be better expressed as: *Don't fidget when another actor is speaking*.

The examples throughout are of my own composition, often based on remembered and in some cases recorded improvisations. I have not used any of the very limited number of documented examples as they are well represented elsewhere, and in most cases tend to be unworkable before today's audiences.

Although roughly dividing information into categories – costume, face-mask, movement, etc. – I have not thought it necessary to stick to too rigid a formula and the exercises are meant for you to use creatively, altering them to your needs and supplying others. Where, for example, I haven't given a 'Mirror' for any of the masks, you may like to write your own. I have also avoided duplicating items, such as the exercises for changing ordinary speech to Mask-speak. That given for Pantalone (see page 160) could equally well be used for Doctor or Captain-speak.

---

2. In Part One there are games which might seem to contradict this rule, but they have to be refined and modified when it comes to the performance.

Pantalone

Pantalone
Il Magnifico
(also a separate mask[1])
Pantaloon
Pantalone de' Bisognosi

21

The earliest mentioned of all the Masks, Pantalone is also the highest in prestige, and when on stage is expected to lead the improvisation. He is a Venetian merchant of aristocratic family; the origin of his name is uncertain, perhaps from 'Pantaleoni', a name given to merchants who 'Planted the Lion' of Venice around the Adriatic. He either has, or more frequently had, money (his family name, Bisognosi, means 'in need'). In any case, he is miserly. He is often the father of the heroine, and it is his efforts to marry her off to his financial advantage that forms the basis of many of the plots. He is conservative, abstemious, and authoritarian. He is given to sudden tirades. He is sly and quarrelsome. His machinations to encompass another's ruin invariably end in his own discomfiture. In extant scenarios he seems to be a man in his late fifties, there being the Masks of Cola and Cassandro to represent really old men. He thinks of himself as being in the prime of life, and much of the humour of his role comes from his attempts to vie with men younger than himself in physical and amorous exploits. He is, however, strong enough for his servants to fear his chastisement and it is only in his love affairs that he is ridiculous. He is not an unsympathetic character; we sense that underneath he has real affection for his family and even for his servants – affection they return, even though he treats them abominably.

Facemask

Half-mask of muddy or reddish brown with a prominent nose. Grey wispy hair from under his hat. Thin grey whiskers and a narrow beard, pointed or divided at the end.

Costume

A close-fitting jacket in dark red. His nether garments, to which he gave the name pantaloons, can be thought of as either baggy hose or narrow trews, in the same red. In the eighteenth century these were sometimes exchanged for breeches and hose. Over these he wears a loose coat (*zimarra*), which, under the sumptuary laws[2] of Venice, had to be black. On his head he has a red woollen skullcap or a brimless black hat, shaped rather like a fez. A purse and a dagger hang from his belt. He wears Turkish slippers in black or red. Early illustrations show that he sometimes wore an exaggerated codpiece to suggest an erect phallus; another indication that he was not so old that he wished it thought that his virility had passed.

Speech

His accent is upper-class Venetian, and Oxbridge English is a satisfactory substitute, or alternatively something like an educated Scottish. His tone

---

1. Pantalone is sometimes referred to as ' Il Magnifico' which may mean 'The Magnificent' – or ironically 'The Munificent', as John Rudlin suggests in '*Commedia dell'Arte* – an Actor's Handbook'. In some scenarios 'Il Magnifico' appears alongside Pantalone as a separate Mask.

2. Laws to curb extravagance – the gondolas, still subject to this rule, are all painted black.

is one of authority, only breaking into a childish treble when he is angry, or when he is aroused to amorous excitement. Though not as pedantic as The Doctor, he is fond of metaphor and classical allusion. He is prone to giving advice, and at least one such *'consiglio'* would be included in each performance. Polonius's speech to Laertes (Hamlet I, 3) is an example, which also shows a similar fondness for antithesis ('Lend everyone thine ear, but few thy voice').

Movement

Pantalone's walk is deliberate, picking his feet up rather more than is natural, feet turned out, knees relaxed. He need not be bent forward, like a child acting Grandpa, but flexible with an exaggerated bend backwards in indignation, and forward in accusation. As one of the 'masters' he employs the upper-class deportment and courtesies of the time (see pages 55 and 65). None of the engravings show a walking stick, but should he carry one, he is more likely to use it to hit people than to lean on.

> . . . The sixth age shifts
> Into the lean and slippered Pantaloon.
> His youthful hose, well sav'd, a world too wide,
> For his shrunk shanks. And his big manly voice
> Turned to a childish treble, pipes
> And whistles in his sound.
>
> *As You Like It*, II, 7

Shakespeare's description seems to contradict the evidence of both scenarios and engravings; possibly even as early as 1600 an English tradition of him as a really old man had been established and was to continue into the Harlequinade. If an older Pantalone is called for in an early scenario, his movement can be similar to that of the Victorian Pantaloon (see overleaf): bent body, small mincing steps, piping voice, and even the walking stick! Even then, I find no precedent for playing him as if rigor mortis had set in, or like the hideous Nosferatu of the 1922 German film, as some teachers seem to advise. It might only work if the rest of the Masks were to be played in similar inhuman style.

22

English Pantaloon from c. 1800

The character of Pantaloon, as we judge it from countless printed pantomimes and Harlequinades, is woefully two-dimensional: essentially a very old and unpleasant dotard. He is presented as an unrepentant skinflint, who uses the 'Clown' to perpetrate the crimes and cruelties for which he no longer has the strength. His voice squeaks, his hands shake, and he is almost always in a rage, unless he is counting his money; he leans well over his stick and walks in short fast steps, frequently stopping to catch his breath. His knees are bent and his toes point straight forward.

A white face with clown-like features replaces his mask. He has a white beard, but no moustache. He has a white wig with a pigtail, which curves upward. The only attractive thing about him (apart from the fun for an actor of playing so objectionable a being and basking in the boos and jeers of an audience of children) is his strange and colourful costume. Mainly in red, with blue trimmings, there are usually short pants over coloured stockings and a jacket decorated with jester-like points. This seems to have developed from the late eighteenth-century pinned-back frock coat, and the pigtail from the eighteenth-century queue – the whole costume a parody of an aged and outdated 'Macaroni' dandy.

A Mirror for Pantalone

This exercise is done progressively in three ways:
Visualisation – Mime – Improvisation.

a)   **Visualisation**[3]
     The following is first read aloud by a student or instructor to the class who sit or lie, with eyes closed, visualising the situation described.

b) **Mime**

It can then be read again, with suitable pauses, while an individual student mimes out the scene, preferably performed in the Pantalone mask. The aim is to find Pantalone's character through the movements made.

c) **Improvisation**

It is then used as a basis for a solo impro, in which the narration is omitted. The performer repeats the mime but now gives Pantalone a voice, and in soliloquy takes over the 'story', retelling it and adding to it as he thinks fit.

23

Pantalone Dressing

The Narrator: Firstly you pull on the dark red pantaloons, so distinctive that the world has borrowed your name for the tight-fitting nether garments. 'Pantalone' – you bear the name with pride, derived perhaps from 'Piantaleone' – to plant the flag of Venice at trading posts throughout the Adriatic. This appeals to you as you deem yourself a merchant prince. Your family name de' Bisognosi means 'in need'. An aristocrat, you live in a palace, though small and already in decay by 1600. The family once had money but it's long gone. No money for heating, so you shiver as you put on the pantaloons; it's five o'clock in the morning. The floor is cold, so you hurry to put on your Turkish slippers, rather worn now, but once very splendid. On with the red jerkin matching the pantaloons – which, although you've worn it for twenty years, fits you like a glove. Looking in the cracked mirror you congratulate yourself on your figure, as slim as in your youth.

In fact you are rather thinner than ever. 'Old? No you're good as ever . . . Well nearly . . . That young widow, Brunettina, smiled at you on Thursday, or was it Friday? – or was it at that young coachman? Bah! hold yourself

---

3. The 'Visualisation' aspect is based on a suggestion by Mark Rand, a student at the Bath Summer School, 1999.

upright.' Your hair's looking thin; cover it up with the brimless black hat you always wear. You pull on the *zimarra* (a long black coat). Just as well the sumptuary laws of Venice insist that they be made only of plain black cloth, as now you could afford little else – The gondolas have to be black too, what's that to you? – you don't run one. Your servant Arlecchino and the maid Colombina cost you enough in food and lodging. Heaven forbid that they should ask for wages!

'Can't do anything about the thin grey straggly beard. Should I shave it off? Certainly not! Always had a beard. Well, today I have to see that old devil Graziano, and he needn't think he's getting any dowry from me. Well . . . go down I suppose . . . face the . . . Santa Lucia! I am getting old – I nearly forgot my belt.' You put on your belt with its small dagger, and . . . moneybag. 'My purse!!!! Thought I'd forgotten you my precious, my own sweet little money moneybags: I'd never do that . . .'

Advanced Exercises for Developing the Mask of Pantalone

1. **Seek out or invent aphorisms like the one from Polonius** (see page 157):

   Example: 'He is long of limb and short of temper.'

   'He's a man of means but a mean man.'

   Or ones with a 'punctured' end:

   > 'She was a most beautiful woman, and clever too; wise as an owl; voice like a nightingale; neck like a swan; moved like a gazelle; playful as a kitten – but stank like a polecat!'

2. **Relate a short incident in ordinary speech:**

   Example: 'I was walking along the street, rapt in my own thoughts, so I was really startled when a man came from nowhere and put his hand on my shoulder. He looked a real villain, but he called me by name and I recognised him as my old servant Zan Padella.'

   Repeat – elaborating it in Pantalone's language (Pantalone-speak):

   > 'I was perambulating at a leisurely gait, my mind concerning itself more with the eternal verities, than

taking cognisance of the surrounding scene, when I was startled from my reverie by a violent hand upon my shoulder. I turned and found myself confronting a visage of villainy. I reached for my dagger with my right hand and my purse with my left, while the assailant stretched his hand towards me. "Are you not going to shake hands with the friend of your youth, your father's faithful servant Zan Padella?" And in truth it was he.'

3. **Improvise (or prepare) a monologue addressing the audience on:**

(a) Money (shrewd, mean, ruthless).

(b) Love (from lewd to lyrical).

(c) The Younger Generation (contemptuous and reactionary).

4. **Improvise a scene with another mask:**
Pantalone originating

(a) He proposes marriage to a young maiden (Isabella).

(b) He proposes to a wealthy widow (Harlequin – in drag).

(c) He gives advice on life, marriage, or money to –

   His son (Lelio).

   His daughter (Isabella).

(d) He argues over a dowry with –

   His intended father-in-law (The Doctor).

   His intended son-in-law (The Captain).

(e) He gives a servant instructions for –

   A feast (Harlequin or a Zanni).

   An assassination (Brighella or a Bravo).[4]

---

4. Bravo: any of the Zanni in bandit guise – the forerunner of the Robbers of British panto.

Examples, Exercises and Games involving Pantalone

24

The Doctor
Il Dottore

Dottore Graziano de Violoni
Dottore Spacca Stummolo
Dottore Baloardo
Dottore Balanzone, etc

The Doctor is *Commedia's* second *'vecchio'* or 'old man'. He is a counterpart to Pantalone, whether as his confidant or as his rival, being similar in age and social standing. In the plot he is frequently the 'other' father who must be outwitted in the matter of the marriage settlement. He is known usually as 'The Doctor' but is also given various personal names, the most frequent being that of Graziano, or Baloardo, while others like Stummolo, Bombada, Lanternone and Partesana were mainly associated with specific interpreters.

He comes from Bologna, the seat of a famous university, of which he claims to be a graduate. He was in the early days a Doctor of Law, rather than of medicine, but then there was hardly any sphere of human knowledge upon which he would hesitate to pontificate; and a *Commedia* troupe was hardly likely to miss the opportunity for

25

the sort of *Carry On*-type obscenities provided by the patient–doctor relationship illustrated above. However, the mainspring of his humour was the continuous outpouring of high-flown nonsense, mispronunciations, misquotations, atrocious puns and chop logic with which he attempted to hide his total ignorance of the subject under consideration. He is the caricature of the pedagogue, the pedantic windbag. We laugh at him to revenge the miseries of our school days, and it is likely that at least part of his origins are to be attributed to the students' portrayal of their masters at Bologna University.

Certain aspects of his character may be best revealed by comparing him to Pantalone. Their motives are frequently the same: to avoid spending money, to marry off their progeny to the best financial advantage, to seduce the maidservant and to make a catch of a wealthy heiress. However he has a larger share of the usual human qualities, as well as human failings; a greater affection for the rest of mankind; a certain bonhomie lacking in Pantalone; and an appreciation of good living, food and wine, in which he might on occasion overindulge. Physically he tends to a corpulence contrasting with Pantalone's lean and scrawny aspect. A role cannot amuse us, in my view, if it is totally without our sympathy, and so The Doctor, even in his greatest pomposity, should gain our understanding, if not our respect; for, though his knowledge is bogus, his love of learning is genuine. It is of course evident that the actor beneath the mask should be well read, and have at least a passing acquaintance with other languages, some familiarity with classical mythology, and a mind packed with otherwise useless information.

Facemask

This is unusual in being a quarter rather than a half-mask. It is black, and only covers the forehead and the nose, which is large and bulbous. The mask is said to originate from a birthmark, which disfigured the face of a much-hated member of the judiciary. As the mask only covers part of the face there is no problem here of the mask being too dark. Extra comic 'mileage' can be gained by making him myopic, with spectacles on the end of his nose.

Costume

A black academic gown, which can be long to the ground or short (to the knees) over breeches and a knee-length black jacket (full in material so that it sometimes gives the appearance of a skirt). On his head, a skull-cap, beret, or a wonderful wide brimmed hat (like a cardinal's but in black) which should be carried and played with, as well as worn. The all black costume can be relieved by white stockings, a wide white neck ruff, and a white handkerchief in the belt at his waist.

Speech

He tends to huff and puff in his pomposity. When he speaks, he expects undivided attention from all about him, and uses every device of rhetoric, varying volume, pitch and the speed of delivery until his manner of speaking is as ridiculous as the nonsense he imparts. Originally his accent was that of Bologna; in Britain he is usually played with 'received pronunciation', but it works well if he is given one of the harsher provincial accents – Birmingham, Liverpool, or Belfast. There is a tradition that he pronounced 'S' as 'Sh' but I haven't found this particularly rewarding when applied to the English language.

Movement

Being corpulent and the most voluble of all the masks, his movements tend to be ponderous and deliberate. He walks with feet apart, toes straight forward to support his bulk. He uses large sweeping gestures, and postures in statuesque poses. He makes much of his academic gown, thumbs holding the 'lapels', or putting his hands behind his back, under the gown, swishing it as he turns. He is fond of his large belly and taps it affectionately.

In contrast to this extrovert interpretation there is an alternative, springing from a later period (early eighteenth century) – a quieter, more elegant, hesitant pedagogue, finicky and pedantic in speech and manner. He will often stop in midstream, either to consider a point of logic, or just because his mind has gone a complete blank. The glasses help in this version.

A Mirror for The Doctor
Visualisation – Mime – Impro

Important note: see pages 158–9 for the way of working the Mirror exercises.

The Narrator: You are standing before a full-length mirror. What a fine figure of a man you consider yourself! Of ample girth, not like that mean, lean and slippered Pantaloon. The world is spherical, so that is also the shape to which a man should aspire. You pat your paunch approvingly: you turn your back, and, looking over your shoulder, you see the graceful folds of your academic gown in the mirror. You turn to face it, with slow deliberation, and grasp the lapels of your gown, in the time-honoured manner of all pedagogues. You pronounce your name, rolling the rrr's and accenting the t's with relish – 'Il Dottore Graziano . . . Dottore Graziano . . . Dottore Graziano'.

(*Adopting a different voice.*) 'My lords and gentlemen of the academy of Arts and Sciences, I have the honour to present Il Dottore Graziano of Bologna University'. You bow to the assembly with a mixture of assumed humility and appropriate profundity. You launch yourself into a speech of total gobbledegook while striking poses of impassioned rhetoric, carefully copied from antique statues of Greek and Roman orators. You pause, awaiting the plaudits of the crowd. No applause comes. You realise you are not at an academy of learning but standing before a mirror in your dingy apartment. For a moment your bubble bursts. The mirror reveals the truth: a fat, ageing man with a disfiguring birthmark darkening your forehead and nose. You are not an MD nor D of L, not a D of Ph, not a D of Lit; you are a D of P: a Doctor of Pretence. The certificates you show are your own pathetic forgeries. You did go to Bologna University – once – when its halls were open to visitors on payment of three soldi; when you were young and lean and three soldi would have bought a meal. Yes, you would dearly have liked to have studied at Bologna . . . But things are not so bad: 'nil desperandum! Dum spiro spero!' You are a fat cat, and never now go short of a meal, and you are held in such esteem that you are to be affianced to Pantalone's delectable daughter, half your age; and tomorrow you must outwit old Pantalone on the matter of the dowry. 'Caveat Pantalorum!'

*Note: after the **Visualisation** the Mirror exercise should be repeated by first miming out the scene to the narration, and then without the narration the student enacts the scene adding his own monologue, which can be as alike or as different from the narration as the student wishes.*

The Doctor Demonstrates a Little Etymology

What is the *'Real'*?
Real is that which is *Actual*.
Actual is formed of two syllables – *Act* and *Yule*.
To *Act* is to perform, to appear in a play.
Yule – the season of good will, So *Act-Yule* is to put on a Christmas
    play – that is, one that is referred to as a *Pant*omime.
To *pant* is to be out of breath, and you have to mime because you
    are so out of breath, you can't speak.
Mime is *Movement*.
Movement is the part of a clock that goes tick-tock, showing that
    Tempus Fugit, or time *'Flies'*.
Fly; a device for deceiving fish into taking the hook, and in paren-
    thesis, Hook is part of Holland, so that's where the Double
    Dutch comes in.
However the fish is brought in by winding the Reel and of course
    the *Reel* is *Actual*.
Actual is of two syllables *Act* and *Yule*, and so we have this, as well
    as last Christmas.

Game: devise similar etymologies for The Doctor.

The Ancient Mariner Impro

So called because one character buttonholes another, who then can't get away. This 'impro' mechanism can be used for different Masks, but suits The Doctor especially as he is so verbose.

Example

> *Flavio, a native of Padua, finding himself in Venice, seeks the residence of Pantalone. He has the misfortune to ask the passing Dr Graziano for help.*

Flavio: Sir, could you possibly direct me to the house of Signor Pantalone de' Bisognosi?

Doctor: Would you repeat your question?

Flavio: (*speaking loudly*) Could you possibly . . .

Doctor: There is no need to shout. I'm not deaf! It is not a question of volume but of clarity! (*Assuming his Doctor of Logic Mode.*) As I understand it, you ask me if I can *possibly* point out the domicile of a certain . . .

Together: Signor Pantalone de' Bisognosi . . .

Doctor: (*continuing*) . . . and after due reflection and consideration of your enquiry as to whether I can possibly direct you to the house of the, er . . .

Together: Signor Pantalone de' Bisognosi . . .

Doctor: I can assure you that the answer is 'yes – it *is* possible'. However to do this it would be required, a) that I should know such a person as . . .

Flavio: (*getting anxious*) Pantalone de' Bisognosi.

Doctor: Exactly, but please don't interrupt my train of thought! And b) that I should know where that person lived. Are you following me? And furthermore it would be necessary for me to have the ears to hear your original question, a voice with which to reply, with such additional body parts as arms to extend and fingers to point out this direction, or that, in this street or that, or five leagues hence.

Flavio:	But can you tell me?
Doctor:	The answer is again in the affirmative. As to point a) I have long been acquainted with Signor Pantalone; point b) – Yes, for I have been at his house this very morning to bleed him for the jitters; and finally c) I have all the needed bits and pieces, so to speak, to pass the inform-ation to whosoever should request it, in this case your-self. So to answer your query: Yes, it is possible – yes. Good day to you . . .
Flavio:	Sir, will you not tell me where the house is?
Doctor:	Ah, now this is most interesting . . . You use the word *will*, which is of the future tense, and who of us would presume to know the divine will as to what *will* happen? Had you asked me *would* I tell you, being naturally of a friendly disposition to my fellow man, I would have willingly acceded to your request.
	Etc . . . etc . . .

Advanced Exercises for Developing the Mask of The Doctor

1. Relate an incident in everyday style, then repeat it in 'Doctor Speak' (see Pantalone Advanced Exercise 2, page 160).

2. Improvise (or prepare) a monologue addressing the audience on:

   a) a learned subject   The Peloponnesian Wars.
   The movement of heavenly bodies.
   The lesser-toed Mongolian weasel.

   b) a trivial subject   The importance of pepper in the
   manufacture of sausages.
   Correct table manners before the Grand
   Sultan.

3. Improvise a scene with another Mask, The Doctor taking the lead:

   a) Propose marriage to Isabella.
   b) Make an indecent proposal to Colombina.

    c) Argue with Pantalone about a business
        venture.
    d) Discuss the proposition 'the pen is
        mightier than the sword', with Captain
        Spavento.

4.   Improvise (or prepare) a speech in which The Doctor, returning
to his early days as a mountebank, attempts to sell a cure-all elixir
to the crowds in the market place. A Zanni can be called upon as
an assistant.

Examples, Exercises and Games involving The Doctor

27

28

The Captain
Il
Capitano

*Il Capitano
Matamoros*

*Il Capitano
Giangurgolo*

*Spavento da
Vall'Inferno*

*Il Capitano
Coccodrillo*

The Captain is the eternal stranger. Usually of Spanish origin, he is a parody of the hated soldier of occupation who strutted the Italian cities. He is always new to the town in which he finds himself; and he likes it that way, for no-one is likely to challenge his version of the past, which he paints in the vivid colours of his imagination, with stories of his unsurpassed valour, deeds of daring and destruction. If he was ever in battle, he fought as a mercenary, having no home or country to defend. His goal now is to find a cushy billet, and his tragedy is that he never will. Like the bogus 'major' of more recent times, his plan is to con some gullible investor out of his money, or swindle some widow out of her savings. Should he fail (unlike the smooth-talking major, he is not skilled in the art of deception), his hopes are that he will find an heiress, and he usually manages to persuade Pantalone or The Doctor that he is a wealthy and suitable son-in-law, though the Zanni aren't so easily fooled. By the play's dénouement he is invariably unmasked (metaphorically of course) for the penniless scoundrel he is.

There is wide scope in the way The Captain can be played, partly depending upon what age you choose to play him. It can range from a brash thirty-year-old to a decrepit septuagenarian. The young Captain can be dashing, handsome, moustache-twirling: ridiculous but not yet wholly contemptible. At forty he becomes a bully, loud-voiced and space-consuming, strutting and posturing till real danger sends him running. At middle age, he is a little less sure of himself, retreating more often than advancing. He spends more time recounting the fictional exploits of his past than in taking any action in the present. His cowardice has become prodigious; a mouse can send him running; a child holding a stick can make him tremble at the knees. The old Captain is just a shell of his former self, full of stories of daring that he is beginning to believe himself. He thinks he was there when Athens fought Sparta, and Rome fought Carthage. His nightmares are full of fearful Moors (Matamoros means the Moor slayer).

Facemask

The Captain's mask is one of the most interesting and evocative. It varies considerably, principally in the length of the nose, being longish for Captain Spavento, longer for Matamoros, and positively stupendous for Coccodrillo. There is also a wide choice of colour. Originally probably flesh coloured, the Captain's flamboyant personality can cope with an outlandish range of tints: pure white, bright pink, red, light blue, and my favourite, bright yellow; but please, please, not black or dark brown. Where there is more than one Captain, they can each wear a similar mask in a contrasting colour.

Costume

This is conditioned more by the period in which the production is set than most of the other male Masks. It should represent a military man of that period. For example the early Callot pictures show a late sixteenth-century peascod doublet, with large pompom buttons, slashed trunks and sleeves, hose, hat with a feather, all in a delightfully ragged state, and a sword at his belt, whereas a seventeenth-century engraving by de Geijn shows him with full coat, breeches, and carrying a musket.

Speech

His voice, like his bearing, is of military stamp. Loud and commanding, it is used to parade-ground and battlefield. As he is a 'foreigner' to the other Masks, a Spanish accent is acceptable. An alternative is an English upper-class twang, lapsing into cockney in moments of anger or fear. Although he is physically rather than vocally motivated, he relishes words, particularly those that involve a threat:

> 'If you *evvv*er cro*sss* my path again, I shall *sss*lice you into rashers, and *ffff*ry you for breakfast!!!'

Movement

The Captain in movement can be one of the joys of *Commedia dell'Arte*. The Callot engravings alone supply a whole range of startling images, and also provide source points for a vocabulary of eccentric movements.

There is no excuse for playing The Captain (from any period) like a slightly irritable bank-clerk! The head, shoulders, chest, hips, legs and feet, should never be allowed to rest in their normal alignment. There should always be counterbalance and contrary direction (see the 'Callot Captains' routine below). The Captain's gestures are broad and powerful. He is a coward, but he is not physically weak; in fact he is a world-class athlete - when he's running away.

He will need several rehearsed Lazzi of sword-play, and it will be more pleasing to the audience if he has some competence in duelling and striking the correct fencer's stance (or a juggler's dexterity to make ineptitude amusing). If there is only one Captain in the piece, the Innamorato is his natural rival, but any of the Zanni may take on disguise and challenge him. A traditional scenario is for Colombina to appear 'en travestie'[1] and put the Captain to flight.

---

1. Dressed in male attire – also known as a 'breeches part'.

A Mirror for the Captain

Visualisation – Mime – Impro

Important note: see pages 158–9 for the way of working the Mirror exercises.

The Narrator: Captain Spavento lies in a strange bed. As he has no money whatsoever, he naturally puts up in the best hotel in town – 'might as well be caught for a sheep as a lamb.' Not that the best hotel has that much to be said for it; but he has a bed to himself in a large, sparsely furnished room. The heavy and dust laden drapes of the four-poster bed are tightly drawn round the sleeping Captain. He dreams of battle and snores mightily like the cannons of his dreams. He dreams that all around him are the dead and dying. He thinks himself safe but a powerful hand suddenly pulls him from his horse, and he finds himself over-towered by a Turkish adversary of evil ferocity. He reaches for his sword but it is no longer in its scabbard and he is defenceless. The Turk raises his scimitar to cleave the wretched Captain's head from his shoulders. The Captain awakes in a cold sweat.

He pokes his head between the bed curtains. The first rays of dawn faintly illumine the room. He slips from the bed and goes in search of the chamber pot. The boards creak as he creeps round the massive bed.

He looks up suddenly, and to his horror discovers that he is not alone in the room. He perceives a figure crouching in a corner. He leaps into bed covering himself with the bedclothes. He lies there shivering with fear, and tries to reassure himself: 'Bah, I must have been dreaming again'. He takes his sword from its place under his pillow and alights from the bed. He listens: not a sound. Stealthily he creeps round – then he sees it again, in the same corner: a menacing, creeping figure with a drawn sword in its hand. The Captain makes a threatening gesture, and the figure across the room threatens back. The Captain shakes his fist, and so does the enemy. He tries an insulting movement, by putting his hand to his nose. The adversary duplicates it exactly. He circles his blade above his head; the figure does the same. In terror he retreats, and the enemy retreats likewise.

A cold gust of wind from the open window sweeps the curtains aside, the light revealing that the Captain is facing a full-length mirror in which his reflection is now clearly to be identified.

A cuckoo clock mocks the Captain as it lets him know that it is now six in the morning.

29

A Captain's Monologue

My own view is that the Captain is often too full of his own importance, his own goals and problems to communicate freely with the audience. He is the one Mask who doesn't individualise the audience (see page 126). Mostly he sees them as a mob and addresses them as if they belong with those on stage whom he wishes to impress, or threaten. So a monologue like the one below is perhaps best directed to a single on-stage character. It might well be a woman, or one of the lower Zanni.

The Ambush

'Twas some days before the fearful battle of Trebizone, and I was riding alone through the infamous Vall' Inferno to rejoin my regiment at Kastamou. The heat was stifling, the silence oppressive; no sound but the clomp, clomp of my steed's hooves on the baked earth, and the occasional screech of a solitary vulture as it circled expectantly above. Clomp, clomp, clomp, 'Onward, my trusty Bucephalus III'. Bucephalus III, my charger, who had seen me through so many encounters. 'Onward, we shall have rest before nightfall'.

Suddenly the end of my beard starts to curl upwards, and my eyebrows to quiver. Danger! From long years of campaigning, my beard and brows have become sensitive to unseen threats. So I am not surprised when I espy, behind a distant rock, an upright feather. No bird, this I know! I take my crossbow, wind back the bow, insert the bolt and aim at the feather, which soon raises itself

to reveal a turban, and below, the fearful visage of a fighting janizary. I release the bolt, gaining a direct hit to his forehead. His scream alerts his fellows. Some *thirty* swarthy brutes come yelling from their hiding places, brandishing scimitars and cracking firearms. Another bolt from my crossbow passes through one of my assailants and also kills three men behind him. I draw a brace of pistols from my belt; bang, bang – another six of the *forty* dealt with. But a shower of arrows rains down on me. However, by rapid evasive action, ducking and diving, as it were, none finds its target. For me that is! But, alas, one hits my poor horse, the noble Bucephalus III, and he falls beneath me.

Now I have only my sword and the fiends are upon me. Slash, slash, thrust, parry, riposte. They fall, one by one, to my mighty blows; there are but *sixty* left. Slash, thrust, chop, circle, down they go.

There is but one giant left, and as our blades meet, both shatter to a million fragments under the power of our mighty strokes. I leap for his throat and strangle him with my bare hands. Silence – and a *hundred* lie dead around me. I survey the desolate scene. Not a sound stirs.

Then, faintly, a feeble whinny from my wounded charger. He's still alive, and attempts to rise when I go to him, but alas, he has no strength and sinks again to the ground. 'Bucephalus, my friend, do you think that I, Matamoros da Vall'Inferno, would leave you here to die? No, now it is my turn to carry you'. So I pick up his limp body and throw it over my left shoulder, I tie the severed head of a Turk to my belt – to substantiate my story – and leaving the scene of desolation and destruction, walk, with Bucephalus on my shoulder, the thirty odd leagues to Kastamou and a night's rest.

Advanced Movement Routine
based on the Callot engravings

This exercise should be worked with a colleague. The dialogue should be memorised and the moves choreographed and learnt. The purpose is to 'train in' a highly developed movement capacity. Some indication of

31

suitable moves is given but the intention is for you to invent the choreography, inspired by the extravagant attitudes depicted in the Callot engravings, above.

The Narrow Defile

Captain Giangurgolo meets Captain Coccodrillo in a narrow defile. There would be in fact room enough for them to pass each other but neither is willing to move from the centre of the pass. They start as far apart as the acting space will allow and shout (almost singing) at each other across the divide.

Each line should be matched by a single held position, giving visual support to the meaning.

Dialogue	Examples of movement
Giangurgolo: Hey! You!	Pointing move; express distance.
Coccodrillo: Eh?	Hand to ear.
Giangurgolo: Yes, you!	New pose. Point, shaking finger.
Coccodrillo: Who, sir?	New pose. Surprise.
Giangurgolo: You, sir.	New pose, indicating 'are you stupid?'
Coccodrillo: Me, sir?	New pose, pointing at self.
Giangurgolo: Yes, you sir.	New pose – exasperation.
Coccodrillo: What, sir?	(*Continue to improvise similar moves.*)
Giangurgolo: Move, sir.	
Coccodrillo: Move what, sir?	
Giangurgolo: Your arse, sir.	
Coccodrillo: No, sir.	
Giangurgolo: What!	
Coccodrillo: No. Move I will not, sir.	
Giangurgolo: Know sir, that I am Captain Giangurgolo!	The single poses change to a swagger.
Coccodrillo: So what, sir? I am Captain Coccodrillo!	Bigger swagger.
Giangurgolo: I am on business of military import and can brook no delay.	They move closer.
Coccodrillo: I am on an errand of mercy, to rescue a maiden. She can afford no delay.	
Giangurgolo: Out of my way, I say.	Powerful movement.
Coccodrillo: You can say what you please, I stand on my guard.	Legs apart, arms akimbo.
Giangurgolo: Out of my way fool, dolt, I stand. Do you understand?	Extravagant movements then freeze. They are now close together.
Coccodrillo: Cretin, pig's bladder, idiot. I stand. Do you comprehend?	Nose to nose.
Giangurgolo: You have insulted me!	Step apart. Hand rotation, outward to point 'You'. Inward rotation and point 'Me'.

Coccodrillo: Oh, can a tiger insult a flea?

Giangurgolo: You shall taste my sword.

Elaborate gesture to draw sword which he takes halfway from its scabbard, but seeing that Coccodrillo has his sword at the ready, slams it back in its scabbard.

There, let that be a lesson to you!

Turns away, bum sticking out.

Coccodrillo: Gurgolo, you coward, turn or I shall run my sword up your . . .

Giangurgolo: Aaarrh – you would cross swords with the fearful Giangurgolo?

The confrontation

They back up and face each other, then advance in Callot lunges. This is a movement in which the back foot, with the knee well bent, bears most of the weight. The front leg held stiffly straight is thrust forward and advance is made by alternating the legs. Swords held straight in front of them, they lean perilously backward until the swords meet. They both become so terrified that they turn away from each other, though their blades, clattering away, are still in contact. They creep away from each other with the previous leg movement, but now with their upper bodies leaning forward. They turn and renew the approach and this time come into a close clinch – revolving a half circle round each other as they do so.

Giangurgolo: Let me pass!

Coccodrillo: Never! Wait! Which way are you headed?

Sudden drop of tension.

Giangurgolo: To Treviso; and you?

Coccodrillo: To Bassano.

They have changed sides.

Giangurgolo: In which case, nothing is in your way. I bid you good day, sir.

They bow to each other and go on their way.

Examples, Exercises and Games involving The Captain

Arlecchino

Arlequin
Harlequin

Harlequin is, in the popular imagination, primarily
a visual symbol – an icon,
known more for what he
looks like than for what he
is or does, so we'll break
the usual format and des-
cribe his costume first,
which will also help to distinguish his four incar-
nations.

Costume: first period: the suit of irregular patches

The first known illustra-
tion we have of Arlecchino

32

dates from 1572 – a painting by Paul or Frans Probus, which shows a performance by a mixture of aristocratic amateurs (among them, Charles
IX of France) and professional actors, including the representation of
Arlecchino. In it he wears a light coloured suit, loose, but not so baggy
as the usual Zanni, covered with irregular patches of other colours,
principally red, yellow and green. He has a dark mask, and a white cap
(possibly a bald cap) with a feather, and is clean-shaven. He looks a thin
and callow youth. Undated, but from only a few years later, comes the
'*Recueil Fossard*', a series of engravings showing many of the *Commedia
dell'Arte* figures in action. Arlecchino is represented in a similar costume
with the patches clearly shown. He has a small cap, the same dark mask,

but sports a full moustache and a pointed beard. A third confirmation of this costume comes from pictures, dated 1601, of one of the earliest Arlecchinos, Tristano Martinelli. The outfit is almost the same. The mask however, is clearly seen to be moulded and he has a short stubbly beard.

This, his first costume, lasted for almost a hundred years, surviving long after the introduction of his second form of dress.

33

Second period – the suit of triangles

Somewhere in the middle of the seventeenth century the irregular patches were stylised into triangles (occasionally diamond shapes) separated by white bands. Illustrations of this costume are frequent, though usually of unnamed Arlecchinos, and sometimes given another Mask name (Truffaldino, Tracagnino, Trivelin). Perhaps the most famous Arlecchino to wear this costume was Evaristo Gherardi, who was one of the Italian troupe to be banished from Paris in 1697. During the eighteenth century the costume tended to refine, but remained basically the same, occasionally introducing the diamond or lozenge shapes, which were sometimes very elongated.

Third period – Arlecchino becomes Harlequin

This period heralds a transfer to the English pantomime and Harlequinade. The period lasts from the mid-seventeenth century through to the nineteenth century – from the Regency to late Victorian. The triangles persist, but the suit becomes a tight-fitting leotard,[1] more suited to his new role. A wide black belt pulls in his narrow waist. The slapstick, or wand, replaces the more usual wooden sword. The whole effect is crowned by a large bicorne[2] in black or red and on his face the black unmoulded mask, often with a black chin-strap. The costume, generously bespangled, is well represented in the illuminated 'Twopence Coloured' prints of the time.

---

1. Leotard: here indicates a tight one-piece costume covering arms, legs and torso.

2. Having two points, like the hat worn by Napoleon.

Fourth period – Harlequin Dancer

This came at the beginning of the twentieth century, largely as a result of the influence of the Diaghilev Russian Ballet's '*Carnaval*', and the slightly later Art Deco craze. Some of the extravagances of the Victorian costumes have been stripped away, the triangles uniformly becoming diamond shaped, the spangles disappearing, the bicorne being reduce to a skull cap, or bandanna.[3] A soft collar or silk bow is worn at the neck instead of the ruff, the mask becoming no more than a small black domino, sometimes painted on the face.

The Facemask

The earliest mask is black, and covers the upper part of the face. As far as one can tell, those before Martinelli look more like an unsculptured flap, with just the nose shape moulded in. The grotesque mask with deep furrows, a flat nose and pinhole eyes, often bordered with dark hair and with full eyebrows, started with Martinelli and continued through to Gherardi and beyond into the eighteenth century. Most present-day performers who essay the Arlecchino role wear a mask based on an original created by Sartori in the 1950's. It gives a laughing, pugnacious character, with a broad nose, high cheeks, and thick upper lip. It is a good mask, and is nice to play in, but not very like most of the pictorial evidence. This doesn't matter at all, but I wish it were not considered by so many as the one and only Arlecchino mask.

The English Harlequin of Regency and Victorian times favoured a mask less grotesque than the earlier examples and in time it became a black domino with minor variations. By the Art Deco period it had become a domino of minimal size.

Origins and Character

Trying to find the origins of the individual Masks and seeking the derivation of their names is a complicated, sometimes bewildering pursuit, and although worthy of the intensive study required, I have not considered it essential for our present purposes, nor within the scope of this book. Arlecchino/Harlequin is an exception because, although he is

---

3. A headscarf tied tightly at the nape of the neck.

the most famous of the Masks, his origins are the most obscure and to some degree they influence the way the part is played. There are three possibilities:

a)   That his origins are African – a servant or slave.

b)   That his ancestors are French rather than Italian, and connected with the comic representation of a medieval demon.

c)   That he had always been what he became, a stage presentation of a dimwitted, lazy, greedy but not unamusing Zanni, born in the crowded, working-class streets of lower Bergamo.

Each theory has its champions who put forward a good case for their favourite claims. At first view, the Martinelli mask could be considered to represent a black servant: Venice was the world centre for trade with the Arabs, who were the great providers of African slaves. Here, more than anywhere else, a good-looking young man or boy could be acquired to add an exotic element to one's establishment. However, once having got your blackamoor, the next thing was to dress him in the richest silks and brocades, bestowing on him earrings of gold, bangles of silver, and ropes of pearls, as so many of the Venetian paintings show – nothing like the poor patched suit of Arlecchino. It's true that there might have been a less fortunate black fellow thrown onto the streets of some north Italian town, and obliged to make a living there, but there is not the slightest indication of any ethnic background for him in any of the scenarios.

There is much I like in the second proposal. French popular legend boasted a demon called Herlequin. An early document tells of a priest of Saint Aubin de Bonneval who claimed to have seen a troupe of demons led by the Devil Herlequin driving the souls of the damned to Hell. A later step in the humanisation of this fearful demon, documented in the fourteenth century, was to be impersonated by local youths at a wedding feast, dressed in outlandish costumes, going round the town scaring the wits out of the old and impressionable. This Herlequin then became part of French medieval mystery plays (in which 'hell's mouth' was known as 'la chappe d'Hellequin')[4] and, as he no longer had the capacity to terrify, he developed the ability to make people laugh. A professional player may have taken on and adapted this role to fit the requirements of the *Commedia dell'Arte*. Again, the mask

---

4. See K. M. Lea, 'Italian Popular Comedy', p. 74.

fits well with this theory: the medieval devil was traditionally represented in a black mask, of similar aspect to that of Arlecchino.

There are two movement-related items, which I can add to support this theory. They are that in early representations Arlecchino is shown striding on demi-pointe – the goat-walk (described on page 185) and *'Arlecchino's cabriole'* (see page 188). The word *'cabriole'* means 'goat kick' and of course the goat was associated in the popular mind with the Devil. The dress is again a stumbling block; there are spotted demons, and ones with flaps of material representing scales or flames, but not surely on a near white suit!

Finally there is the version which says that Arlecchino is no more than a development of the stupid Zanni; his costume suits this theory well; again the near white Zanni suit, which for Arlecchino, the poorest of servants, had become full of holes over which he – or more likely some kind Servetta – had stitched patches of any material to hand, but this still leaves the problem of the name, whose derivation is quite unlike that of any other of the characters.

Speech

We British are so indoctrinated into the idea of Harlequin as a silent mime that it is difficult for us to make him speak at all. The first great English Harlequin, John Rich, known as Lun, was aware of his own ugly and uneducated voice and chose to be silent. Many followed this tradition, though there were others, like the great Garrick himself, who spoke, and the later Victorian Harlequinade gave rhymed lines to all the characters including Harlequin himself. Getting back to Arlecchino, we need to find a suitable substitute for his Bergamese accent. Dominique (1640-88) had a high piping voice, said to be like that of a parrot, and so successful had he been that he set a tradition for the actor playing Arlecchino to speak that way. Today's actor can either use it or not as he thinks fit. The best accent seems to be that of a light and chirpy cockney, whose nature has some affinity with the Bergamese servant.

Movement

The attribution of animal characteristics is surely a late concept, and would I feel sure have been alien to the *Commedia dell'Arte* players. This doesn't necessarily mean that there is nothing to be gained from the notion. The idea has been to attribute certain characteristics to each Mask: Brighella – fox, Isabella – gazelle and so on. In the case of Arlecchino we do have a likely affinity with a goat, and it is possible to see other animal characteristics brought into play at various times: the faithful dog, the mischievous monkey, the sly cat, and so on.

The Arlecchino Menagerie

This exercise incorporates some of these elements, and is based in traditional movements. It starts with the goat walk already mentioned.

Practise this first

Stand as high as possible on the balls of the feet, and then make as big a stride as you can with the right foot, still on the balls of the feet, and with as little bend at the knees as you can achieve. Continue left, right, left, right, etc. The steps should be as smooth and as swift as possible covering as much distance as you can.

Stand ready to enter U.S.L. Hips face the way you're about to travel [dir. 2]. Shoulders face [dir. 8] (Egyptian position). Both hands, right arm across the body, rest on the hilt of the wooden sword or slap-stick, on your left hip. Lean forward, right shoulder leading. Head faces front [dir.1].

The Goat

Count **1**/ to 8.   Eight 'goat' walks towards [dir.2] R, L, R, L, R, L, R, L. Maintain the body and arm position.

Count **2**/ 2,   Lower heels suddenly, turning the feet out, to form a well crossed 4th Position left foot crossed in front and increase the lean forward. Head juts forward (lateral move) [dir.1] (see Fig. 15a).

Figure 15a

185

The Twist (*follows after a short pause*)

Figure 15b

Counts 3,4, Swivel round three quarters of a clockwise circle so that you duplicate the stance to the left. Your hips will then be facing [dir.8], shoulders [dir. 2]. Head to the front again. Feet in crossed 4th Position, right leg in front.

The movement should be very rapid. To accomplish 'the twist' some may find it necessary to momentarily lift the right foot just before replacing it in the crossed 4th Position. The emotion is aggressive and the stare goat-like (see Fig. 15b).

Count 5, 6, 7, 8. Hold position. Then into 'The Cat':

The Cat

Figure 15c

Harlequin thinks he'd better propitiate the audience, and becomes kittenish, and makes the following '*pas de chat*' (almost the ballet one).

Count **1/ 2** With the back leg (left) of the 4th Position take a leap sideways [dir. 7] landing on the ball of the foot, knee bent.

Count 3,4, Right leg follows and is placed crossed in front of the left. Both legs slightly bent. The position is on the balls of the feet with the knees turned out. The whole body now faces [dir. 1].

Count 5, 6, 7, 8. Both hands do a '*politesse*' finger roll, close to the shoulders. Head tilts sideways right and left, appealing with a kittenish smile (see Fig. 15c).

Then comes 'The Giraffe':

The Giraffe

Early Arlecchinos would not have heard of the creature but in about 1700 a player known for his long neck was renowned for the effect on which the following is based.

Count **2**/ 2,3,4, Harlequin sees something or someone in the audience to displease him. Hands curve upwards and inwards, (right hand anticlockwise, left hand clockwise) till the backs of the hands rest on the waist, elbows bent and turned out.

Count 5,6,7,8. The shoulders hunch up and the head sinks in between them. *The hands now raise about 4 inches, to the lower ribs.* The knees increase their bend.

This last is one of a number of Commedia 'illusions'. Its aim is to give the impression of an unnatural lengthening of the body and neck.

Figure 15d

Count **3**/ 2,3,4, The head rises from between the shoulders slowly, the head tipping slightly from side-to-side. To aid the effect of growing upwards, *the hands are pushed gradually downwards at the same time, to below the belt level.*

Count 5,6,7,8. Hold position, neck extended as much as possible (see Fig. 15d).

The audience tend to think that the body is stretching, rather than the hands moving down! The effect is helped by Harlequin's expression of surprised indignation.

Then finally 'The Monkey':

The Monkey

Figure 15e

Count **4**/ 2, 3, 4, Suddenly he returns to the lowest position, knees bent, as at the end of 'The Cat'. Arms raise and spread wider; the head juts forward and the tongue sticks out and down like a gargoyle.

'Ha!' he ejaculates.

Count 5, 6, 7, 8. Hold position (see Fig. 15e).

End of sequence.

The Arlecchino Cabriole (A)

Figure 16

1.   Stand with the feet in ballet third Position, right foot in front.

2.   Bend the knees keeping the heels on the ground.

3.   Leap straight into the air, keeping the knees *slightly* bent. The right foot just crossed in front of the left foot, toes sharply pointed.

4.   Land back in the original position (3rd Position). The arms cross in front of the chest on the leap and open out on landing. Final position: arms straight [dirs. 2 and 8], palms of hands up. The position is like an invitation to embrace (see Fig. 16).

The Gherardi Bow (B)

Figure 17

The left leg steps back, into a lunge, left knee bent and taking most of the weight . . . The right leg stays in position: foot on the ground, knee straight. The body leans forward from the hips. Keep facing [dir. 1].

At the same time, the arms cross in front of the chest and open out in a similar movement to those of the cabriole, but with the body forward in a bow to the audience. The head can remain upright (see Fig. 17).

A single cabriole (A) can be done to precede the bow (B) to make a lively obeisance.

A Mirror for Harlequin
Visualisation – Mime – Impro

Important note: see pages 158–9 for the way of working the Mirror exercises.

The Narrator: You – *the actor*, stand before the mirror. It is the mirror of your imagination; one of glass would be less than useful. The image it reflects is not you as your everyday self, but you as the quintessential Victorian Harlequin of popular imagination. What do you see? A slim, elegant dancer's figure. Your motley of tri-coloured lozenges, bespattered with spangles, covers your shape from the white frill at your neck to the black dancing pumps at your feet. A bicorne on your head, a domino across your eyes, and in your hands the wand of your magic, or the slapstick of your humour.

You strike the 'Harlequin attitudes', ending with a deep lunge to the side and putting your hand to your ear to listen. You draw your feet together, put your finger to your lips in a gesture asking for silence. You take a few paces and, shielding your eyes with your hand, look into the wings. 'Yes, it's old Pantaloon'. You shake your shoulders in silent laughter. You run up-stage; then you cross your left arm across your chest, the palm of the hand facing forward. The right arm is held in a similar position but just above your head, so that you are looking through – between – the arms. All you have to do now is to close the arms in front of you and by a convention of the Harlequinade you are invisible to the approaching Pantaloon. As he passes by, you catch the old man by the coat-tails and swing him round, so that he continues his walk in the direction he came from, unaware of what has happened. You lunge, pointing in the opposite direction and run off in laughter.

You sneak back, and look into the mirror. There is no reflection, only the mists of a celestial smoke machine. You thrust your thumbs into the belt set low on your hips. You stand in a firm 4th Position, raise your shoulders and stare into the mirror. Through the mists the figure of an early Arlecchino in a suit of rough patches appears before you.

You speak to him in the half-pompous, half-mocking tones Martinelli himself used in addressing Henri IV of France:

34

'I recognise you, most honoured Signore, as Tristano Martinelli, first and greatest in the line of famous Arlecchinos. Founding father and progenitor of our calling, which you were the first to illumine with your wit, charm and skill, and elevate from mere buffoonery to artistry worthy of the praise of kings and the adulation of the populace. Great Savoyard, or was Mantua your birthplace? . . . Or are you *truly* the spirit of *Commedia*, who descended to earth, already clad in your suit of patches, to show what the role could be? I kneel before you, as you are shown kneeling to King Henri IV in the *'Compositions de Rhetorique'*.[5] I beg you, Signore to bestow on me the gift of Comedy. Take your wooden sword and dub me Dominus Arlecinus'. But the reflection only copies your every move. 'Yes, I was told that mimicry was one of your talents!'

You turn away and receive a blow from a slapstick on your behind! You turn back but Martinelli has gone. You call after him: 'By the way, did you ever get your gold medal?'

You distance yourself from the mirror, but still face it. You rise onto your toes and walk towards the mirror, crossing one leg in front of the other as you advance. Through the mists comes another performer. A most elegant figure: the suit of diamonds fits him closely, a buckled belt at his waist, a soft frill round his neck, a chin-strap, and a close fitting skullcap. Ah yes, here is the perfect model for an Art Deco statuette. But there are two odd things

---

5. A document published in 1601, in which Martinelli addresses Henri IV of France in comic and intimate style. He is asking for the gift of a gold medal and chain which, apart from monetary worth, was valued by players as proof that they were under noble or, as here, royal protection.

about him; an unusual white broad brimmed hat above the scull-cap, and he is not wearing a mask! Then you notice he is holding aloft in his left hand, the traditional Arlecchino mask of the seventeenth century – a quite barbaric visage surrounded by curly dark hair, and with full curly eyebrows. You are puppet master to this vision, so when you put your right hand to your face, the reflection dons the mask. You speak for him and notice that your voice is high and parrot-like: 'Here I stand before you, Domenico Bian-colelli (see illustration), known to my adoring public as Domi-nique. Beloved of Sa Majesté le Roi Soleil Louis XIV de France. You see how easily the French language rolls off my tongue. Yes, at first I found it difficult, and my native Italian was not popular, so I relied on my skill as a mime to perfect my role. As

35

I mastered the language, the actors of the Comédie Française tried to prevent our company from playing in French, but when we stood before the king, I asked in what language I should put my case. The king replied, 'Any you choose'. 'That settles it then, your Majesty. My case is won.' As Dominique laughs to himself the vision fades.

Suddenly with a leap, in springs Evaristo Gherardi, in his suit of triangles, with his grotesque mask and dark curly beard. He takes one look at you and turns to go. 'Signor Gherardi, please have you anything you can teach me?' 'Much, but I have been banished from Paris and must seek my fortune elsewhere. Remember that Harlequin, like me at this moment, is always in a hurry, always running after a bright tomorrow, the eternal optimist. But never hurry your bow. With me now, *cabriole* – arms stretching forward to embrace the audience, then the bow, arms welcoming the

36

applause. Don't move yet, they're still applauding. Another bow, hold it, hold it. Listen the applause is just beginning to fade, now off stage as quick as you can.' He vanishes. The mirror has also gone, until we call upon it again.'

Examples, Exercises and Games involving Arlecchino/Harlequin

Brighella

Brighella Cavicchio di Val Brembana
Flautino
(variant)
Buffet
(variant)

37

Brighella is the principal surviving example of the crafty servant from the Zanni pair of earlier years. On stage he enjoys the highest status of the servants and will lead the *impros* in the absence of one of the Masters. In the later scenarios he gets separated from his twin, but will still pair up with Arlecchino when the occasion presents itself. In some ways as First Zanni he tends to be the 'straight man', to the stupid Zanni's 'comic'. From recent times one could cite Abbott and Costello, Costello being the stupid and Abbott the clever one, or again Dean Martin and Jerry Lewis in their early partnership. Like Dean Martin's straight man, Brighella and the other First Zanni tend to be musicians and singers.

The story is that Brighella comes from Bergamo, a town on two levels, and from the upper district, whose denizens consider themselves quicker and craftier than those, like Arlecchino, from the lower town. In the scenarios he usually attaches himself as servant to Pantalone, The Doctor, or the Captain, but will lose no opportunity to better himself by means fair or foul, and will sometimes find himself as innkeeper, shop owner, messenger, and even soldier. He will have temporary scrapes but will usually end up just where he started. He is very smooth, very seductive, macho, dangerous. He has all the charm of the shiftless character he is; lazy, sauntering, but capable of sudden speed and agility.

Facemask

Olive green frontal mask of saturnine aspect; broad nose, sloe-shaped eyes. The expression is half-mocking, half-threatening. He has a plentiful supply of dark unruly facial hair, with a short curly beard, and a full moustache.

Costume

If we consider the basic Zanni costume – the loose off-white suit, made of rough weave – we can see how this was decorated and personalised in various ways: the early Arlecchino's coloured patches of varied shapes; the stripes of Mezzetino; the little ribbons of Burattino; and for Brighella the green frogging down the front of his tunic and the sides of his trousers. This is decidedly a type of livery, but to what affluent household did it belong? I'm not sure that even Brighella remembers. He doesn't seem to take any pride in his uniform, which he wears like an unwilling conscript, or an organ-grinder's monkey.

Speech

If Arlecchino has by tradition a high squeaky voice, Brighella's is low, either gruff or seductively melodious. There is not much excuse for giving the *Commedia dell'Arte* Masks Italian accents. Brighella is perhaps the exception. He seems the nearest to our stereotype of an 'Italian' and it is hard to find an Anglo-Saxon equivalent. A slow drawling London or Essex accent has worked well, and a Glaswegian actor using his native brogue was superb. I found two of the best ever Brighellas in Scandinavia (one of them a woman) speaking in English with a Swedish accent.

194

Movement

Brighella's philosophy is:

> Why run when you can walk?
> Why walk when you can stand?
> Why stand when you can sit?
> Why sit when you can lie?

But it is the philosophy of a 'big cat'. When he needs to move, it is so quick you barely see it. He is very powerful, but unlike Arlecchino, who is ever on the move, Brighella conserves his energy. So he stays still, or he slinks (again like a big cat), or he pounces.

We can see him leaning against a doorpost cleaning his nails or teeth with his knife. This act of hygiene is a threat. We know the knife could as easily be at our throats. Or he sits in a distant doorway softly playing his guitar. The music stops and within a second he is an inch from you, breathing garlic into your face and offering to guide you round the city. We can see him lying by the fountain. Is he asleep? Watch him and you will see one eye open. He has a great talent as a spy, this Brighella. He knows everything that passes, and you can gain that information for a price! Brighella is a salesman. He will sell anything at a price. His sister? His grandmother? The Rialto Bridge? The bones of St Mark? A Canaletto? Certainly, signore!

A Mirror for Brighella
Visualisation – Mime – Impro

Important note: see pages 158–9 for the way of working the Mirror exercises.

The Narrator: Brighella lies sleeping, dreaming of his boyhood in the hills above Bergamo. He is playing with his brothers. He is the youngest, and they are taunting him. They push him to the ground and as he tries to get up, someone gives him a great nudge in the back . . .

He awakes with a start to find himself staring into the muzzle of a horse: the horse among whose hay he had made himself a bed for the night. Now he remembers; he had crept into the stable in the early hours. 'Bon Giorno, Signor Cavallo. I thank you for your hospitality, but was there any need to wake me so brutally?' The horse snorts by way of an answer. 'I accept your apology.' Brighella rises and makes a most elegant obeisance to his equine host. 'Allow me to introduce myself: Brighella Cavicchio di Val Brembana, lately manservant to a certain Capitano Matamoros. As you are doubtless a scholar, you will know that Brighella means "trouble" and Cavicchio, chicanery. But *I* am meant to give the trouble not be in it, and I am expected to trick others – not be tricked by them. I'm not boring you, am I?' The horse stifles a yawn but Brighella continues.

'So this captain spins me a story about his man being drowned as they forded the river; how all his luggage was lost, but for this great trunk, containing his valuables. Would I help him carry it to the inn? So he engages me as manservant, and I spend the next three weeks eating well, doing light duties, like helping the captain get kitted out in new clothes, acquired on credit, and hoping each day to see something in the way of wages. Yesterday he vanishes, having paid nothing for our keep at the inn. "But his trunk is still in the room," I tell the innkeeper. We break it open – nothing but stones wrapped in old rags. The innkeeper was not to be persuaded to extend my residency in his establishment; so that is why I have presumed upon your hospitality.'

'Now I must seek employment elsewhere. I hear that a man is sought in the household of La Signorina Fiorinetta. But I will have to make a good impression.' Brighella brushes the straw from his trousers, takes off the jacket he has been sleeping in and shakes it, to rid it from the debris of the stable.

On a ledge he finds a piece of broken mirror. Brighella doesn't often seek his own image. It is not that he is free from vanity; rather, he is so confident of his masculine allure that he rarely has need of the mirror's confirmation. 'Today, I must impress; create an image of honesty, reliability, and efficiency. Such attributes are not ones that come naturally to me, so I must rehearse them before the glass,' he explains to the horse. He tries to see himself in the fragment of mirror, but the trouble is that however he holds it, or wherever he places it, he can only see glimpses of himself; a bit of his green and white braiding here, his worn shoes there, his cap all awry, his black matted beard. He polishes his brilliant white teeth with his finger; tries to untangle his beard, straighten his cap, re-button his jacket. He smiles into the mirror and tries to assume a dignified humility and look less like the villain he knows himself to be. He poses and gestures: 'Yes, Madam I was long in the service of the duke . . . Well, Signor Cavallo, how will that do? Do you think I look honest?' A small snort from Signor Cavallo. 'Reliable?' Another snort. 'Efficient?' Quite an affirmative whinny. 'I thank you, Signor Cavallo, and should Signorina Fiorinetta require a reference, I will give her your name. *Grazie tante* – but do try and get a new mirror for your guests.' Brighella slips out into the early morn.

Arlecchino and Brighella

38

We have given examples of the Zanni pair relationship; the crafty Brighella dominating the simpleton Arlecchino, but as always the rules are there to be adapted, twisted, given a new angle. This can be applied with profit to any of the status relationships. Isabella finds herself in love (temporarily) with a Zanni (*A Midsummer Night's Dream*). Lelio is bewitched by Colombina. Pantalone is forced to be a servant to Pulcinella. In the following short example, Brighella finds himself subservient to Arlecchino, but both retain their own natures.

Arlecchino enters carrying a sign 'Rooms to Let'. He addresses the audience.

Arlecchino: Not bad, eh? Arlecchino no longer in service, but his own master. Proprietor of a refined lodging house. And I have a servant of my own . . . (*Calls.*) Brighella.

Brighella: (*entering*) Yes Master?

Arlecchino:	(*introducing Brighella*) My man Brighella. Brighella . . .
Brighella:	Yes Master?
Arlecchino:	Fetch that ladder.
Brighella:	. . . That ladder?
Arlecchino:	And carry it over here . . .

Ladder Lazzi in which Brighella with the pretence of getting the instruction exactly correct, in fact does nothing at all, and Arlecchino in demonstrating what he wants, actually does it himself.

Brighella:	I see, and what would you like me to do next, Master?
Arlecchino:	Climb up and fix this sign up there.
Brighella:	This sign up there?
Arlecchino:	Yes, up there.
Brighella:	Right, master. (*Brighella starts to mount the ladder with the sign, then thinks better of it.*) Oh no, it would not be fitting.
Arlecchino:	Wouldn't it?
Brighella:	Oh no, you're the Master, I'm the servant. A servant must never be higher than a master! You must go up the ladder, and I will wait humbly below.
Arlecchino:	(*climbs the ladder*) I'm glad you pointed that out. You see I haven't been a master before.

Examples, Exercises and Games involving Brighella

Pierrot
Pedrolino

Pierrot doesn't belong to the *Commedia dell'Arte* proper, and even Pedrolino from which he is said to have sprung, was a very minor Mask. But Pierrot is a very important part of the communal psyche and there is no reason why he should not be embraced in the new *Commedia*. There are, however, dangers; the spirit with which he has been imbued since his inception is so powerful, so all-pervasive, that there is a chance that he can infect the other Masks with a virus of melancholia quite alien to their bright natures.

Pedrolino

Pedrolino was one of a number of 'useful' Masks, who could be called upon to fulfil various requirements of the scenario. These could be anything from the lowest of the Zanni – introduced when Arlecchino's native intelligence took him up a rung or two, leaving a space at the bottom of the ladder – to the role of a respected upper servant and companion to the Innamorato. Of these two extremes the doltish Zanni is the more rewarding for the actor to play.

39

40

Pedrolino's Costume

For the more stupid Pedrolino, the costume is as if it had been handed down to him by a much larger Zanni than he. It is too big for him and the sleeves cover his hands, indicating the genesis of Pierrot's famous costume. He wears a short-brimmed soft hat, he has no mask, and his face is white, giving real meaning to the term 'en farine',[1] i. e. looking as if he has just fallen into the baker's flour bin.

Speech

Pedrolino is either mute, or limited to noises and the vocabulary of a two-year-old. This, of course, only applies to the ultra simple-minded version. At the other end of the scale Pedrolino can have a facility for language exceeding most of the other servants.

Movement – as the Stupid Zanni

He walks with his legs apart, toes straightforward, picking his feet up as if he were walking in a muddy field (or as if he'd wet himself). He uses the stare and sudden head movements of a baby, and will arrest his

---

1. 'Floured'. The origin of the mime's white face is said to have originated with the baker's guild's contribution to the mystery plays.

movement, freezing, often for a long stretch, in awkward but stable balances.

The Chain (A)

This is a status game, in which Pedrolino (or Pierrot) takes the lowest status but the leading comic role. The Masks of the *Commedia* (as are available) stand in line, in order of precedence. At the top end stands Pantalone, and next to him, his daughter Isabella, then The Doctor and his son Lelio, then The Captain, Brighella, Arlecchino, Colombina, Zanni perhaps, and finally Pedrolino.

Pantalone blames his daughter for some mishap or error, and walks off the stage. Isabella accuses The Doctor, who in turn puts the blame on his son, Lelio. Each character leaves the stage after passing the blame to the next person. As it goes down the line, the accusation becomes more abusive and more physical, with Brighella knocking Arlecchino about as he tells him off, and when it comes to his turn Pedrolino getting the full treatment. When he looks around there is no one left; the buck stops here.

The Chain (B)

The routine is as above, but this time involves a large cake or other edible. In workshop conditions it would be mimed.

Pantalone enters carrying a large cake and a knife. He cuts it in two, gives one half to Isabella and goes off eating the other. She cuts it in half and gives one part to The Doctor, and so on, with the portions getting smaller and smaller. The Zanni, or whoever is before Pedrolino, eats his small piece with greed on stage. Pedrolino looks for his share. 'All gone,' says Zanni. Pedrolino starts to cry. Zanni, finding a last crumb stuck to his finger, gives it to Pedrolino and exits. Pedrolino, left alone, is all smiles till he drops the crumb and can't find it. He collapses in despair.

The Chain (C)

In this version Pantalone gives a task to his daughter – one suitable to her status: 'Would you put the flowers in water so that they are fresh for the wedding?' He leaves her and she makes an excuse and asks The Doctor if he'd be so kind as to water the flowers *and* close all the windows. The Doctor also delegates to the next in line, adding an additional task. Each Mask adds a further chore to the previous ones, and they get more numerous, more onerous, and more roughly demanded as they go down the scale, until Pedrolino is left alone with labours of Herculean proportions.

The Chain (D)

In this version Pantalone is not present, so we start with The Doctor at the head. He gives a verbal message to be delivered to Pantalone asking, say, for the return of a book. As the message is handed down the chain it gets altered little by little, until a confused Pedrolino asks Pantalone, who has now entered, to give the bearer of the message a good thrashing. Of course Pantalone obliges.

Note: in a workshop, the above formula, with all the characters standing in line, is a good exercise to start with. Later, and in performance, the Masks can enter one at a time in the same status order, so there are only two on stage at the same moment.

Pierrot

41

From this stupid Zanni developed the Pierrot of dreams. We can locate certain milestones in the popularisation of the myth.

In 1697, King Louis XIV banished the Italian players from Paris. The company disintegrated, a few of its members seeking work in the 'theatres of the fairs', where prohibitions against spoken dialogue encouraged the development of silent performances. These reached their pinnacle in the early nineteenth century with the mime dramas of Deburau (1796-1846). He, more than anyone else, was responsible for the transformation from a half-witted Zanni to a creature of dark shadows, introversion and longing. The scenario of his *'Old Clo' Man'* is worth recounting again to show the extreme darkness of the interpretation.

Pierrot, lonely and wandering the cold streets, stops to watch the affluent guests arriving for a ball, among them a young woman with whom he immediately falls in love. He tries to enter but in his poor clothes he is instantly repulsed. Walking the streets again, he passes an old clothes man (the '*Old Clo' Man*' of the title) who carries a pole from which hang the costumes, hats and so on that he has for sale. Among them Pierrot notices the resplendent uniform of a dragoon, whose sword also dangles from the pole. Having no money to offer, and feeling compelled to have the uniform, he takes the sword and runs the Old Clo' Man through the back. Leaving him dead, he takes and dons the uniform and is welcomed at the ball. He eventually succeeds in asking the young girl to dance, but as he takes her in his arms and begins to dance, she turns into the ghost of the Old Clo' Man who won't let him go, but presses him closer and closer until Pierrot is pierced by the sword still in the Old Clo' Man.

It is probable that the adoption of Pierrot by poets and painters at the end of the nineteenth century, as a symbol of their own lowly position, sprang from less elegant interpretations than that of Deburau and his successor Legrand, but unfortunately the 'Art' gradually stuck to Pierrot and he became dangerously 'Arty', as he was absorbed into every art form, culminating in the graphic and plastic arts of the 1920's, and the rash of Pierrot dolls, complete with painted tears, of the 1970's.

Mention should also be made of the 1943 film '*Les Enfants du Paradis*' which told the story of Deburau, and in which Jean-Louis Barrault performed some exquisite mime scenes, setting a style for mime artistes that still influences today's performers. Watching the film again, I find the set 'mimes' rather too sentimental for us and I think they would have been too sentimental for Deburau, but Barrault's mime of the stealing of a watch on the Parade is an absolute masterpiece.

Pierrot Movement

The Pierrot movements are completely individual and among the most beautiful of any theatrical convention. Perhaps this is why the character is so beloved of mimes and dancers.

Pierrot Movement Sequence

This is similar to the Pierrot crossing described in Part One (Game 28a, page 59).

Practise these arm movements first.

a) Start by gently raising the right arm to the side and above the head, then lowering it till the hand takes a position shielding the eyes, in the mime of *'looking'*. It is held briefly in this position as the left hand is lifted to the side, and above the head. The right hand is then lowered, its place being taken by the left hand in the same 'looking' gesture. This is repeated: right, left, right, left in a continuous movement of inward flowing circles. As you carry the hand down in front of you, from the looking position, make a small bend of the knees – straightening them again as the other arm reaches its highest point.

b) An alternative is to use the back of the hand in an *'aside'* gesture (whispering behind the hand), the right hand held just to the left of the mouth and (after completing the circular movement) the left hand just to the right of the mouth.

c) *'Shush!'* In this version, the hand, with the index finger pointed, presses against the lips. (Shush! don't make a sound.)

d) Another variation is to hold a clenched *'fist'* in front of the teeth in a gesture of anxiety.

   Invent others, always keeping the inward circular arm movements going.

Leg Movements

Stand with the right foot in front (4th Position). Rise onto the balls of the feet and bend both knees. Lift the left (back) leg and carry it high to the side, and complete a half circle, bringing it high to the front. Then put it down in front of the right foot (4th Position) still on the balls of the feet (*ballet: grand rond de jambe en dedans*).

Repeat, lifting the right leg.

It is like the dance movement with these important differences: the supporting knee is bent throughout; the working leg also bends a little, the toe well pointed; and lastly, we want *'muscular disbalance'* rather than well-placed symmetry, i. e – little wobbles, side leans and hesitations, helping to establish the Pierrot idiom.

Another element that makes Pierrot movement interesting is an effect of reversed gravity when possible. In the foregoing step any other character would make the accent *down* (onto the floor) on reaching the 4th Position each time. Pierrot will give an *up* accent, even a pause, at the *height* of the movement, when the leg is in the *air*. As is usually the case in music, the accent is given to the first beat of the bar: **1**/ 2 3 4. **2**/ 2 3 4. **3**/ 2 3 4. **4**/ 2 3 4.

So Pierrot's movement will be: **Up**/ 2, 3, 4. **Up**/ 2, 3, 4. **Up**/ 2, 3, 4. **Up**/ 2, 3, 4. but should retain a soft and flowing quality.

The arm movements are now combined with the step, the left leg making the inward *'rond de jambe'* as the right arm lifts to the side, and lowering as the hand makes the 'mime' gesture. A routine, starting well up-stage, could be made from the following combination:

> Two steps with the 'looking' movement (a).
>
> Two steps with the 'aside' movement (b).
>
> Two steps with the 'shush!' movement (c).
>
> Two steps with the 'fist' movement (d).
>
> Stop. Stand feet together with knees turned in, miming fear.
>
> Sudden run away in panic.

A Mirror for Pierrot
Visualisation – Mime – Impro

Important note: see pages 158–9 for the way of working the Mirror exercises.

The Narrator: Pierrot walks and walks. He walks in a dream world. At first there is nothing but the moon in his dream. He is walking towards it.

> How many leagues away is the Moon, can it be more than ten?
> Will I get there before she wanes, and hides in the clouds again?

Pierrot walks and walks. In his sleep he breathes deeply, and his dream moves in slow motion, slower and slower. He starts to run but each step gets slower and slower, till he is almost suspended in the air on each movement.

Gradually dark and baleful shadows cross his path: shadows of giant trees, which he tries to leap over. He changes to a walk and as he walks he feels that there is someone following him. He turns and is frightened by his own shadow, cast by the moon. It is long and sinister. He tries to shoo it away. He shakes his fist, and it shakes back. He tries to frighten it away by pretending to be a tiger, but it too shows its claws and tosses its head. He tries to kick it and sees that it somehow has hold of his feet. He tries to shake it off. Then he jumps – the shadow jumps. He dances and the shadow dances. He dances a soft and lyrical dance which the shadow copies. Pierrot has found a friend. He plays games. He pretends he is a chicken, then a monkey and then a great bird: an eagle spreading its great wings. He is flying, flying over great open spaces, but the shadow is getting fainter, fainter. The moon is going down and the sun rising. Now his friend has gone and he is the only bird in the sky. Pierrot is lonely again.

Now he is just walking along a country lane – walking – walking. It is early morning, and the sun is shining. He comes to a little bridge, overlooking a still millstream. He looks down and sees himself. 'That's Pierrot,' he says, 'Poor Pierrot, who walks all by himself. I'll go and see if I can keep him company'. He walks down to the edge of the stream and kneels close to the water, and looks at the reflection. But it is not Pierrot, it is Columbine, the beautiful Columbine. Will she run away this time as she always does if he goes closer? He lowers himself down to the water. No! She is coming closer, she purses her lips to kiss him, and he falls into the . . . 'Ow! That hurt!' No, he hasn't drowned, he is not even wet, he has just fallen out of bed. Pierrot picks himself up, and gets back into bed. Perhaps he can go to sleep again and get Columbine's kiss.

Examples, Exercises and Games involving Pierrot

Pulcinella

Pulcinella Cetrulo

Polichinelle

Mr Punch

Whereas most of the other Masks stem from northern Italy, Pulcinella comes from Naples, and he is a very different sort of creature. As Arlecchino was to become the 'star' of the northern *Commedia dell'Arte*, Pulcinella was the 'star' of the southern companies.

When the actor Charles Laughton, who could well have made an excellent Pulcinella, was working on the never to be completed film '*I, Claudius*', he was having difficulty with the role and is reported as saying, 'I can't find the man'. Pulcinella is also difficult to find. There is plenty to provide the visual image. Domenico Tiepolo's numerous drawings from '*La Vita di Pulcinella*' are among

42

the best illustrations of the *Commedia dell'Arte*. They show various troupes in wonderful acrobatic and dancing poses: grotesque, with their paunches and humped backs, hooked noses and tall hats. Although clearly indicating the costume, mask and build of Pulcinella they are not, however, as useful as the Callot engravings of Captains and Zanni, as each of the Pulcinellas is almost a clone of the others. Here we have, I believe, a company of acrobats who chose for their costumes the garb of a popular comic figure of the time, and not the character of Pulcinella himself. Later illustrations are mostly useful for showing the costume

207

changes adopted by the French Polichinelle and the English Punch. If we seek him in existing anecdotes, the information is conflicting. One tells us he was quick-witted, another that he was a dolt. One that he was cruel and malicious, another that he was kindly, sharing his last loaf with a stranger. The information to be gathered from the extant scenarios is more helpful, but still difficult as he is given so many roles – servant, master, innkeeper, baker, dentist, schoolmaster, soldier.

There are various stories of his origins; his first interpreter was likely to have been Silvio Fiorillo (fl. 1585-1632) who was also the creator of Captain Matamoros, and who may have developed the role of Pulcinella from a Neapolitan peasant turned actor, a certain Puccio D'Aniello, or perhaps, just from observation of the peasant types of the area. Either way, Pulcinella is a peasant – but just what is that? He is not part of our culture. He is perhaps like a mule: strong, obstinate, stupid in the eyes of the world, but capable, very capable of managing his own survival. Pulcinella represents closeness to the earth: a country Zanni rather than a town one.

He survives as our Mr Punch, and some writers would have it that his extremely nasty character is a British invention, but the traditional story told in fairgrounds and at children's parties is an almost exact survival from a popular Neapolitan scenario. He murders his baby and then his wife; he is apprehended by the law and sentenced to be hanged. He persuades the hangman to demonstrate just how his head should go into the noose, and with great glee hangs the hangman. He later cheats the Devil (in recent times replaced by a crocodile) – an amazing thing in a Catholic country!

In a sort of time warp, he starts the whole sequence again at the next performance – perhaps this is his punishment.

In the northern scenarios, the evil plans of Brighella, Pantalone or The Captain always come to nothing or rebound on their own heads, but the machinations of Pulcinella invariably succeed – he gets away with murder and the affection with which he was held by the populace (he was never taken up by the gentry in the same way as Arlecchino and his fellows were in the north) was based on the sneaking admiration for a villain who gets away with his crime. He did all the things his audience would like to have done if they were not afraid of the consequences. He treats all women abominably, especially his wife (unlike most of the other Masks he is usually married) and he is the male chauvinist pig of all time: a lecher without the slightest attempt at courtesy. What he

43

wants he takes, not covertly like Brighella, but by sheer force and brutality. But . . . because he represents revolt against all established order and decency, he is also a symbol of Liberty, albeit a dangerous one to follow.

Facemask

A black or dark brown mask (which for indoor use is better with some highlights) with a very pronounced Roman nose, and heavily wrinkled, with a large wart on the forehead. This seems to have remained standard until, in the case of Polichinelle and Punch, the mask was abandoned. Except in the very early days, the rest of his face was clean-shaven.

Costume

The early, all-white costume consisted of wide trousers and a loose blouse without a collar, held in by a belt or rope with a purse attached, set on the hips to allow for his paunch. He has a row of big buttons down his front. He has a large hump on his back – occasionally two!

Various types of headgear appear, until in the mid-seventeenth century he acquired the distinctive sugar-loaf hat.[1]

By the end of the seventeenth century, and in following years, a new version of his costume developed which never entirely replaced the old. In several Watteau paintings we see a very elegant version of this: a costume of pastel-shaded silks. Whether this was ever seen on stage is doubtful and may have been an invention of the artist to match his lyrical idealistic paintings (see Appendix). It does have similarities to the French Polichinelle who, both as live performer and as puppet, wore a brightly coloured outfit, with a bicorne hat. Though a ruddy complexion had replaced the dark mask, he was otherwise much the same fellow and always boasted the large hooked nose. It is only a small step from his costume to that of brightly clad Mr Punch.

Speech

The name Pulcinella is most likely derived from 'little chick', which may have come about from his 'squawky' manner of speech, a tendency to be perpetuated in the Punch and Judy master's 'swazzle'.[2] Unlike Brighella or Arlecchino, or in fact any of the other servants, he is highly talkative, and loves to chatter to the other characters, the audience, and failing that, himself.

He is particularly apt to use 'alienation' – coming out of character to talk to the audience, comment on the play, the acting, the weather, the price of eggs, or to excuse himself by urinating in front of the audience.

A Suggestion for Playing Pulcinella

See him as a juvenile delinquent in an old man's body. He is hunch-backed and pot-bellied, but very strong in the arm. Establish the hump and belly, bright squinting eyes, and all the nasty aspects of old age, but with all lust, both sexual and digestive, undiminished, then give him the behaviour of an equally nasty ten-year-old boy. He likes to pick quarrels, cause trouble, avoid responsibility and put the blame on others.

---

1. A tall cloth hat, shaped like the conical sugar-loaf.

2. A device which the showman inserts into his mouth to produce the distinctive Punch croak.

Movement

Taking the cue from above will find him fond of skipping, and other child-associated moves; running, dashing about, kicking, and doing silly dances, often as he chants some obscene ditty.

Sometimes he pauses to get his breath back after such unsuitable activities for a grown, even old man. His gestures on the other hand tend to be broad, heavy, laborious. Pantalone and The Doctor, with occasional lapses, attempt to maintain their dignity. The Captain is frequently 'on his dignity'. Pulcinella doesn't know the meaning of the word.

There were Pulcinellas, notably Vincenzo Cammarano (1720-1809), who presented a much more literate figure, and this possibility is always open, but I have so far found this less of a contrast to the other Masks and to offer less comic potential.

Example of a Scene from a 'Punch' Scenario.

> *Pulcinella enters holding a bunch of wild flowers. He sings to himself, and skips about gaily, gathering more flowers with exaggerated delicacy.*

Pulcinella: Oh, pretty, pretty, pretty! Aren't they pretty?

(*To audience.*) As you see good people, I am picking a few flowers for my sweet wife. Did ever man have such a wife? What a beauty! Wait till you see her. What a beauty, and such a cook, such a mother to our dear baby. There's a white flower for her hair. A blue one for her skin, and red for her eyes! What a beauty, she has quite the reddest eyes I ever saw. But you'll see for yourself. I'll call her. She'll come running, the minute I call her. (*Calls.*) Rota . . . Rota. She'll be here before I finish her name. Rota . . . (*Stops to listen.*) Rota . . .?

(*Getting no response, he bellows*) Rotalinda![3] Rotalinda! Come here at once you baggage, old cow, whore . . . when your husband calls you!!! Rotalinda . . . !

Rotalinda: (*entering*) What do you want?

---

3. The name usually given to Pulcinella's wife. The origin of the name 'Judy' is unknown.

Pulcinella:	There she is, my darling, my heart's beloved. Come and show yourself to my guests.
Rotalinda:	(*scowling at the audience*) More of your good-for-nothing cronies. I'm not wasting my time on them. I've the washing to do.
Pulcinella:	Come and give me a kiss, you beauty.
Rotalinda:	Kiss you? I'd rather kiss a dog's arse.
Pulcinella:	Isn't she a tease? (*She shakes her fist at him.*) Oh, she's so bashful, so delicate. Go fetch the baby. It's such a beautiful baby; the image of its father.

Rotalinda exits and returns immediately, carrying the baby.

Give the sweet thing to its Dadadadadada!

They fight over it, Pulcinella winning.

Give your Dada a kiss.

Baby starts screaming. Pulcinella throws it to Rotalinda.

Make it quiet. Make the little bastard shut up. If there's one thing I can't stand it's a baby. Always watering from one end or the other.

Rotalinda tries to comfort the baby but it goes on screaming. Pulcinella snatches it back.

You faggot, don't you know how to rock a baby to sleep? There, there, there.

Rocks baby gently at first then more and more furiously.

'Rock a bye baby on the tree top
The more the wind blows the . . .'

Baby howls more and more.

Shut up, you little varmint – or I'll shut you up! I'll teach you to cry when your loving Dada sings to you!

He gets the baby by the legs and begins to swing it violently bashing its head against the floor.

There we are! That's made it shut up. Good little fellow, he's not making a sound now.

Rotalinda:	You beast, you villain, you murderer, you've killed my baby!
Pulcinella:	Just as well, it ate too much. Throw it out the window.

They have a tug-of-war with the baby, Pulcinella gaining possession in the end.

	Out the window, out the window. Look out down there, dead baby coming down!
Rotalinda:	You killed my baby. I've lost my dear baby.
Pulcinella:	Stop carrying on so . . . It's only a blasted baby. We'll make another one, right now! The people here won't mind, they know what goes on. Come on my beauty, up with your skirts.
Rotalinda:	Oh no you don't . . . (*Chase.*)

Another Scene for Pulcinella

Pulcinella has a special gift for turning the tables, particularly where there is a chance to shift the blame from himself to another.

Pulcinella, not for the first time, finds himself up before the bench.

Judge:	Give me your name.
Pulcinella:	*Give* you my name? Certainly not. Have you not one of your own. Besides I may need it . . .
Judge:	No more of your nonsense. It is essential that I have your name, so that you may be accused of grievous bodily harm against your neighbour Pasquariello.
Pulcinella:	Oh, very well. It's Pulcinella Cetrulo. (*Pause as judge writes.*) Have you got my name now?
Judge:	Yes, I have it.
Pulcinella:	Very well, as *you* have *my* name, you can accuse yourself of anything you wish and sentence yourself to a fine, or flogging, or to be hung drawn and quartered, for all I care. So I'll say good day to you.
Judge:	Stay where you are. What's your address?

Pulcinella:	Address, is it? Do you think I'd give my address to you, so that you could come round when I'm out, and rape my wife and steal my chickens? Your face is familiar, and a more villainous face I never saw. Ladies and gentlemen of the Jury, I put it to you that this is the man who caused bodily harm to poor old Pasquariello.
Judge:	How dare you? Do you not know that I am Merlino Pulpettone?
Pulcinella:	I knew it. Officer of the court, tell us what is known against this man. Is he not one of the infamous Pulpettone gang of chicken thieves and wife rapists? I demand his arrest. Are we safe in our beds with such a fiend on the loose? Lock him up before he steals your wives and rapes your chickens!!!

44

The Lovers

The Innamorato

who might be named
**Flavio, Lelio, Leandro
Cinzio, Ottavio
Aurelio Florindo**
or **Orazio,** etc.

The Innamorata[1]

who might be named
**Isabella, Flaminia Lavinia,
Camilla Silvia, Lidia**
or **Auralia,** etc.

45

Although in the Lovers we have the hero and heroine of the story, or heroes and heroines, because there can be more than one pair of lovers, they are frequently pushed onto the sidelines by the more purely comic Masks. This is a shame because, in their way, they are of equal importance, and offer equal opportunities for both dramatic and comic excellence. Their comedy is subtler: more wit than wisecrack. We laugh more at their predicament than at their antics. Historically, of the two lovers, it was the Innamorata who drew the public to the shows. Partly because of the novelty of seeing a woman on the stage, but also frequently because of her beauty, intelligence, wit and culture. The *Commedia dell' Arte* suffers from the lack of female character roles – there are really none to parallel those of the men – but one may remember that it was a new thing for a woman to tread the boards, and the woman herself was not yet confident enough to 'make a fool of herself' in public. I do not think it was a matter of male suppression to any great degree. The women of the companies were held in the highest esteem by their colleagues and at least two of the great companies were run by women. There is also

---

1. The Italian form is useful in distinguishing the female from the male 'Lover'.

the example of Isabella Andreini, an actress, poet and playwright so esteemed inside and outside her profession that she was celebrated by poets, made an honorary doctor of the Academy of Padua and had a medal struck in her honour. When she died giving birth to her seventh child, her distraught husband disbanded the company and devoted his life to editing her writings. Such was one of the women who played the part of the Innamorata.

Facemask

None, though they would on occasion disguise themselves with a domino (or loup) as would any upper or middle-class Venetian.

Costume

46

The Lovers have no identifying guise, and so were more subject to the fashions of the day than any of the Masks. The richness of their apparel denoted the status of the company in which they worked, and those groups enjoying patronage would frequently be given the hand-me-downs of their noble protectors. The objective for a modern company would be to use The Lovers to help establish the period of the piece,[2] to make both the actors and the costumes as attractive and as accurate as possible, and to fit in with the colour scheme of the production. (Yes, there should be one!)

2. The other Masks, apart from The Captain, all being less subject to the vagaries of fashion.

Speech

The rule is perfect English (R. P.), as perfect Tuscan was the ideal of the old *Commedia dell'Arte* companies. The rule is there for you to break if you wish, and quality of sound is more important than accent. But here is a chance for the actor to put his voice training to use, displaying diction, tone, variety in speed, volume and inflection. As with all the roles, it is necessary to have some practice in finding a vocabulary that is neither tediously archaic, nor disturbingly anachronistic.

Movement

The Masters' movements, described in Part One (pages 55 and 67), should provide a basis for those of The Lovers. The aim should be towards elegance, but need not be anaemic, I would suggest that anything in the way of parody, like the piss-taking usually displayed in playing Victorian melodrama, should be eschewed. Although the situation is comic, I don't think the movement should be. The Innamorato should be something of a swordsman, and if the Innamorata is as well, this opens up considerable impro possibilities. Simple routines, based on the slower period dances, can be choreographed, learnt and used within an improvised love scene.

Courtly Dance for the Lovers

There are only two movements: a) the *pas*, a slow and stately step forward on the heel pausing briefly before using the other foot; b) the *swivel*, a change of body direction as you draw the back foot to join the other, with a gentle rise onto the balls of the feet but without transferring the weight.

The Sequence

The pair stand side by side facing front [dir. 1], the man on the woman's left. He holds the woman's left hand in his right hand.

The man makes three '*pas*', starting with the left foot. The woman does the same starting with the right foot. They both then do the '*swivel*', the man closing his right foot in to his left foot and turning inwards (clockwise) till he faces up-stage (weight still on left foot) [dir. 5]. The woman does the same movement closing her left foot to her right, making a half-turn anticlockwise to also face up-stage. Man now holds woman's right hand in his left.

They take three **pas** up-stage; man R. L. R., woman L. R. L. The *man* does a **swivel** to face down-stage [dir. 1], closing left to right in an anticlockwise direction, changing his hand so as to have her right in his right. The woman pauses and remains facing [dir. 5]. They then take three **pas** round each other to complete a half circle (Man L. R. L. ends facing [dir. 5] Woman R. L. R. ending facing front [dir. 1]), followed by an *inward* **swivel,** which gives a change of direction and of hands (left in left). Then they take three **pas** to return. The man takes three **pas** R. L. R. and a **swivel** to face front. The woman, after the three steps (L. R. L.) is already facing front, so just draws right foot in to the left foot.

Repeat from the beginning.

Exercise: learn the routine, then improvise a dialogue of love and intrigue; you can make pauses after each **swivel** for the words, or make the dialogue continuous throughout the dance.

Uscite (Exits) and Chiusette (Endings)

These are both types of memorised 'tags', usually rhymed couplets; *'uscite'* (plural) are used by a character before making an exit, and *'chiusette'* (plural) to end an otherwise improvised scene. They can be employed by any of the characters, but are a particular help to The Lovers. The Italian words (unlike **lazzi**) are not in common use, and the English *'exits'* and *'endings'* will suffice just as well.

Examples

Uscite (exit lines)

If the Innamorato has been banished from the city, he might use the following before quitting the stage:

> 'For a strange and distant land I must straightway depart,
> Leaving nought behind, except my heart!'

Or when his true love (or a false hope) dashes his aspirations:

> 'Oh, if t'were but a dream, that my true love bids me go,
> Then might I wake and find it were not so.'

The Innamorata, having been lectured by Pantalone on the dire consequences of refusing to comply with his commands, sinks under the
strain:

'To my father's command, my weaker will must bend,
There duty lies, but duty, my broken heart won't mend.'

Chiusette (ending lines)

The **'chiusetta'** (singular), to close a scene or even the play, tends to be
longer. The following has been preceded by an improvised lovers'
quarrel in which they threaten to part forever. In this case it is the
Innamorata who must choose when to introduce the **'chiusetta'**.

She: Then farewell, though fare well I do not intend,
      For one whose love had but an idle hour to spend.

He: I protest, my love was like the sun, constant, bright,
      Yours but a candle flickering in the night.

She: Then go, why do you linger? Why do you stay?

He: I go. Adieu, I'm on my way. (*He exits.*)

She: Lelio . . . Lelio . . .

He: (*he comes back*) You called me?

She: Called? What more would I want from you?

He: Isabella! Isabella!

      She turns away. He exits again.

She: (*too late*) Yes? Yes? Lelio? He's gone. Farewell my love.

      She exits.

He: (*returning*) Isabella? – She's gone. Adieu my dove.

      He goes.

      A moment's pause and then both dash on and call out together.

Both: My darling!! (*They rush into each other's arms.*)

Lidia, the Innamorata, has sent Flavio packing, and now regrets her action. This time the 'chiusetta' is played by Lidia and her maid, Franceschina.

Lidia: He's gone Franceschina; he's gone.

Franceschina: Yes, he's gone. Yes, sent him packing, didn't you? Well it's no good his hanging round if you don't care for the fellow, is it?

Lidia: But I do care for him.

Franceschina: No good his wastin' his time, if you think him all those things you told him. What was it you said? He was too big for his boots?

Lidia: I never said that!

Franceschina: Well, it was something about boots, or was it about fish? That's it – a fish out of water.

Lidia: Did I say that?

Franceschina: Something about fish. No, I know, you called him a poor fish.

Lidia: Franceschina, you were listening!

Franceschina: Well, you were shouting.

Lidia: Oh? Franceschina, what have I done. I love him. I want him.

She now starts the 'chiusetta'.

Not tempest wild, nor raging sea,
Has cast my lover far from me.
Nor tyrant's anger sent away,
To distant land, there to stay,
Away from all that he holds dear.
But *I* myself in selfish pride,
Have cast my dear one from my side,
And now forever must dwell in sorrow

She exits.

Franceschina: (*to audience*) Not if I know the boy, he'll be back – tomorrow. (*She exits.*)

A Scene for the Innamorato and His Manservant.

Bertolino, an 'upper' Zanni, playing a valet, is dressing his master, Ottavio:

Ottavio: Well, Bertolino, what news for me?

Bertolino: News, Master?

Ottavio: News, man, what have you discovered?

Bertolino: Me? Discovered?

Ottavio: Discovered, discovered, discovered . . .

Bertolino: Would Master mean about a certain lady?

Ottavio: Certainly about a certain lady – what can you tell me?

Bertolino: Well – she is very young and very beautiful.

Ottavio: This I know. Do I need you to tell me she is young and beautiful? Have I not seen her for myself at church and in the street? She is the most beautiful woman in the world.

Bertolino: That I wouldn't know, never having been away from Venezia.

Ottavio: Bertolino, you are most provoking!

Bertolino: Yes, Master.

Ottavio: What have you found out? For mercy's sake tell me, I hang on your every word.

Bertolino: She is on a visit to Venice.

Ottavio: Of course she is on a visit to Venice, otherwise I would have seen her before. Have you found out her name?

Bertolino: I did hear it. I think it begins with an L . . .

Ottavio: Lavinia, Laura, Leonora, Licetta???

Bertolino: No, It must have been a C . . .

Ottavio: Claudia, Cornelia, Cintia, Celia??

Bertolino: No . . . It must have been a Z . . .

Ottavio: You are teasing and tormenting me. Just because I condescend to treat you as a friend as well as a servant,

	you presume on my good nature. You go too far. I demand her name.
Bertolino:	Flaminia.
Ottavio:	Flaminia, Flaminia, Flaminia, Flaminia (*ad lib.*). My true love, my dearest . . .
Bertolino:	Flaminia de' Bisognosi!
Ottavio:	Flaminia de' Bisognosi. De' Bisognosi? Are you sure? It's not possible. She – related to that skinflint, that monster, to whom I'm in debt, who threatens me with banishment or worse?
Bertolino:	Pantalone de' Bisognosi. She is his niece, his ward, returned from the court of France, and to be paraded by Pantalone before the nobility of Venice, for the greatest marriage contract.
Ottavio:	Oh my despair, my despair; he will never let me see her. There is no hope for me.
Bertolino:	From where we're looking not a lot, but as the philosophers proclaim; 'nil desperandum' – and where there's a Bertolino . . . who has a certain way with the wenches . . . and has already caught the eye of a pretty little miss called Spinetta.
Ottavio:	I wish you well, but I fail to see how your lascivious gallantries concern me in my despondency.
Bertolino:	Maybe not a lot, but Spinetta happens, by the merest chance, to be maidservant to . . .
Ottavio:	What care I whose maidservant you seduce . . .
Bertolino:	Not at all, unless, unless you were interested to know that her mistress is Flaminia de' Bisognosi!
	Exits, quickly slamming door behind him.
Ottavio:	Come back here at once. Bertolino! Bertolino!
Bertolino:	(*putting head round door*) Did you call, Master?

Version B

A similar scene can be improvised between the Innamorata, Flaminia, and her maid, Spinetta (Juliet and the Nurse!)

Version C

A split stage impro with Flaminia and Spinetta stage-right, and Ottavio and Bertolino stage-left. A strict order in the lines of the dialogue has to be established first, e. g.:

a) Flaminia, b) Spinetta, c) Ottavio, d) Bertolino . . .

Example

Flaminia: (a)   At last we're alone – What have you to tell me?

Spinetta: (b)   About what, Ma'am?

Ottavio: (c)   Now we're together, what news?

Bertolino: (d) News, Master?

Flaminia: (a)   You know full well, what I want to know.

Spinetta: (b)   About a certain gentleman would it be?

Ottavio: (c)   You know exactly what I mean!

Bertolino: (d) Would it be about a certain Lady?

　　　　　　　　Etc, etc.

Ottavio and Bertolino must initially paraphrase (parrot) lines improvised by the two women.

Examples, Exercises and Games involving the Lovers

Innamorata

Game 26	'A Lover Confides . . . ', page 55
Game 49	'The Two Suitors', page 102
Game 52	'A Proposal Scorned', page 107

Innamorato

Game 26	'A Lover Confides . . . ', page 55
Game 49	'The Two Suitors', page 102
	'The Ancient Mariner', page 168

Colombina
Columbine

and other servants

Servette, Zanne
Fantesche

whose names might be

Franceschina, Spinetta,
Licetta, Smeraldin,
Oliva, Nespola

47

48

So far we have only considered one female role, that of the Innamorata; now we examine her essential supporter, her maid, known as the **Servetta** or **Fantescha**, and also by the female form of **Zanni – Zanne**. This last is perhaps not a good term, as her standing and function varies considerably from theirs. She is a lady's maid, not a lower servant, and unlike them her comedy never springs from some deformity of body or character; neither is she greedy, miserly, cowardly, nor stupid. In fact she is very bright, and perhaps the only one in the play to behave at all in a rational manner. She is also unique in the scenario. There are at least two **Zanni** in a company and often many more, but even when there are two **Innamorate**, there is rarely more than one **Servetta**. Her stage business, for much of the play, is with the Innamorata, although in the case of Colombina she is usually coupled with Arlecchino and often ends by marrying him (heaven help her!). Prior to that, she is frequently pursued by Pantalone, or The Doctor, and sometimes briefly by the Innamorato himself.

224

Mostly about Costume

We can get something near to an understanding of how the male Masks performed because we have such a wealth of iconographic material on how they looked, stood, even related to one another. But there are few early pictures of the *servette* and none that fulfil the generally held conception of Columbine (or Colombina). We have to expel from our minds certain hard-held misconceptions; these are so pervasive that otherwise conscientious historians, having worked hard on the male Masks, largely give up on the *servetta* and describe her only as she was in her latter days of the eighteenth and nineteenth centuries, giving her short skirts, frilly blouses, mob caps and 'operatic gypsy' movements. The result is that we quite frequently see a *servetta* costumed and behaving in a style some hundred years later than the rest of the cast, so I think it would be as well to survey the admittedly scanty information we do have, and put it into some kind of order.

Let us establish first the all-important matter of hemlines! No, there were no short skirts prior to 1730, by which time the *Commedia dell'Arte* proper was in decline. Before that, the dresses of upper-class women, both in real life and those represented on the stage, trailed on the ground. The rest of womankind wore hers perhaps an inch or two off the ground. It was in 1730 that the dancer Camargo raised her skirts to allow her ankles to be seen. You will be relieved to know that as a result of this daring innovation she considered it incumbent upon herself to start wearing knickers (*caleçon*): as far as we know, the first dancer to do so.

Our earliest pictures of a *servetta* are shown in the *Recueil Fossard*, a collection of pictures made by a Mons. Fossard for Louis XIV, showing actors from a slightly earlier period (c. 1585). They are lively engravings displaying a lot of the action between the Innamorati, Pantalone, Arlecchino, Zanni, etc. Among them are two *servette*, who are named Licetta and Francisquina (*sic*). Nothing could be more different from our ideas of the later *servette*, such as Colombina, than these two solid looking matrons, plainly dressed, with full skirts to the ground, voluminous aprons, and severe coifs covering their hair. In spite of the austerity of their attire, Licetta is shown revealing much ample bosom, and in one of the prints, Francisquina is putting up no resistance to Arlecchino's libidinous caresses. She has removed her apron and it is worth noting that her bodice, unlike that of her mistress, is laced at the front, as she would have had to dress herself.

49

Over thirty years later (1622), we have an entirely different Franceschina, from the hand of Jacques Callot – a joyous dancing figure striking a tambourine above her head. The skirt of her dress is flying about and seems rather shorter, but if we look closely we can see that she has hitched it up at the waist by using a second girdle. This is much more what we expect and desire of the *servetta*, although she may represent either a ballerina or a *cantatina* (either seem to have both sung and danced), who would have appeared in musical interludes between the acts, rather than an actress involved in the play itself.

Still no actual Colombina. For her first appearance in pictorial form we have to go to the engravings showing Caterina Biancolelli (1665-1716), daughter of the great Arlecchino, Dominique, and granddaughter of Isabella Franchini Biancolelli, an actress who herself had played Colombina. Caterina Biancolelli, described as dark haired, petite and vivacious, was the first to become a 'star' in the role. In the late seventeenth century, we find that many of the advertised attractions included either

50

'Arlecchino', or 'Colombina' as part of the title. *Arlecchino, Emperor of the Moon'*, *Arlecchino, Doge of England'*, or *'Colombina, Advocate For and Against', 'Colombina, a Woman's Revenge'*, etc. The Arlecchino was Gherardi; the Colombina, Caterina Biancolelli.

So what did Colombina look like at this date? Again a surprise; she wore the full and heavy court dress of a lady of the time complete with the high *'fontange'* head-dress.[1] The only concession to the lower status of lady's maid was the diminutive apron she sometimes wore – not a costume one would have thought of as expressing the vivacious, spirited, provocative, creature suggested by the scenarios. One thing that would have helped would have been the many disguises, often into male attire, with which she enlivened the proceedings. When women first appeared on the stage, the influence of the classical tradition kept the length of time which a high-born heroine actually exposed herself to the gaze of the public to a minimum. Many of the Innamorata's scenes were, for that reason, conducted by the lower status *servetta*, as proxy. This greatly enhanced the *servetta*'s role and established many of the themes of substitution, disguise and intrigue that remained her contribution to the plot, even when restrictions on the Innamorata no longer held sway.

In the eighteenth century there are more frequent illustrations of *servette*, and we have pictures of Camilla Veronese, who would have worn the post-Camargo length dress, and seems to have had those qualities we look for in vain before her time.

So to the thorny question of how you should dress and play the *servetta*. If the production is to be set during the sixteenth or early seventeenth century, when Arlecchino would be wearing the early 'patched' suit, the more solid, plainly dressed mature woman of the *Fossard* pictures would be called for: overtly sexual, and somewhat coarse in speech and gesture, possibly influenced by the fact that at this period the part of Franceschina was sometimes played by a man.

For the late seventeenth and early eighteenth century one could try the style of Caterina Biancolelli, varying it with 'disguises' where appropriate, or one could take inspiration from the Callot *servetta*, which, although dating from the first quarter of the seventeenth century, need not look too much of an anachronism, if the length of the gown is there but made of soft and flowing material with a minimum of petticoats, to give greater freedom of movement.

---

1. A tall lace head-dress supported on a wire frame, also known as a Commode.

By the middle and late eighteenth century – Goldoni, rather than *Commedia dell'Arte* – we are on clearer ground: shorter skirt, laced bodice, bright colours, and even a mob cap; but remember the rest of your cast should also be in this period. In the early nineteenth-century Harlequinade, she has the flimsy, high-waisted Regency look. For the rest of the century she seems to retain the slightly bell-shaped dress and puff sleeves first seen in the 1840's.

Speech

The earlier *servette* (like those in *Receuil Fossard*) give opportunities for country dialects, with tones varying from the warm and maternal to the coarse or vulgar. It is a good idea to search for the less obvious, by using contradictions, e. g., obscenities rendered in a sweet innocent voice, or the most innocent remark delivered like an innuendo.

From the end of the seventeenth century the pace would have been quicker, lighter and more charming, with much laughter and bantering.

Movement

The older, plainer *servetta* would have had slow earthy movements, enlivened by swift movements of arms or feet in defence or attack, and perhaps unexpected acrobatic skills.

From the date of the Callot pictures onwards, we can, I think correctly, see Colombina as a dancer. From the age of Biancolelli until the end of the eighteenth century the guiding gesture would have been Baroque, and in the following century balletic (Cecchetti or Bournonville rather than a Russian or British model).

If the performer playing Colombina is a dancer, she starts off with an advantage, but she must also invest the part with an actor's sense of timing, restraint and composure.

A Mirror for Colombina (c. 1690)
Visualisation – Mime – Impro

Important note: see pages 158–9 for the way of working the Mirror exercises.

The Narrator: Colombina, maidservant to La Signorina Isabella de'
Bisognosi, stands in her mistress' boudoir surrounded by cast-
aside dresses, shoes, jewellery, head-dresses. She has just gone
through the usual palaver of dressing Isabella. In her anxiety to
appear irresistible to her beloved Lelio, whom she was to meet
again at tonight's ball, her mistress had been more fractious and
indecisive than ever. Nothing would do: the blue, the silver, the
pink ball gowns were all tried and rejected, till she settled on one
of pure white in which, it had to be admitted, she looked
enchanting. Now Colombina must clear up. Old Pantalone is
supposed to be broke, and she hasn't been paid any wages in
months, yet Isabella never seems to go short of anything.

As Colombina looks round at the scene of chaos she notices a pair
of gloves on the dressing table. She takes the gloves, rushes out of
the room and calls 'Isabella'. Too late: she has gone! Colombina
comes back into the room and throws the gloves back on the
dressing table. She sits on the very edge of a chair and leans back,
her shoulders resting against its back, but with her whole body
straight. (Except when she is impersonating somebody else, she
never sits.) She stretches out her arms and legs and points her
dancer's feet. She yawns, crosses her feet in a series of *entrechats*.
Does a *developpé* with each leg in turn. She stands, stretching her
arms upwards, then, bringing her arms down again, she caresses
herself voluptuously. She relaxes, takes a big breath, and lets it out
with a weary 'hurrr . . . '

She looks around the room and becomes her workaday self. 'Clear
up, I suppose', she says to herself, picking up a shoe thrown here,
a stocking discarded there. As she is putting them away she catches
sight of herself in the mirror.

'You, Colombina,' she says to her reflection, 'are a fool'. She puts
the shoes in the chest and the stocking in a laundry basket, and
goes back to the mirror. 'You could be living a life of ease and
indulgence, with a servant of your own to bring your meals to you
in bed, and to empty your chamber pot, if you had only said "Yes"

or "Si" or even "Oui". What other girl in your position, would have refused an offer of marriage – yes marriage – to Il Dottore Baloardo? Yes, he's an old fart; fat, smelly, and idiotic. But he would have been easy to handle, and you know him to be impotent, so demands in that direction would have been 'little', but you had to say "No" ... "Nein", "Non" ... and even "Niet" for good measure, and so you find yourself six months later stuck in this miserable house of Pantalone, and still fetching and carrying for Isabella, stupid love-sick girl, kind enough but with a mind filled only with her Lelio and what a dumb cluck he is proving to be! And why did I say no?

'For Arlecchino! – so who's the dumb cluck now? If I'd have married Baloardo, *I'd* be going to the ball!' She picks up one of the rejected gowns, holds it against her and dances round the room. She stows it away and returns to the mirror. She takes a brisk step to the right,[2] stands stiffly, doffs an imaginary cocked hat, and adopts a male voice. 'Donna Colombina, allow me to present myself, Il Barone Pezzo di Cretino. May I have the honour of this dance?' She moves to her left to be herself again, 'Barone? Then I fear not, sir, I never dance with anyone less than a Duke.' (Moves back to her right.) 'Then perhaps we could walk. Will you give me your arm?' (Moves again to the left.) 'Give you my arm? No sir, I would only give my arm to he who offers me his hand!' She tires of this game and returns to her work, till everything is cleared away. All that remains is a gown of silver brocade that Isabella, in the last of a series of changes of mind, had rejected. Colombina is about to put it away, but instead lays it on the chair and quickly slips out of her own dress and into the silver ballgown. She goes to the mirror. She is really very pretty, she admits to herself. True, she hasn't Isabella's fashionable white complexion: her hands are rough from the work she has to do, she is fuller of figure; but men like that.

The gown is undone at the back, and although she can't do it up as she would for her mistress with all the lacing and pinning involved, she pulls the lace round to the front and tightens them so that the dress is pulled to fit her, She finds the head-dress and fan to match.

---

2. See Part One, Game 50 – 'Split Personality', page 103.

Suddenly she hears Pantalone's voice downstairs, raging and ranting, and Isabella crying and protesting. They have come back early! Colombina pauses to listen; Pantalone must have caught her with Lelio, and demanded that she return home at once. Colombina takes off the ball dress and has just about got it and its accoutrements into the chest when the crying Isabella enters the room.

The Letter: a Short Scene between Colombina and Arlecchino

Arlecchino suddenly appears and scares Colombina, who is returning from the dairy with two jugs of milk.

Colombina: Now look what you've done, made me spill my milk.

Arlecchino: No use crying over spilt milk, my pretty maid.

Colombina: Don't you pretty maid me! And stop staring at my jugs. A face like yours might turn my milk sour. Off with you! (*She turns to go.*)

Arlecchino: (*calling her back*) Colombina!

Colombina: Don't you call me that.

Arlecchino: What shall I call you then?

Colombina: You needn't call me anything – for I have no intention of having further concourse with you.

Arlecchino: Concourse?

Colombina: Of course, concourse.

Arlecchino: What's that mean?

Colombina: I don't know – but my mistress is always refusing to have it with people.

Arlecchino: Oh, come on, let's have a bit of concourse. Well, give us a kiss, then.

Colombina: Stop it. You'll bring old Pantalone running.

Arlecchino: Listen, I've got a letter for Donna Isabella.

Waves sealed letter.

Colombina: She doesn't want a letter from the likes of you.

Arlecchino:	It's not from me, it's from my master, Lelio.
Colombina:	Show it to me (*She snatches it from him.*) Where does it say Donna Isabella?
Arlecchino:	There! (*Pointing to the inscription.*) 'To Donna Isabella.'
Colombina:	It doesn't say that. It says (*Reading slowly.*) 'Alle-basi . . . Annod ot.' Though it is writ funny.
Arlecchino:	No it says . . . (*Staring at the writing.*) ' To Donna Isabella.'
Colombina:	You can't read
Arlecchino:	Yes I can, my master's learning me,
Colombina:	Well my mistress is learning me better. It says 'Allebasi Annod ot.' Here she comes. Now you'll see. (*To Isabella, who has just entered.*) Mistress, what does Allebasi Annod ot mean?' See, 'Allebasi Annod ot.'
Isabella:	Very good, but if we turn it the right way round it might say . . .
Colombina:	(*reading it*) . . . 'To Donna Isabella!'

Exercises and Games from Part One involving the Servette

51

Some Lesser-Known Masks

Arlecchina (Mlle Harlequine)

The limited scope of female Masks, particularly comic ones, was being felt by the end of the sixteenth and early seventeenth century, and attempts were made to introduce female versions of the principal male Masks. Many of these are to be found in *'The New and Curious School of Theatrical Dance'* published in Nuremberg in 1716, the work of a visiting Venetian dancing master, Georgio Lambranzi. The book has nearly a hundred engraved plates, which show dances and comedy mime scenes (about half being of *Commedia dell'Arte* Masks), with the music, and some basic description of

52

steps and action. They do not represent part of a scenario performance, but novelty routines that would have been presented as interludes in a variety of entertainments. Each of the principal Masks has a female counterpart wearing a woman's version of the male costume. Sometimes these roles are given a name like 'Pandora', who was partnered with Pantalone, but mostly they are just referred to as 'The Doctor's Wife', 'Scapino's Wife', 'Pulcinella's Wife', and so on (see Appendix).

Arlecchina seems to be the only one of the gender translations to appear with the *Commedia dell'Arte* proper, and it was Caterina Biancolelli who was probably the first to take on the role, when she presented it as an alternative to Colombina in 1695. As characters, there seems to be little difference between the two roles. The beautiful costume, however, has been popular ever since, sometimes being appropriated by other *servetta* names (see the illustration of Rosetta with The Doctor, page 170).

Bertolino

A useful Zanni – one of several that can be helpful where one of the better known Masks would be unsuitable, or involved in other essentials of the plot. He is usually considered one of the 'brighter' servants, although he is sometimes paired with Coviello in which case he would take second place. No costume or mask is specified so he can appear as a typical Zanni or with variations on Brighella-type livery. (Example: 'Bertolino and his Master' p. 221.)

Burattino

This Mask has similarities to Pedrolino, in that he can be played as a bottom of the pile '*stupido*' or a higher Zanni to be cast as valet, inn-

53

keeper, tradesman, and so on. If the first, he wears the Zanni costume and mask of mid-brown with a shortish nose. He tends towards heavy and slow movement and drawling speech. Like others at this level, he has an insatiable hunger and, unlike the sympathetic Pedrolino, he tends to be vicious when not getting his own way.

There is an unusual illustration, of early date, showing little bows or tags of material sewn all over his costume. I have re-created this costume using multi-coloured bows and it proved an effective and unusual costume for the more urbane Burattino. At the end of the sixteenth century Burattino was adopted from the *Commedia dell'Arte* by the Italian marionette theatre and became their most popular puppet.

Cassandro and Cola

Cassandro is an old man, a friend or rival to Pantalone, usurping The Doctor's place when he is not present. Cola is also an old man: a ludicrous figure, whether servant or master. An opportunity to introduce a really old man, if Pantalone is played as being in his middle years.

Coviello

Something between a Zanni and a Captain. In the Callot illustrations, he is seen as a wild dancing figure with a long nose, a sword dangling from his belt and his cloak flying in the air. He seems to have originated in Calabria, travelling northward to become part of the Neapolitan *Commedia dell'Arte*; soon his name was to be found over a wide area. Maurice Sand says he was 'famous for his grimace and confused language'. If he wore the large prominent-nosed mask depicted in a print by Bartelli, there wouldn't have been much face left to grimace with! He is variously described as witty, shrewd, adroit, supple and vain. 'He's a Coviello' is an old Italian phrase referring to any boastful fool. In several scenarios he appears as a doctor, which would fit in with the 'confused language'; but whether he wore anything like the costume given him by Maurice Sand on those occasions is doubtful. Sand's version is based on that in the Bartelli picture, and shows a tight one-piece costume all in blue, with large buttons down the centre, and with bells at his ankles and wrists; a tight fitting hood surmounted with a feather, and an interesting two-tone mask, with reddish cheeks and a dark nose and forehead. In a similar costume he is occasionally used by modern companies as a decorative and amusing Master of Ceremonies.

Fiorinetta

It is perhaps surprising that, for all its reputation for bawdiness, the *Commedia dell'Arte* rarely calls on courtesans or prostitutes in its scenarios; Fiorinetta is an exception. She has the education, cultivation and wealth of an Innamorata, but not the same prerequisite of chastity. She will be beautiful, but a little too extravagantly dressed, bejewelled and befeathered.

She is a very useful addition to any modern cast, providing an excellent foil for Pantalone and The Doctor.

Mezzetino

A Metzetin is to be found among the Callot Zanni, and there were Mezzetinos throughout the sixteenth century, but it was an individual actor, Angelo Costantini (1654-1727), who introduced the red and white striped costume familiar to us from the Watteau paintings, and made the name his own. The actor's life story is rather more interesting than anything we can glean of his performances. He was born in Verona, the son of a *Commedia* player, Costantino Costantini, and performed in Italy until invited to join the Hôtel de Bourgogne company in Paris in 1683, taking the part of the unmasked Mezzetino. A few years later, on the death of Dominique, he was given the role of Arlecchino in an on-stage ceremony in which Colombina presented him with the costume and bat. He accepted the challenge, but the public, having grown fond of his expressive face, refused to let him wear the mask. 'No Mask', they chanted. He played Arlecchino for a year or two, without a mask, and even more oddly under the name of Mezzetino, until in 1689 Gherardi joined the company, when Costantini reverted to the proper Mezzetino role.

In 1695 he wrote a scurrilous 'Life' of his co-star 'Scaramouche'. When the company disbanded, he was fortunate in being asked to form a company for the Elector of Saxony, who was also King of Poland, and was so successful that he was ennobled and showered with gifts.

54

However, he didn't know where to stop and made amorous advances to the Elector's own mistress. He was promptly stripped of his assets and thrown into the prison of Königstein castle, where he languished for twenty years. On his release he made a triumphant comeback in a scene in which the actor playing Arlecchino promises the audience a new novelty. He introduced an aged cloaked figure, who soon threw off the cloak and presented himself, Costantini, a youthful figure of 75, in his Mezzetino costume. He then told the audience that he had had a dream in which he stood before his beloved Paris public and in it his guitar had risen from the ground before him. By a mechanical device this then happened, and he went on to entertain them in song and patter. After packing the theatre for five jubilant performances he returned to Italy and died later that year.

Some of his scenes are included in Gherardi's *'Italian Theatre'* (1697), a book giving 'written' French language scenes which had been interpolated into the performances. They don't read very well in this day and age. In one scene, after a long discourse between Mezzetino and Isabella, in which he proposes that she should marry him, she replies:

Isabella: I can see only one little difficulty to our marriage, and that is that I am already wed.

Mezzetino: Married? That's no problem. Me too. Nothing could be easier to arrange. Five sous of rat-poison will do the trick!

His legacy is the beautiful costume and an easy, flowing relationship with the audience. I have used his persona as compère and narrator in performances of Handel's opera *'Atalanta'* and felt comfortable and honoured to wear his mantle.

Pasquariello

Another old man, said to be a variant of Pulcinella and the original of the French Polichinelle, rather than Pulcinella himself. He too came from Naples. He wore a black costume and red stockings! Neither a Callot engraving, nor a later French print, which show him in a variation on the Zanni suit, have any semblance to this. (He is referred to in the Pulcinella sketch on page 214.)

55

La Ruffiana

Another boost to the very limited number of female roles: her name indicates that she was a procuress, and so was sometimes cast as Fiorinetta's mother, but she also fulfilled other roles where an elderly peasant woman was needed. In character she was talkative, pig-headed, stubborn, and of limited intelligence. She wears the costume of a Neapolitan peasant woman. The one picture of her that exists shows her shrouded in a full cloak and what appears to be a mask and so could offer a good precedent for a female character to wear one.

Rosaura / Rosetta / Rotalinda

Three names for a more mature *servetta* from the second half of the seventeenth century. The first can be married to Pantalone on the rare occasions he has a wife, whom she may cuckold for The Captain.

The last two are names given to a similar *servetta* who takes the role of Pulcinella's much-abused wife. The costumes would have been those of the *servette* of the appropriate period, but an engraving of the late seventeenth century shows Rosetta in an Arlecchina dress of triangular patches (see page 170).

56

Scapino

Scapino – from *scappare* to escape. An attractive and apt name for this close relative of Brighella. He flees from danger, he evades the consequence of his misdeeds, he eludes the objects of previous romantic entanglements, to embark on yet more escapades. Callot's engravings show him dressed as the standard Zanni – loose suit in off-white, belt with a wooden sword, wide brimmed feathered hat – and this is how he was probably portrayed by the originator of the Mask, Francesco Gabrielli (1588-1636). Gabrielli was a multi-instrumentalist and most inheritors of the Mask have presented Scapino as a musical Zanni.

In character he is similar to Brighella, though a little less vicious and a lot more cowardly. He is an arch intriguer, and can be considered one of the 'crafty' zanni. By the late seventeenth century he wears a green striped livery, indistinguishable from that of Brighella, the only difference being that at that period Scapino dispensed with his mask, appearing 'en farine'. It was this character that Molière used for *'Les Fouberies de Scapin'*. Later, his costume is sometimes changed for an eighteenth century-style one when he appears in white breeches and jacket frogged with green braid and a green cloak. The Maurice Sand illustration shows him with blue trimmings and cape, which would be a useful distinction from Brighella, were it not almost certainly a mistake of the original hand-colourist of the print.

His manner of speech could be studied from Molière or from Otway's English version, *'The Cheats of Scapin'* (1676). There is no information on how he performed or how he moved, except the interesting possibilities in the 'slipperiness' implied by his name. Someone grasps hold of him, only to find that they are holding nothing but his cloak, and he has made good his escape!

Scaramuccia (*Scaramouche*)

57

This is one of a number of Masks that are to be found at their most distinctive and identifiable in the work of a single interpreter. There had been Scaramuccias as early as the end of the sixteenth century. Callot presents him masked, long-nosed, a beret with great feathers on his head, a close-fitting costume and a long sword; in fact one of the 'standard' Callot Captains. Scaramuccia means 'little skirmisher' and in the early scenarios he plays either a Captain or a Zanni, or something between the two. He was associated with Naples, and is sometimes paired with Pulcinella.

It was the Neapolitan, Tiberio Fiorilli, who developed the 'Scaramouche' (French spelling) that became famous throughout Europe at the end of the seventeenth century. He was said by Garrick to be the greatest actor of the day. He danced, played the guitar, and was a considerable acrobat even in old age; he was still performing at 87! He was also the first great mime as we now understand the term, and along with the later developments of Deburau's Pierrot, set the basis for our present mime traditions.

He dispensed with the facemask, using a white make-up with dark eyebrows and a small pointed black beard. He dressed entirely in black: jacket, breeches, a short cloak and a large beret (possibly to suggest a Spaniard), the only relief being a narrow white ruff round his neck.

There is a popular conception of a totally different Scaramouche: a brightly clad and masked carnival figure of mercurial temperament, sparkling wit, and astonishing swordsmanship, which entered our culture in the twentieth century with a Rafael Sabatini novel, which was made into a silent film with Ramon Novarro, and then into the Stewart Granger swashbuckling film 'Scaramouche'. The Commedia has always been a thing of popular imagination, so there is no reason why such a swordsman/player, which might after all bear some resemblance to the Callot Captain, should be rejected from the Commedia pantheon.

Playing Scaramouche

One would be unlikely to choose the Callot Captain, as there are many other names to fulfil this category;[1] leaving aside the Carnival Scaramouche just discussed, the most interesting to a modern performer would be the Fiorilli version, giving opportunities for traditional mime skills. But Fiorilli was also a remarkable acrobat and contortionist, specialising in effects made possible by his remarkable strength and suppleness. It is not uncommon for a circus performer to have such skills but it is very rare, if not unknown, for this performer to be also a great actor and mime. Only his contemporaries can attest to Fiorilli's greatness, but a few of his startling feats have been recorded. The 'Pas de Scaramouche' was a kind of walk in which he would go down into splits and then, drawing his legs together with the weight on the front foot, come to an upright position and drag the back foot through, to repeat

---

1. See Appendixes for notes on Callot's Mask names.

the splits on the other leg, continuing until he had rapidly crossed the stage. He could also change his apparent size, walking about on his haunches, his cloak hiding his knees so that he looked like a dwarf. He was also an illusionist and would use tricks and doubles of himself to make himself grow into a giant, or even 'dismember' himself about the stage. There is a description of one of his mime scenes in which an unseen Pasquariello touches him on the shoulder and then exits. This was the cue for a long 'Haunting' sequence, which was probably the origin of the pantomime routine still performed by traditional comics. (See Game 30c, page 64.)

Stentarello

A mish-mash of a character for whom I, myself, can find little enthusiasm. He doesn't arrive upon the scene until the middle of the eighteenth century and was then referred to as a *'caratterista'* role. This meant a comic personage, usually characteristic of some specific region, and having nothing to do with the plot, who would come on and fool about or 'gag'. Stentarello was from Florence, and described by Sand and Duchartre as a simpleton; lazy, absent-minded, a glutton and a blackguard. He was identified by the gaudy ill-matching colours of his costume, odd stockings and shoes, and with his hair or wig in a long pig-tail, like the Victorian Pantaloon. He had no mask, painted his eyebrows with an upward curl, and – this was the important bit – he was always missing his front teeth. The bigger the gap, the more successful one was in the part!

Tartaglia

This is an 'as required' Mask, introduced when the role of a 'lawyer' or similar pedantic personage was needed. He is to be found in the earliest scenarios in a number of capacities: as servant, innkeeper, apothecary, lawyer, even father of an Innamorata. His name indicates 'one who stutters' and that is about all the certain information we have. There is to my mind a very unsatisfactory delineation of him by Maurice Sand, wearing a costume of wide green and yellow horizontal stripes, and a wide frilled collar. He is fat with a large belly. He hasn't a mask, but wears large green-rimmed spectacles, which almost answer the same purpose. Most other illustrations seem to be derived from this picture by Maurice Sand.

His is a particularly interesting example of how limited information can be widely interpreted. I myself used the character in one of my first *Commedia* productions, and, with a background of English theatre and literature behind me, from Ben Jonson and Dickens to Chaplin and the silent films, saw him as a brow-beaten figure, whose stuttering was prompted by a conflict between fear and a need to use the law for his

58

own or his client's purposes. He was presented with a pale mask, almost hidden by large wobbly spectacles. Plot-wise and theatrically it was very successful, if different from the Sand conception.

Even further from Sand is a beautiful mask by Sartori made for Mario Gonzales (1952), who saw Tartaglia as a tragic figure, stuttering through his tears: a pathetic mask with a small upswept nose and sunken cheeks; no glasses.

Another possibility is the 'stupido', who, in his stammering, pauses on what sounds as if he is about to utter an obscenity, with an innocent word substituted, either by him or another, at the last moment.

Some of the scenarios offer still another choice, in which Tartaglia stutters with anger. 'How d–d–d–dare you, s–stand in my w–w–way'. So Tartaglia stutters, and has large spectacles; otherwise, make of him what you will!

Trivellino / Trivelin / Truffaldino / Tracagnino

These four Masks are each, for the most part, Arlecchino under another name. The most famous interpreter of Trivellino ('Little Gimlet') was Domenico Locatelli (1613-1671), and he is depicted in a costume closely duplicating the early 'patches' of Martinelli. A later Trivelin, performing in Paris in the last part of the seventeenth century, wears a costume very similar to that of Gherardi.

A third costume is described and illustrated by Maurice Sand: a delightful creation shared by no other Mask. It consists of small triangles along the seams of the trousers and the arms of the jacket, with the rest of the costume bespattered with stars and moons. Duchartre mentions this alternative but gives no source.[2] All three variations wear the Arlecchino face mask.

Opportunities for reviving Trivellino are limited, unless one wants two 'Arlecchinos' in the production, or a new zanni Mask based on Sand's costume of stars and moons – possibly as a musician, vocalist or Master of Ceremonies.

Truffaldino and Tracagnino are two further exact Arlecchino duplicates. I can only surmise that actors who wished to cash in on the Arlecchino bandwagon used the mask and costume when they didn't feel free to use the name.

---

2. There is an eighteenth-century water-colour showing a costume decorated with stars and moons which is assigned to an unlikely Brighella.

Zanni

as an individual mask
who can also be known as

Zan Cornetto, Zan Paolo
Zan Ganasso, Zan Padella,
Zan Mortadella,
Zan Muzzina, etc

As previously mentioned, the word *Zanni*, the form being the same in both singular and plural, can be used in a generic sense to refer to any or all of the male servant Masks of the *Commedia dell'Arte*. In many of the early scenarios and references, however, it can also be applied as a name for an individual character, sometimes with a distinguishing additional cognomen added, so that he became Zan Cornetto or Zan Ganasso, etc. Here we will just call him 'Zanni'.

The English word 'zany' is taken from the Italian *Zanni* and is defined in the dictionary as 'crazily idiotic' and carries an implication of lively buffoonery, a description very suitable for Arlecchino but not for the Mask of Zanni himself; he does not have what we might call a 'zany' nature. He seems lethargic, weary from a life of hard physical work, and tends to be fairly advanced in years; certainly not a youth. In fact he sometimes seems to be of an age with Pantalone, with whom he often has an easy familiarity, as if he had served the family for several generations.

He has a husky voice that comes from life on the streets and market squares, and from the physical strain of carrying the city's burdens, from a sack of flour to a sedan chair, along the narrow lanes and across the wide piazzas of Venice. Bearing this weight has given him arms that hang low by his sides, and hands that turn backwards, his shoulders pulled down and his knees bent. Even so he is not taciturn, and his head, arm and hand movements can be rapid and expressive.

He is the original of both the 'stupid' and the 'crafty' Zanni, into which he later divided, so can have either of their natures, or a mixture of both. From the scenarios, and also from pictorial evidence, it seems that frequently he could not only read, but could read music as well. He is mostly trusting and trustworthy. We know his costume well, and though it is simple, it can be very beautiful to look at and a pleasure to wear. It is nicest when it is fairly full and loose. The hat should be large and the feathers long.

The mask, of medium to reddish brown, looks good if accompanied by a generous growth of facial hair. The nose can vary in size and length. The tradition is that the bigger the nose, the more stupid the fellow. The mask can thus vary from almost a **frontal** one to a pronounced **profile**.

His movement should spring from the character itself, depending firstly on how bright or how stupid, how young or how old, and so on, you want to make him, and secondly on his emotional and physical state at that moment in the play.

Before giving an example of a scene between Zanni and Pantalone here is a traditional movement, which suits the physical nature of the opening sequence.

Zanni Pas de Basque

The rhythm is in threes **1/** 2, 3. **2/** 2, 3. **3/** 2, 3. **4/** 2, 3. etc. (music ¾ or ⅝).

Start with the weight on the left foot, with the knee slightly bent. Place the right foot on the floor in front of you, without any weight on it.

Count:	**1/**	Drop the weight on to the front foot (right foot).
	2,	Take a step straight forward on to the heel of the left foot.
	3.	Draw up the right foot to join to the left, taking the weight onto the right foot.
Count:	**2/**	Dropping on to the left foot, and shooting the right foot forward.
	2,	Take a step forward on to the heel of the right foot.
	3.	Draw up the left foot and join to the right, taking the weight onto the left foot.

Repeat ad lib., alternating the feet.

Old Friends
Pantalone and Zanni Meet Again after Twenty Years [1]

> *Pantalone crosses from stage-right towards stage-left [dir. 7]. doing '**The Triplet Walk**' (r/l/r pause l/r/l pause), ad lib (see page 62).*
>
> *Zanni crosses from stage left to stage right [dir. 3] doing '**The Pas de Basque**' (see above) in the same rhythm but progressing more rapidly than Pantalone. He passes up-stage of Pantalone and stops; then does a few more steps and stops again, and looks round. Pantalone looks round furtively. Turns away again, and does '**The Quick Rhythmic Walk**' (see page 56), trying to get away but actually staying almost in place. Zanni, moving very rapidly, runs and intercepts Pantalone just before he makes an exit. Pantalone, without stopping, turns to face the opposite direction [dir. 3] and continues his '**Quick Rhythmic Walk**'. Zanni stays stage left and calls after Pantalone.*

Zanni: Pantalone! (*Pantalone continues to walk away.*) Pantalone! (*Pantalone still walks, but on place.*) Pantalone, you old fool, (*Pantalone turns round.*) it's me! And I know it's you! (*Pantalone is doing the '**rib focus**': Game 23, page 51.*) It's me! Zanni!

Pantalone: Zanni? Can't be!

> *Both do a series of broad welcoming gestures, which Pantalone improvises and which are copied by Zanni. Pantalone then leads into the embrace lazzi which is:*
>
> a) *Spread arms out wide (facing each other).*
>
> b) *Pantalone raises his right arm and lowers the left about 1 foot. Zanni does the same. (As they are facing each other, this is a reverse not a mirror image.)*
>
> c) *They then run towards each other keeping their arms extended, until they embrace; the arms go round each other and their left leg lifts behind them. They pat each other on the back in rhythmic motion, with suitable ejaculations of greeting.*

---

1. Inspired by an account of a performance given in Trausnitz Castle, Bavaria, in 1568. See Giacomo Oreglia '*The Commedia dell'Arte*', Methuen, 1968.

d)   *They step apart looking at each other, extend their arms sideways to a horizontal position. This time they raise their left arms and repeat the embrace and back-patting over the other shoulder, as they raise the right leg behind.*

Repeat d) ad lib.

Pantalone: Zanni, my old friend, let me look at you.

They step apart a few paces to look at each other. They speed towards each other and in an excess of friendly emotion Pantalone jumps up with his legs round Zanni's waist. Zanni whirls him round, and puts him down. They part and have another look at each other. Then it's Zanni's turn to leap round Pantalone's waist and be spun round; they continue their antics, laughing and calling out each other's names until exhausted they fall to the ground.

Pantalone: So how have you been, eh? Still doing the old . . .

Zanni: Yes still at it, and you've still got the . . .

Pantalone: Oh, yes, yes – I don't think I could manage if I hadn't Mind you I get a touch of the . . .

Zanni: So do I.

Pantalone: Do you? Where in the . . .?

Zanni:	No, just in the winter . . . Good times we had, eh?
Pantalone:	Yes, good times . . . and bad.
Zanni:	Yes, good and bad. Those were the days.
Pantalone:	(*looking at Zanni*) But my poor Zanni – you look so – er – old!
Zanni:	Well it is twenty years since we last met. (*Pause.*) You on the other hand, haven't changed a jot.
Pantalone:	(*preening*) I try to look after . . .
Zanni:	When I first knew you, you looked ten years older than Methuselah; so twenty more years haven't made much difference.
Pantalone:	Yes, tempus fugit.
Zanni:	Yes . . . What?
Pantalone:	Tempus fugit . . . Time flies.
Zanni:	Yes and that as well. And how's Pandora?
Pantalone:	Pandora? Oh my poor Pandora. Died this three years since. (*He breaks into uncontrollable wailing.*)
Zanni:	Pandora dead? It can't be. It can't be.
	He joins in the crying. After a time, Pantalone suddenly stops.
Pantalone:	What are you crying for? She was *my* wife.
Zanni:	Well she was your wife, but she was my mistress.
Pantalone:	Oh, yes I forgot that. So she was, so she was. In that case my condolences old fellow.
	They embrace again and dissolve into floods of tears.
Zanni:	I think we should drink a glass to her memory and to our long friendship. What do you say?
Pantalone:	Yes, yes a glass to our beloved Pandora. (*With sudden change of tone.*) Who's paying?
	They look into their purses, which are very empty. They turn to each other, and both say at the same time:
Both:	Dutch?

Rather appropriately, Z for Zanni brings this book of studies to an end.

Now upon this final page,
Like a bare and almost empty stage,
None but I, Zanni, left behind
To bid you, a fond farewell.

A simple fellow I, of modest wit,
A mere buffoon, hardly fit
To find words in verse or prose
To close this book. So I propose

Just my obeisance now to make,
And in these final words to take
The chance of wishing – if I may –
Well, to all who would *Commedia* play!

61

APPENDIXES

BOOKS

Bibliography being a bit too pompous for the following subjective and incomplete notes, giving my thoughts on some of the books dealing with our subject; it is for those who want to look into the history of *Commedia dell'Arte* in greater detail. Except where otherwise stated all the books are out of print. Most can be ordered from a library, or consulted in a major reference library. If you are in London, many can be examined at the Pavlova Library, which is part of the Westminster Reference Library.[1] They can occasionally be found at secondhand bookshops and book fairs, but can be expensive; for example, the current price for '*The History of Harlequin*' by Beaumont is around £150 according to the condition.

Beaumont, Cyril: 'The History of Harlequin', London, Beaumont, 1926

This is a beautifully produced book, the type of thing they were so good at in the 1920's – handmade paper, fine illustrations in colour and black and white, a pictorial cover, and specially designed vignettes. There is a forward by Sacheverell Sitwell, in which Gordon Craig was to find a number of errors, but the text by Beaumont is accurate and useful, particularly in the part dealing with Harlequin in England in the nineteenth century. I knew Mr Beaumont in his later years, visiting him in his tiny shop in Charing Cross Road – an elegant Edwardian gentleman who was very tolerant in answering the endless questions of an eighteen year old.

Craig, Edward Gordon: Articles in 'The Mask', especially that of January 1912

Gordon Craig (1872–1966) was the son of the actress Ellen Terry. He spent some years as an actor before devoting himself to the designs and productions, which were to greatly influence subsequent staging. He published and wrote most of the articles

---

1. 35 St Martin's Street, London WC2H 7HP.

in 'The Mask', under various nom de plumes. He was one of the first to realise the importance of the Commedia dell'Arte, historically and as a source for the revitalisation of the acting of the time. The issues of the periodical are scarce but can be found in bound volumes in some reference libraries.

Duchartre, Pierre L: 'The Italian Comedy', London, Harrap, 1929, reprinted London, Dover, 1966

The most widely read book in English (originally published in French) on the Commedia dell'Arte and one of the few still in print, and deservedly so. There are some minor factual errors and discredited theories but it is still about the best introduction to the history and the characters, and a useful reference book to always have on hand. One can learn much of the style and even the technique from careful perusal of its numerous illustrations.

Lambranzi, Gregorio: 'The New and Curious School of Theatrical Dancing', Beaumont, London, 1928

This is another luxury book. Edited and published by Beaumont, it is a translation of the German original published in Nuremberg in 1716. It consists of fifty engravings of theatrical novelty dances, about half of which are of Commedia dell'Arte characters. There are brief descriptions of the routines and a top line of the music to which they were performed. As is so often the case with Commedia dell'Arte pictures we are getting them 'once removed': by that I mean that these are not the Commedia actors themselves, but other performers cashing in on the popularity of the characters created by them. That being said, they provide useful information on the novelty aspect that more and more became part of popular entertainment, including the Commedia dell'Arte itself, during the eighteenth and early nineteenth century.[2] There are several plates, however, that illustrate a scene between Arlecchino and Scaramouche that definitely seems to owe something to the work of Gherardi and Fiorilli from the 1690's.

Lea, Katherine M: 'Italian Popular Comedy', Oxford, 1934, reprinted Oxford, Russell and Russell, 1962

This is, I think, the best of the more serious accounts of Commedia dell'Arte. While giving a mass of accurate and documented information, the author successfully brings it to life with anecdote and description of performances, and extracts from contemporary written plays that give an indication of what the style might have

---

2. This demand for novelty also manifested itself in large and spectacular stage settings, transformations, trick scenery and a greater reliance on props.

been like. She gives accounts of the elements of Commedia dell'Arte, the contributory factors in its origin and evolution, a description of the individual Masks, information on the collections of scenarios, and where they are now housed. Miss Lea is very good on the management and economy of the troupes and the careers of the principal actors. The second volume of the book (of two volumes in one) is devoted to the influence of Commedia dell'Arte on the English stage and on the written drama. The appendixes give specimen scenarios from different collections, a handlist of scenarios, and a list of actors and Mask roles. Beg, borrow, or steal it!

Nicoll, Allardyce: 'Masks, Mimes and Miracles', London, Harrap, 1931, reprinted, Cooper Square, 1963

Although only the second half of the book is devoted to the Commedia dell'Arte, it might nonetheless be considered to challenge Miss Lea's 'Italian Popular Comedy' as its standard history. It is accurate and entirely free from the romantic speculation into which it is so easy to fall when trying to tell the story of Commedia dell'Arte. He gives the alternative theories on origins and development before telling us those he favours. Numerous and detailed footnotes give the sources of his information. There are good illustrations, many being different from those in Duchartre, if they are not so numerous. There is an amazing appendix giving: 1) A list of Mask names (roles), over 300 of them! 2) A list of the most famous actors and actresses, and 3) A list of the principal extant scenarios and where they can be found. It is Nicholl's spelling of both characters and actors – which otherwise tend to vary wildly from book to book – that I have considered the most reliable and followed throughout.

Nicoll, Allardyce: 'The World of Harlequin', Cambridge, 1963, paperback edition, 1976

Nicoll came back to the subject of Commedia dell'Arte more than 30 years later, and the treatment is somewhat different. Here he gives us less facts and allows himself more comment. What he says is always interesting, sometimes enlightening, and the book is a valuable addition to Commedia studies. It is not, I think, as essential a work of reference as his previous work.

Niklaus, Thelma: 'Harlequin Phoenix', Oxford, Bodley Head, 1965

This is a romanticised, almost fictionalised account, presenting Harlequin as a sort of guiding spirit rather than just a role, which many actors have impersonated. The author's intention is to engender in the reader something of her own interest in the old Commedia all'improvviso, and this she does most successfully. One would have to be very blasé not to be carried along by her enthusiasm, and as it is our job, as entertainers, to be creative and imaginative, we are not in a position to condemn her for filling out and enlivening the narrative. In any case she is well versed in the historical evidence and makes no factual errors, apart from the one referred to on page 260. Read it if you can get hold of a copy.

Oreglia, Giacomo: 'The Commedia dell'Arte', London, Methuen, 1968

This is an excellent little book. I understand that Oreglia worked with actors in Sweden so had some practical knowledge of performing. Though the book is principally a history, it defines the characters clearly and gives examples of *lazzi* and surviving dialogue. Short, clear, very well illustrated, and free from debatable theorising, it is an ideal first introductory book. Too bad it is out of print.

Rudlin, John: 'Commedia dell'Arte: an Actor's Handbook', Routledge, London, 1994

This is one of the very few books, other than my present work, which also tries to give the actor some practical help in portraying the Masks. Not surprisingly, in a subject so open to speculation, there are areas in which I differ from Mr Rudlin. Nevertheless, I find it is a book of much interest and value to the performer. The first half of the book is devoted to a brief history and then a description of each of the major Masks. The second part is devoted to some of those who made attempts to revive Commedia dell'Arte or incorporate it in their productions during the twentieth century. Mr. Rudlin has gathered together information on Gordon Craig, Meyerhold, Copeau, Dario Fo, and others, which would be very time consuming to study otherwise. I find it comforting and inspiring to read of others who have trod the same somewhat perilous path before me.

Sand, Maurice: 'The History of the Harlequinade', London, Martin Secker, 1915, reprinted as 'The History of Harlequin', Oxford, Blom, 1958

These books (I say books because the 1915 edition is in two volumes) have had tremendous influence, mostly for good, in reviving interest in the ancient comedy of skills – but also bad, in giving a romantic nineteenth-century cast at odds with the vitality of the original. He is very fond of anecdotes about the performers, many of which are probably apocryphal. Not the least of its attraction, and also of its

256

disservice to later generations, is the hand-coloured re-drawings from earlier engravings of many of the masks. Many recent writers have found it convenient to reproduce these, rather than the less clear, confusing and sometimes non-surviving originals. I have tried to resist the temptation in my present book.

Scala, Flaminio: 'Scenarios of the Commedia dell'Arte', trans. Henry F. Salerno, London, University of London Press, 1967

This is a translation of fifty scenarios collected by Flaminio Scala, first published in Venice in 1611. Scala was with the famous Gelosi Company playing the role of Lelio. Using a convention we are familiar with, from Boccaccio, Scala gives us a different scenario for each one of fifty 'days'. Titles like The Twin Captains, The Disguised Servants, The Fake Mad Woman, The Dentist, *tell us the sort of story to expect. They all have excellent dramatic potential and one can well imagine a company such as the Gelosi bringing them to life.*

Smith, Winifred: 'The Commedia dell'Arte', New York, Blom, 1964

The author starts the book with a description of a farce given in a Pennsylvania barn sometime in the 1950's, to promote the sale of a certain brand of soap. She draws parallels with Commedia dell'Arte performances of four hundred years earlier. This is useful, as it clearly points out that so much style, method and technique arises in response to the demands of the public to which it is played and the physical environment in which it takes place. There is therefore no need for attempts such as the one that tries to connect Commedia dell'Arte with the Roman mimes. The whole book is a lively but scholarly account, with chapters on definition, on the mountebanks, and the travels of companies outside Italy, with a particularly interesting section on the Commedia dell'Arte in Elizabethan and Jacobean England. There is a final section devoted to some less commonly seen illustrations.

Smith, Winifred: 'Italian Actors of the Renaissance', Blom, New York, 1930, revised, 1968

This is interesting to compare with Thelma Niklaus' 'Harlequin Phoenix'. Here is a book of careful scholarship dealing with the personalities of the major Commedia dell'Arte companies, and what a tedious lot she makes of them. Undoubtedly for much of the time that's just what they were, with their squabbles, jealousies, their insincere flatteries, and their begging and whining letters to their patrons. Apart from an interesting chapter on Giambattista Andreini – an author, designer and deviser with a talent and enthusiasm for elaborate scenery and trick effects very much at variance with the Commedia dell'Arte style of his famous parents Francesco and famed Isabella Andreini – there is little about actual performing and little to enlighten or motivate a present-day performer.

Storey, Robert F: ' Pierrot, a Critical History of a Mask', Princeton University Press, 1978

Another American publication of exemplary scholarship. Its sphere is perhaps as much literary as theatrical, but if you are not in a hurry to get before an audience and present your Pierrot, you should be able to absorb much that will be of value in performance from the detailed, constantly shifting perspectives of Pierrot's history.

PICTURES

I have always thought that the various pictures of the *Commedia dell'Arte* Masks give us greater insight into how the players performed than a mass of description and information even from the players themselves. However we should carefully weigh up exactly what we are looking at, for even with the greatest of all *Commedia dell'Arte* draughtsmen, Jacques Callot, there are a number of uncertainties. First to be considered are the names of the characters that frequently appear under the figures themselves, They seem a bit arbitrary. Callot often depicts a Zanni, and you will see him named Fricasso, Metzetin, Zerbino, Gian Farina, or Pulliciniello, although his costume is almost exactly the same for each of them. Others, sporting slashed doublet and hose, and a third type who appear to be almost nude, are hard to distinguish from the Captains like Mala Gamba, Bellauita and Scaramuccia, Coviello, Bello Squardo, Cardoni, Coccodrillo, etc. There is a series of splendid full-length portraits and these are clearly identifiable as Pantalone, the Lover Fabio, Scapino, etc.

Allardyce Nicoll discusses this problem and suggests that they represent Carnival figures and not 'faithful portraits of actors performing on a stage'.[1] It may be that Callot was careless about naming the characters, or that Neapolitan *Commedia dell'Arte* was itself vague in apportioning names to the Masks, but I cannot accept that these were mere Carnival revellers. No, these are professional performers of great skill and discipline, performing familiar *lazzi*. My guess is that Callot, having made himself familiar with the performers of one or more *Commedia dell'Arte* troupes, later invented a series of 'Capricios', faithfully translating the images from his memory.

If the Callot pictures are, as I maintain, theatrical, there are many others that are not, a prime example being the dreamscapes of Watteau (1684–1721) It is unlikely that Watteau ever saw a *Commedia dell'Arte* performance, as he didn't come to Paris until 1704, by which time the company had been banned from the city. He studied under Claude Gillot, and the numerous sketches of *Commedia* players he found in his master's studio are said to have inspired him to create the many pictures involving

1. 'The World of Harlequin', pages 75/78.

players. Gillot's own work most likely portrays the actors as they appeared, in the correct costumes and showing some of their poses and actions, though perhaps he gave them a languid grace that they didn't possess, and robbed them of much of the vitality that other illustrators make evident.

The paintings and drawings of Tiepolo are discussed in the section on Pulcinella (see page 207), but another example of what one might at first think to represent a performance is the well-known picture owned by the Comédie Française. Thelma Niklaus reproduces it in 'Harlequin

61

Phoenix' – captioned 'with Molière and members of his company on stage at the Theatre Royal in 1670'.

Molière shared the theatre with the *Commedia dell'Arte*, but most of the actors represented were never to work with Molière, nor to appear together at the same time. The picture is in fact a composite made from other images, engravings and paintings of actors, spanning almost fifty years. Centre stage we see Arlecchino, who is almost certainly Gherardi, and to the far right the unmistakable figure of Tiberio Fiorilli as Scaramouche. Compare the figure of Brighella to the extreme right of the picture with the engraving on page 197.

There is still a lot of interesting work to be done on the pictorial records of the *Commedia dell'Arte*. But this is not the place . . .

How to make
A PROFILE PRACTICE MASK
from cardboard

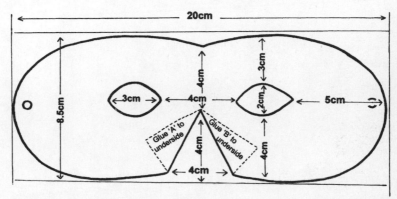

Measurements in centimetres are for medium size. Adjust to larger or smaller as necessary

Nose-Piece

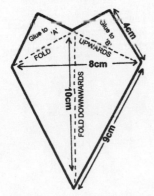

1. Draw out face and nose-piece on flexible card.
2. Cut along edge of the mask & inset for nose.
3. Cut out holes for eyes.
4. Cut out nose-piece.
5. Make downward fold in centre of nose, and upward on the two flaps.
6. Glue flaps to back of mask to attach nose.
7. Use eyelets or reinforce edge of mask to take cord or elastic.

If required, a frontal mask may be made in the same way by shortening the nose to about half the length.

The basics of making

A MASK IN PAPIER MÂCHÉ

Using artist's clay, model a
face that approximates to
the proportions of the performer.

Add clay, to create the characteristics
of the role within the mask area.
Allow the clay to dry and then
grease with petroleum jelly.

Prepare newspaper by tearing into small
pieces, approx 1" square.

Next, cover the greased area with a
layer of unpasted tissue paper
torn into small pieces. Paste
this over with cold-water
paste and build up about
six layers of the torn
newspaper pieces, pasting
each layer and smoothing it down.

Give it time to dry out. Take the mask from the mould. Turn in the
edges and glue down. Cut out the eye holes. Cover the mask with
several layers of Shellac or P.V.A before painting.

263

The conventional

ON-STAGE LOCATIONS

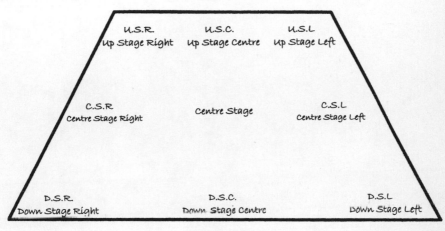

U.S.R.
Up Stage Right

U.S.C.
Up Stage Centre

U.S.L
Up Stage Left

C.S.R
Centre Stage Right

Centre Stage

C.S.L
Centre Stage Left

D.S.R.
Down Stage Right

D.S.C.
Down Stage Centre

D.S.L
Down Stage Left

AUDIENCE

MASK MAKERS AND SUPPLIERS

*Makers of fine individually crafted Commedia Masks
in leather or papier mâché*

Ninian Kinnier-Wilson,
32 Moscow Drive,
Liverpool L13 7DH, UK

0151 259 5422

Fine hand-made masks in leather or papier mâché

I Maschieri ,
Borgo,
Pinti 18 R,
50121 Firenze, Italy

055-265.147

Fine hand-made masks in leather, papier mâché, latex, resin

'Alice le Maschere',
Prof. Agostino Dessi,
Ayalier: V. Faenza 72 R,
50123 Firenze, Italy

055-287.370

Fine hand-made masks in papier mâché

Joka,
104 Harmwood Street,
London N1 8DS, UK

020 7813 0183

www.jokamasks.com

Hand-made masks in papier mâché, and latex. Shop and workshop you can visit

Justin Capp Leather,
4 Moor End,
Oundle,
Northants PE8 5RD, UK

Fine hand-made masks in leather (especially animal, mythic, fantastic)

Jenny Raison,
Harlequin House,
3 Kensington Mall,
London W8

01728 830 582

Importer of Italian masks, shop and exhibition

Stagestruck Costume Company,
41 Brushfield Street,
London E1

0208 174 114

Large selection of imported Commedia and Venetian Carnival Masks

Trylon Ltd,
Freepost,
Thrift Street,
Wollaston,
Northants NN29 7QJ, UK

01933 664275

Supplier of mask-making materials

Curious (Electric) Toad Co.,
92 Foxhall Road,
Forrest Fields,
Nottingham,
Nottinghamshire NG7 6LJ, UK

01159 623 948

Specialist mask and prop-makers for unusual requirements from one-offs to mass production

INDEX

Plautus, 151
Polichinelle, 207-210, 237
Polonius, 157, 160
Porter, Cole, 142
Probus, Paul and Frans, 180
Pulcinella, 207, 213
Punch, 207-211

Rand, Mark, 159
Recueil Fossard, 181, 225, 228
Riccoboni, Luigi, 135, 145
Rich, John, 147, 184
Romeo and Juliet, 6, 108
Rosaura, 170, 238
Rosetta, 233, 238
Rotalinda, 211-213, 238
Rudlin, John, 156, 256
Ruffiana, La, 152, 237
Ruzzante, 135

Sabatini, Rafael, 240
Saint Germain, 143
Saint Laurent, 143
Sand, Maurice, 135, 235, 239, 241-243, 256
Sartori, Donato, 113, 182, 242
Scala, Flaminio, 6, 140, 257
Scapino, xii, 233, 238-239, 259
Scaramouche, 146, 236, 239-240, 254, 260
Scaramouche a Philosopher, 146
Scaramuccia, 239, 259
Servant of Two Masters, The, 113
Servetta, 84, 152, 153, 184, 224
Shakespeare, 3, 9, 146, 151, 157
Sitwell, Sacheverell, 253
Smith, Winifred, 138, 257
Spavento, Captain, 5, 107-109, 169, 171-172, 174

Spinetta, 107-108, 152, 222-224, 232
Stanislavski, Konstantin 10
Stentarello, 241
Storey, Robert F., 258

Tartaglia, xii, 96, 116, 152, 241-242
Tavern Bilkers, The 146
Terry, Ellen, 253
Thomassin, 145
Three-house-set, 6, 141
Tiepolo, 207, 209, 260
Tracagnino, 181, 242-243
Trivelin, 197, 242
Truffaldino, 181, 242-243

Uscite, 7, 218

Veronese, Camilla, 227
Vita di Pulcinella, La, 207

Watteau, Antoine, 210, 235, 259
Weaver, John, 146
West Side Story, 108
Woodward, Henry, 147

Zan Padella, 54, 94, 136, 152, 160-161, 244
Zan Mortadella, 152, 242
Zanni, 50, 53-54, 61, 64, 66, 78-81, 83, 94, 102, 105-107, 116, 122, 129, 137, 140-141, 152, 161, 170, 172-173, 175, 180, 183-184, 192, 194, 197, 199-202, 207, 221, 224-225, 234-235, 237-239, 243, 244-249